SIBLINGS IN SOUTH ASIA

CULTURE AND HUMAN DEVELOPMENT

A Guilford Series

Sara Harkness
Charles M. Super
Editors

SIBLINGS IN SOUTH ASIA: BROTHERS AND SISTERS IN CULTURAL CONTEXT
Charles W. Nuckolls, Editor

Siblings in South Asia

Brothers and Sisters in Cultural Context

Charles W. Nuckolls
Editor

THE GUILFORD PRESS
New York London

A Division of Guilford Publications, Inc.
72 Spring Street, New York, NY 10012

Printed in the United States of America

This book is printed on acid-free paper.

Last digit is print number: 9 8 7 6 5 4 3 2 1

Library of Congress Cataloging-in-Publication Data

Siblings in South Asia : brothers and sisters in cultural context / Charles W. Nuckolls, editor.
p. cm. — (Culture and human development)
Includes bibliographical references and index.
ISBN 0-89862-146-1
1. Brothers and sisters—South Asia. 2. Brothers and sisters—Cross-cultural studies. I. Nuckolls, Charles William, 1956– II. Series.
BF723.S43S53 1993
306.875′0954—dc20 92-30076
CIP

Contributors

Alan R. Beals, PhD, Department of Anthropology, University of California, Riverside

Victor C. de Munck, PhD, Department of Anthropology, University of California, Riverside

Steve Derné, PhD, Department of Sociology, Saint John Fisher College, Rochester, New York

Judy Dunn, PhD, Center for the Study of Child and Adolescent Development, College of Health and Human Development, Pennsylvania State University, University Park

Pauline Kolenda, PhD, Department of Anthropology, University of Houston, Texas

Charles W. Nuckolls, PhD, Department of Anthropology, Emory University, Atlanta, Georgia

Judy F. Pugh, PhD, Department of Anthropology, Michigan State University, East Lansing

Susan Seymour, PhD, Department of Anthropology, Pitzer College, Claremont, California

Thomas S. Weisner, PhD, Department of Anthropology, University of California, Los Angeles

Contents

PART TWO
SIBLINGS IN MYTH, RELIGION, AND ETHNOPSYCHOLOGY

CHAPTER 1

Overview
Sibling Similarity and Difference in Different Cultures

Thomas S. Weisner

Imagine three siblings, all under 12 years old. All three are free of any neurological problems or other diseases that could affect their developmental course. What is the single most important thing that you would want to know about these siblings in order to understand their life course together?

In my view, the single most important thing to know is the cultural and ecological setting—the "cultural place"—in which these siblings are growing up. The essays on South Asia in this volume illustrate the power of the South Asian cultures to influence the lives of siblings. The contrast, for instance, between the Euro-American and South Asian cultures of siblingship makes the power of the cultural place strikingly evident. Studies of siblings in South America (Kensinger 1985), Oceania (Marshall 1983), Africa (Weisner 1987), and comparisons across regions (Zukow 1989) have already demonstrated the influence of cultural places around the world. This volume is intended to add to this literature by applying this approach to the study of sibings in South Asia.

The influence of culture is not central to most North American sibling studies (Weisner 1982; Weisner & Gallimore 1977). Most studies of North American familes mention features of siblings' roles and relationships that sibling researchers working with Euro-American samples have concentrated on: age and gender composition of the sibling group; family circumstances; socioeconomic status; siblings' and parents' temperaments; shared genetic inheritance; schools and educational experiences of the siblings; sibling rivalry; "equal" treatment of siblings by parents; home "stimulation" provided for siblings; or discipline and compliance. Each of these features is important and deserving of study, and each contributes something to the understanding of sibling relationships in any society. Yet the diversity of and other influences on siblings around the world remains underappreciated.

Understanding the Cultural Place: Ecocultural Theory and Activity Settings

There are many useful tools that can assist us in understanding the effects of different cultures on siblings around the world. Nuckolls's introductory chapter to this volume (Chapter 2), provides a useful overview. The additional chapters exemplify a wide range of theoretical approaches—each one of proven value in cross-cultural work. Although choosing which approach to use depends on the questions being asked and the theories and comparative frame of the studies, an *ecocultural* approach, which may be seen as potentially inclusive of the other theoretical approaches has many advantages for doing systematic cultural comparisons (Super & Harkness 1980; Whiting 1980; Weisner 1984).

An ecocultural approach has been applied to cross-cultural studies of siblings (Weisner 1989). It incorporates both the culture (such as beliefs, values, goals, practices, meanings) and the place in which siblings live (including the ecology, subsistence modes and resources, climatic range, threats to mortality and survival, population and demographic characteristics). In any particular cultural place, culture and ecology are interrelated and complementary. Nonetheless, it is analytically useful to distinguish them and compare their relative importance in understanding siblings' lives in that particular environment.

An ecocultural model is comprehensive in that it focuses on a wide range of cultural and ecological conditions that might influence sibling relationships. These ecocultural dimensions include mortality threats to children; demographics of a community; subsistence (work cycles, chores, tasks); personnel around children and the family (division of labor, child caretakers); requirements for the "social replacement" (Goody 1982) of the community through the rearing of children (including family moral and religious training, etiquette and hospitality, social comportment, etc.); roles of women in the community (including support for women and couple relations); and the range of alternative cultural models for conduct (if indeed there are alternatives known and available in a society) from which parents and children may choose.

An ecocultural analysis situates siblings within their everyday world and the local activities and daily routines of life that they share. The unit of analysis that best captures this everyday world is the "activity setting":

> Activity settings are the contexts for action in the everyday routine of life. *Culture is instantiated in local activity settings that shape interaction and thought* (Cole 1985; Super & Harkness 1982; Weisner & Gallimore 1985; Wertsch 1985; B. Whiting 1980; B. Whiting & Edwards 1988).
>
> Activity settings include five components: personnel, tasks, cultural scripts for conduct motives, and goals. To describe activity settings as useful units for comparative analysis, we need data on the *personnel present* in and around sibling groups; information on the kinds of *tasks and social activities* siblings engage in (such as school; home chores; sports and games); the standard *cultural scripts*, or taken-for-granted ways siblings perform tasks and activities (bedtime routines, for example; proper ways of eating meals; rules for going visiting); and the *cultural goals and motives* of children, parents, and significant others in the child's daily life (Weisner 1984; Weisner & Gallimore 1985). (Weisner 1989: 14–5, emphasis in original)

There are other important sources of cultural influence that are more distant from direct participation in whole activity settings (e.g., media exposure). An ecocultural/activity setting theory proposes that children's participation in everyday activities, which are part of a meaningful set of such activities, is the most powerful and important influence in development.

Siblings in South Asia and North America

The many ways in which sibling life in South Asia differs from that in North America is very evident from the chapters in this volume. For one thing, siblings in South Asia participate in shared activity settings *throughout their lives.* As in many other parts of the world, South Asian siblings are likely to live with or near each other throughout life or if not, to feel compelled to produce culturally acceptable reasons why not. They also are likely to share important subsistence resources and decision-making roles regarding the allocation of these resources. Siblings remain involved in decades-long negotiations and interdependent decisions about marriage, wealth, and residence. In such societies, the sibling relationship itself represents a powerful cultural image of an ideal social bond for which culture members should strive (Marshall 1983).

South Asian societies also offer rich and varied sibling roles to children as well as adults. These roles significantly shape the life course. Older sibs take care of their younger brothers and sisters, as described by Beals and Eason (Chapter 4) and Seymour (Chapter 3) in this volume. Siblings participate in decisions about whom and when their brothers and sisters are going to marry. Later on they are agents in their nieces' and nephews' lives, just as their uncles and aunts are in their own lives. Resources are made available to siblings by other siblings for housing, life cycle rituals, and subsistence activities. Examples of this phenomenon appear in this volume in the chapters by de Munck (Chapter 6), Nuckolls (Chapter 8), and Kolenda (Chapter 5). De Munck, for example, points out that one expectable pathway in a culturally desirable life in the community he studied involves moving out of one's conjugal household as one ages and moving into the house of a brother or sister. The cultural career (Goldschmidt 1990) of siblings in these South Asian communities involves substantial interdependence.

Euro-American culture, in contrast, simply does not provide a model of a normal cultural career in which siblings will consistently matter in crucial domains of life, particularly after childhood. This does not mean that sibling relationships are not often rich and meaningful for children and adults, only that such economic and social relationships are not culturally elaborated. If such relationships emerge, they do so on the basis of personal circumstances, not as part of the normal cultural life course. Siblings in the Euro-American context are culturally expected to leave home and separate for life. Important decisions about economic and social life are expected to be made along with one's parents, spouse, friends, or work associates, but not primarily with one's siblings. The parent–child relationship and the couple bond, not the relationship between siblings, represent the cultural relationship ideals Euro-American strive for in life and are the ideals presented in myths and in the popular media.

Although compared to Euro-American societies South Asian societies make explicit culturally the importance of sibling roles, brothers and sisters in South Asia are not simply dutifully enacting customary obligations in a climate of positive, reciprocal social solidarity. South Asian siblings are driven by strategic efforts to attain economic, marital, ritual, or other kinds of benefits. Striking evidence of individuals trying to gain personal advantage by *using* their sibling and wider kin groups is vividly illustrated in many of the chapters in this volume. Although siblings remain in complementary relationships throughout life, sharing many common cultural expectations, they are also clearly different from one another in their personal interests, goals, styles, and life course.

As different chapters in this volume point out, there are many alternative cultural paths that can be followed by siblings in different regions, or within the same community. For instance, de Munck (Chapter 6) describes the strategic manipulation by brothers of senior or junior sibs and in-laws to assist in obtaining housing or providing loans and dowry. Kolenda (Chapter 5) describes the lifelong enmity that results within families when cross-cousin marriage is culturally expected yet not fulfilled because a more financially advantageous marriage is arranged. Nuckolls (Chapter 8) describes the economic situation of brothers in a patrilineal clan: They contribute more and more in the way of material and social resources to their own conjugal families and less and less to the families of their married sisters—eventually leading to patriclan fission. Beals and Eason (Chapter 4) compare sibling solidarity in joint families that are either wealthy or poor; bitterness can accompany economic divisions of the family estate in both situations. The cases in Derné (Chapter 7) and Pugh's (Chapter 9) research frequently include economic conflicts and the attempt to construct a culturally coherent account, a rationale, for family separations that are due to work requirements or economic conflicts among family members. All these chapters suggest common economic and status hierarchy struggles among siblings and in-laws in South Asia—as well as common ideals of sibling solidarity and interdependency throughout life that can aid in the resolution of these struggles.

In this struggle over resources, older sibs in South Asia seem to be favored. They have more dowry available and use authority derived from being at the top of the hierarchy to control wealth. There appears to be both a selective investment effect and an age effect contributing to these widely observed birth-order differences. The selective investment effect is that parents and uncles invest more resources and status in senior siblings, since their marriages and dowry will occur first and thus older siblings are believed to be more appropriate to invest in. The age effect is that seniority itself brings with it deference from others, authority over others, and often enmity as well from childhood on. A number of studies have compared roles of firstborn and later-born siblings across cultures (Fortes 1974; Jackson 1978; Munroe & Munroe 1983, 1988; Sangree 1981; Skinner 1992). These studies have focused on intelligence, personality, mythological representations of siblings, parental relationships, and other topics. Some common patterns based on sibling birth order do appear across a wide range of cultures.

By and large, the siblings presented in this volume stand out clearly as men and women with motives, needs, passions, and desires for wealth and status. It is clear that these South Asian cultures produce bitter personal struggles concerning advantageous marriage alliances, repressed and explicit envy among siblings, jealousy over a sibling's wealth or favored status, and so forth. Both at the level of cultural ideology and rules, and at the level of social interactions in everyday life, sibling conflicts, and struggles over their means for resolution, are continuously problematic. The force of cultural ideology and norms also appears in the shared commitment to cultural customs, categories, schemas, and meanings. The *relative* contributions of cultural ideology, on the one hand, or social interactions, on the other, in resolving individual and family conflicts needs further study, as McGilvray (1988) pointed out with respect to the study of gender in South Asia.

Sibling Similarity and Difference within Families

The situations of South Asian and Euro-American siblings are similar in a number of ways. In both places, individuals attempt to gain personal strategic advantage in a range of possible life careers that their culture and ecology make possible (Weisner 1989). Like Euro-American siblings, South Asian siblings are portrayed in this volume as frequently having very different and conflicting goals within families. Nuckolls (Chapter 8) also suggests that there are similar psychological processes of projection and denial in the world of myths and dreams in the South Asian community, analogous to those found in Western psychology.

There is another similarity between South Asian and North American siblings, and those everywhere else in the world: Any pair of siblings shares on average 50% of their genes. This genetic similarity is itself a reason to do comparative sibling research. Siblings[1] are at least potentially different from other kinds of co-resident, intimate social units (friends, spouses, neighbors) in that they share a very high genetic inheritance. It is not implausible that siblings struggle over *marriages* and are jealous over *differential investment in offspring* because such reproductive matters are important to people who share genes as well as a common culture. It is also possible that siblings always matter—are everywhere culturally important—in part because they share a common genetic inheritance. Furthermore, the extent and nature of sibling similarity and difference within and among families may well be due not only to cultural characteristics unique to South Asia but also to universal processes related to the mutual interaction of genetics and environment.

In most cases, siblings also share a common family experience, live close together for all or significant portions of their lives, and share, at least to some degree, a common set of cultural expectations regarding appropriate conduct between siblings. Beyond shared genes, all of these shared family and cultural circumstances may make siblings in the same family more alike and are plausible reasons for common interests in marriage and property in their community.

It is a common assumption in family and cultural research that there is a high proportion of shared cultural knowledge and experience among siblings *because* they are raised in the same family or community. Thus, it is assumed that siblings reared in the same family are more similar to each other than they are to other community members, and that the family members of this community will produce children more similar than those from another community. Such an assumption is basic to any research design that uses interviews or observations of only one family member to infer the characteristics of the whole family and its socialization practices, or uses interviews conducted with different members of a single family group regarding common community experiences. There would have to be substantial effects on each child or adult of *shared* family and community experiences to make such designs powerful.

Yet there is research that challenges this seemingly self-evident assumption. Plomin and Daniels (1987) and Dunn and Plomin (1990) review evidence from behavior genetics research, as well as from studies of social interaction among siblings, that shows a large contribution of "nonshared" environmental influence. Nonshared family environments are the intrafamilial environments that are unique for each sibling living in the same family setting. For example, if parents act differently toward each sibling (which all parents do to some extent), each sibling has lived in a different family environment unique to that sibling. Or, when siblings in a family each have different abilities and temperaments (which each individual does to some extent) and seek out different environments in which to express these abilities and temperaments, then each sibling will have a unique nonshared family environment. (In addition, some of the "nonshared" component is almost certainly also due to measurement error of such traits and abilities.) Plomin and Daniels (1987) argue that in many North American samples, siblings are not much more similar to each other (using standardized cognitive or personality measures as outcomes for each sibling) than any two individuals picked at random from that culture, even though the siblings grew up in the "same" family environment. A shared family experience, in other words, does not automatically mean siblings share certain abilities or personality traits, as measured by standard assessment scales.

Mechanisms have been proposed that might in fact lead siblings to actively differentiate themsleves from their brothers and sisters. Scarr and Grajek (1982), for instance, argue that genetic or temperamental predispositions are expressed partly through a mechanism whereby individuals actively seek out *different* family contexts for the expression of such predispositions. Other individual predispositions remain latent and appear only when particular eliciting situations occur in the family environment. Schachter (1982) describes the processes of sibling deidentification, in which, for example, the secondborn child identifies more strongly with the parent with whom the firstborn did not identify most strongly.

It is also known that there are cross-cultural regularities in interaction among siblings and cousins (Whiting & Edwards 1988). These cross-cultural regularities mean that siblings are not equally likely to interact with or become close to one another. For instance, children tend to prefer to interact with other children of the same sex. There are more nurturant and prosocial interactions involving girls and between older and younger children, while children nearer in age are more likely to engage in competitive or aggressive interactions (Weisner 1987).

Due in part to such influences, the "family environment" that is actually experienced by each sibling is inevitably socially constructed at least somewhat differently by each sibling. Further, as siblings get older, they are influenced by nonfamilial environmental influences from peers, voluntary association membership, media exposure, and other sources. These nonshared, extrafamilial experiences also contribute to sibling differences. To the extent that these interactional patterns lead to differential experiences of children in their families, they would encourage nonshared family effects, making each sibling at least somewhat different.

Meanwhile, as noted above, genetics conspire to make siblings similar. However, heritability estimates of personality, cognitive, and physical characteristics in sibling studies vary. The order of magnitude is about 50% or less for the contribution of genetic influence for some personality traits, such as extraversion and for adult IQ (Plomin 1989). Height and weight are about 80% and 60%, respectively, due to genetic influence. Many diseases (heart disease, ulcers, etc.) are around 20% genetic (Dunn & Plomin 1990: 46–54).

Genetic effects do not imply a deterministic or invariant influence. Heritability is "merely a descriptive statistic that indicates for a particular population at a particular time the extent to which genetic differences among individuals can account for observed differences. It is not an immutable constant, nor does it tell us how genes have their effect" (Dunn & Plomin 1990: 33). What Plomin, Dunn, and others suggest is that most of the environmental influence on siblings comes not from shared family effects but from nonshared family influences.

Based on their work, Dunn and Plomin (1990) make some strong statements regarding the influence of family environment that suggest that there is little importance in shared family environments, and that influences on siblings—and on development generally—consist primarily of genetic and *non*shared (unique to each child) environmental effects:

> Experiences within the family do not make siblings similar. The only factors important to children's development are those that are experienced differently by children in the same family. . . . siblings resemble each other for genetic reasons . . . not for [shared family] environmental reasons. That is, siblings are similar, but they are just as similar if they are adopted apart and reared in different families. Growing up in the same family is not responsible for their resemblance. What runs in families is DNA, not shared experiences in the family. (Dunn & Plomin 1990: 42–3)

Note that this point of view does not mean that "environment" is unimportant. To the contrary, environmental influences are very important in siblings' development in this approach. But it is the unique-to-each-sibling, nonshared, intrafamilial environment that appears to matter for personality, IQ, and health status—not shared family environment.

The sibling conflicts in South Asia vividly described in this volume could in part be due to such universal developmental mechanisms making siblings different—that is, placing each sibling in nonshared family environments. However, in the chapters in this volume, the authors attribute such conflicts to *cultural* beliefs and practices unique to South Asian culture, and/or to siblings' competition over material resources. Although there is no question of the power of these cultural and ecological factors in human development (Super & Harkness 1980, 1986; Weisner 1984), there also may be universal developmental processes (e.g., the creation of nonshared family environments, as well as genetic influences) making siblings different or similar within a family. These nonshared environments may in turn place siblings inevitably in some conflict with each other.

Although I believe that both genetics and nonshared family environments are important for understanding the sibling relationships depicted in this volume, I also believe that the influence of the culture in making siblings similar within a shared cultural environment is missing in studies of sibling differences in Western sibling research such as Dunn and Plomin's. Nonshared environments are postulated to explain wide *individual* differences within the sibling group. Yet South Asian siblings do *share* to some considerable extent a world view about siblingship, expressed in myths, beliefs about marriages and family relationships, economic obligations, and so forth. South Asia is very different from North America as a cultural place for siblings. North American siblings do not share these cultural beliefs and practices. In this sense of *cultural* similarity or difference, South Asian siblings are far more culturally similar to each other than siblings would be in any North American family selected at random (even granting the importance of the regional and other variations in both places). Similarity or difference between siblings within a family is an important issue, but it is quite a different matter from similarity or differences in siblings' socialization and cultural understandings across cultures.

This is another way of saying (in the language of behavior genetics) that different family environments in a community in a particular cultural place are "correlated"—that is, families share a common set of cultural beliefs and practices to a significant extent. For instance, imagine if we were to ask siblings in South Asia and North America about Hindu beliefs in reincarnation, about certain food taboos, or about ideas of respect for ones' father and mother. Siblings in South Asian families would be very similar to one another, compared to siblings in North American families. Shweder (1991: 190–91) asked children and adults in Orissa, India, and North America about moral judgments—what is right and wrong—and found that by age 5 the children in each culture had very different conceptions of morality, having learned their morality through participation in routine, everyday activity settings characteristic of their culture:

> While there are some areas of agreement between the five-year-olds in the two cultures (for example, that it is wrong to break a promise, destroy a picture drawn by another child, kick a harmless animal), there are just as many areas of disagreement. Oriya (but not American) five-year-olds believe it is wrong to eat beef or address one's father by his first name. American (but not Oriya) five-year-olds believe it is wrong to cane an errant child or to open a letter addressed to one's fourteen-year-old son.

> . . . We assume that moral interpretations of events are expressed through and are discernible in the very organization of routine practices (a separate bed for each child, a communal meal, lining up—first come, first served—to get tickets). (Shweder 1991: 190–91)

Certainly, the families described in this volume, and the authors writing about them, take as a given that brothers and sisters are *culturally* alike in some fundamental ways—that their shared experiences as children and interdependence as adults are real and bind them together, and that this similarity comes from shared family experiences as well as from a common culture. Cultural ideology in South Asia seems to conspire to lead siblings and parents to assert similarities and complementarities among the sibling group, whether or not they are "really" present. And where there are conflicts, South Asian cultural accounts are available in myths, ideology, and beliefs that assert how and why these conflicts arose in the first place. Interestingly, these cultural beliefs basically appeal in turn to the influence of *shared family experiences* among archetypal Indian siblings.

There certainly are cultural and ecological reasons to posit shared experience. In the South Asian cultural setting, as well as in many others around the world, there is a strong emphasis on complementarity of sibling roles in the family, sibling interdependence throughout life, and sibling co-ownership and control of resources crucial for survival and reproduction. It is possible that in such ecological and cultural circumstances, shared family environmental influences *would* be stronger than they appear in studies done in North America. The question is, might the existence of more shared family environmental influence (relative to nonshared environments) within families in cultural places like South Asia be due to the fact that sibling solidarity is more culturally elaborated than it is in North America? This is an interesting and important area for future empirical research.

Taking culture more seriously will also mean measuring sibling characteristics in addition to individual differences on personality and cognitive scales, or standardized measures of psychopathology or health. Most behavioral genetic studies of siblings utilize individual difference measures such as standardized personality inventories or IQ tests. Such measures are important, but they do not capture those aspects of socialization and personality that are embedded in *complementary* sibling and family roles, such as those that exist in South Asia and elsewhere. In fact, Dunn (1985), Mendelson (1990), and others have provided qualitative, self-report, and observational data on such complementary relationships among Euro-American siblings.

This kind of research is embedded in an understanding of family interaction. However, most behavioral genetics research has not used such measures in assessing siblings. Since judgments of sibling similarity are done using individual difference measures such as cognitive tests, rather than more culturally sensitive measures such as customary practices or beliefs, they may have exaggerated differences between siblings within families. This, again, is a question for further empirical research in Euro-American and other cultural places.

Conclusion

The findings of behavior genetics research are striking and important with regard to individual differences within families. The strong conclusion from this work is, "One thing is clear: Siblings growing up in the same family are very different" (Dunn & Plomin 1990: 151). On many measures of health, personality, and intellectual ability, siblings are nearly as different from each other as they are from any two individuals selected at random. However, a cross-cultural perspective requires further expansion, and modification of the conclusion of behavior genetics research: Siblings growing up in the same family may well be different from one another, but only relative to that particular culture, and on measures based largely on individual difference, rather than on embedded complementarity within relationships.

First, there are shared family (and community) effects of an important kind: Families in a particular culture also transmit shared cultural meanings, beliefs, and practices to their children. Indeed, this is an important function of family socialization altogether. From this comparative view, families do make siblings *culturally* similar to each other, compared to siblings in families in other cultures. Now, the extent to which siblings within a culture share cultural meanings, beliefs, understandings, commitments, and practices may be exaggerated in ethnographic work. It *may* well be that siblings in a family from South Asia (or North America) do not share a particular cultural meaning or commitment to a practice any more than *any* two individuals *from within that culture* would share the meaning system or practice the custom. It certainly is true, as we see amply reflected in this volume, that South Asian siblings can be in violent disagreement and conflict over such matters. However, siblings and nonsiblings within a particular culture do seem to share common understandings regarding sibling roles and obligations different from that in other cultural places.

Second, although relatively low sibling similarity may hold true within Euro-American culture, it remains for future research to show to what extent, for example, Euro-American siblings are "similar" to South Asia or East African siblings on appropriately and comparably collected measures. Behavior genetics research proposes that siblings are not much more similar than any two individuals "selected at random." But what "selected at random" usually refers to is a sample selected within a particular culture, certainly not randomly selected from any culture in the world. My prediction is that cultural differences will be profound for cultural matters, and less so (but still present) for individual difference measures.

Studies of siblings done in North America need to take culture more seriously into account. North American culture encourages sibling independence and culturally elaborates the parent–child and couple relationships more than it does sibling relationships. Partly for this reason, siblings may be less similar to one another in Euro-American culture. Siblings may be more similar to one another in other cultures, especially those like South Asia that elaborate the importance of sibling roles more than Euro-American culture does.

However, judging from the ethnographic evidence in this volume, *complementarity* in sibling roles in South Asia, and perhaps in other cultural settings, may be a more powerful effect than similarity across individuals. That is, siblings in South Asian families are more often in similar *patterns* of relationships with each other, as well as in characteristic patterns of personal and cultural identification with one another (e.g., as a result of coresidence arrangements, marriage alliances, dependence on siblings for inheritance, dowry practices). The chapters in this volume describe both patterns: clear complementarity and (at least idealized) similarities within the sibling group. Dunn (1985) and Dunn and Plomin (1990) have explored the subtleties of complementary relationships in their work in England and in North America. And they point out how such complementarity leads to different experiences for each child in a family, and thus to nonshared family environmental effects. Dunn and Brown (1991), who compared children's early social understandings in England and Pennsylvania, found suggestive evidence for cross-national differences in the two places, as well as substantial within-culture variability. South Asian siblings are in lifelong alliances between groups of siblings and other kin that make them highly complementary. Will this make them at least somewhat more similar to one another than is the case in North American studies, or just as different, or even more different, than North American siblings?

I predict that future studies of siblings in other cultures will find

that siblings are not as different from one another as they have been found to be in Euro-American studies. I also expect that lifelong sibling interdependence will make such similarities extend throughout the life span, rather than decline as siblings get older. But I also predict that the effects of nonshared environments in making siblings different will also be found, and that siblings will be less homogeneous than the cultural-level generalizations of many ethnographic studies might have led us to believe. But these are both expectations that need empirical study in many cultural places. To do this will require the active collaboration of developmentalists and anthropologists.

It will also require the active collaboration of members of those cultures, utilizing an approach that focuses on greater understanding of their family experiences. This is a methodological requirement shared both by students of individual development in nonshared family environments and by students of siblings in different cultures. It is the experience of each sibling, and the whole sibling group, in everyday activity settings provided by a culture that matters most for human development. It is the fact that each sibling *experiences* his or her family circumstances differently that limits shared family influences. As Dunn and Plomin (1990) comment regarding the implications of their work on nonshared environments and genetic influence:

> How to make progress towards a more sensitive appreciation of what matters within the family? We will argue . . . for listening to children's and parents' views of what happens with their families—for taking the perceptions of family members very seriously, and also for conducting more naturalistic research. (Dunn & Plomin 1990: 156)

This volume will add to that advice that such research will need to be done in a much wider range of cultural settings than has been done to this point. By focusing on one non-Western culture area, that of South Asia, the chapters in this volume suggest that closely observed studies of social experience and the folk beliefs and perceptions of siblings in the different cultures, using ethnographic and naturalistic research methods, can make a valuable contribution to understanding sibling differences and similarities around the world.

Note

1. In South Asia, as elsewhere in the world, the term "sibling" refers not only to those individuals with the same biological mother and father but also to cousins and other kin of various kinds. This reduces the average percentage

of shared genetic inheritance among the group of "siblings" thus identified, but does not change the fact that the group of individuals so classified still disproportionately share a common genetic inheritance, compared to any two individuals selected at random from the wider community.

References

Cole, M. (1985). The Zone of Proximal Development: Where Culture and Cognition Create Each Other. In J. V. Wertsch (Ed.), *Culture, Communication, and Cognition* (pp. 146-61). New York: Cambridge University Press.

Dunn, J. (1985). *Sisters and Brothers.* Cambridge, MA: Harvard University Press.

Dunn, J., & Brown, J. (1991). Becoming American or English? Talking about the Social World in England and the United States. In M. H. Bornstein (Ed.), *Cultural Approaches to Parenting.* Hillsdale, NJ: Erlbaum.

Dunn, J., & Plomin, R. (1990). *Separate Lives: Why Siblings Are So Different.* New York: Basic Books.

Fortes, M. (1974). "The First Born." *Journal of Child Psychology and Psychiatry* 15: 81-104.

Goldschmidt, W. (1990). *The Human Career.* London: Routledge.

Goody, E. N. (1982). *Parenthood and Social Reproduction: Fostering and Occupational Roles in West Africa.* Cambridge, England: Cambridge University Press.

Jackson, M. (1978). "Ambivalence and the Last-Born: Birth-Order Position in Convention and Myth." *Man* 13: 341-61.

Kensinger, K. (Ed.). (1985). *The Sibling Relation in Lowland South America* (Working papers on South American Indians, no. 7). Bennington, VT: Bennington College.

Marshall, M. (Ed.). (1983). *Siblingship in Oceania: Studies in the Meaning of Kin Relations.* Lanham, MD: University Press of America.

McGilvray, D. (1988). "Sex, Repression, and Sanskritization in Sri Lanka?" *Ethos* 16: 99-127.

Mendelson, M. J. (1990). *Becoming a Brother. A Child Learns about Life, Family, and Self.* Cambridge, MA: MIT Press.

Munroe, R. L., & Munroe, R. H. (1983). "Birth Order and Intellectual Development in East Africa." *Journal of Cross-cultural Psychology* 14: 3-16.

Munroe, R. L., & Munroe, R. H. (1988). Birth Order and Its Psychological Correlates in East Africa. In R. Bolton (Ed.), *The Content of Culture: Constance and Variance* (pp. 271-319). New Haven, CT: Human Relations Area Files Press.

Plomin, R. (1989). "Environment and Genes: Determinants of Behavior." *American Psychologist* 44: 105-11.

Plomin, R., & Daniels, D. (1987). "Why Are Children in the Same Family

So Different from One Another?" *Behavioral and Brain Sciences* 10: 1-59.

Sangree, W. H. (1981). "The 'Last-Born' (*Muxogosi*) and Complementary Filiation in Tiriki, Kenya." *Ethos* 9: 188-200.

Scarr, S., & Grajek, S. (1982). Similarities and Differences among Siblings. In M. E. Lamb & B. Sutton-Smith (Eds.), *Sibling Relationships: Their Nature and Significance across the Lifespan* (pp. 357-82). Hillsdale, NJ: Erlbaum.

Schachter, F. F. (1982). Sibling Deidentification and Split-Parent Identification: A Family Tetrad. In M. E. Lamb & B. Sutton-Smith (Eds.), *Sibling Relationships: Their Nature and Significance across the Lifespan* (pp. 123-151). Hillsdale, NJ: Erlbaum.

Shweder, R. A. (1991). *Thinking through Cultures: Expeditions in Cultural Psychology*. Cambridge, MA: Harvard University Press.

Skinner, G. W. (1992). *Sibling Differentiation: Culture and Configuration in Chinese Families*. Unpublished manuscript.

Super, C., & Harkness, S. (Eds.). (1980). *Anthropological Perspectives on Child Development: New Directions for Child Development, No. 8.* San Francisco: Jossey-Bass.

Super, C., & Harkness, S. (1982). The Infant's Niche in Rural Kenya and Metropolitan America. In L. L. Adler (Ed.), *Cross-cultural Research at Issue* (pp. 47-55). New York: Academic Press.

Super, C., & Harkness, S. (1986). "The Developmental Niche: A Conceptualization at the Interface of Child and Culture." *International Journal of Behavior Development* 9: 1-25.

Weisner, T. (1982). Sibling Interdependence and Child Caretaking: A Cross-Cultural View. In M. E. Lamb & B. Sutton-Smith (Eds.), *Sibling Relationships: Their Nature and Significance across the Lifespan* (pp. 305-327). Hillsdale, NJ: Erlbaum.

Weisner, T. S. (1984). Ecocultural Niches of Middle Childhood: A Cross-cultural Perspective. In W. A. Collins (Ed.), *Development during Middle Childhood: The Years from Six to Twelve* (pp. 335-69). Washington, DC: National Academy of Sciences Press.

Weisner, T. S. (1987). Socialization for Parenthood in Sibling Caretaking Societies. In J. Lancaster, A. Rossi, & J. Altmann (Eds.), *Parenting across the Life Span* (pp. 237-70). New York: Aldine Press.

Weisner, T. S. (1989). Comparing Sibling Relationships across Cultures. In P. Zukow (Ed.), *Sibling Interaction across Cultures: Theoretical and Methodological Issues* (pp. 11-25). New York: Springer-Verlag.

Weisner, T., & Gallimore, R. (1977). "My Brother's Keeper: Child and Sibling Caretaking." *Current Anthropology* 18: 169-90.

Weisner, T. S., & Gallimore, R. (1985, December). *The Convergence of Ecocultural and Activity Theory.* Paper presented at the annual meeting of the American Anthropological Association, Washington, DC.

Wertsch, J. V. (1985). *Vygotsky and the Social Formation of Mind.* Cambridge, MA: Harvard University Press.

Whiting, B. (1980). "Culture and Social Behavior: A Model for the Development of Social Behavior." *Ethos* 8: 95–116.
Whiting B., & Edwards, C. (1988). *Children of Different Worlds: The Formation of Social Behavior.* Cambridge, MA: Harvard University Press.
Zukow, P. (1989). *Sibling Interaction across Cultures: Theoretical and Methodological Issues.* New York: Springer-Verlag.

Photo by Susan Seymour

CHAPTER 2

An Introduction to the Cross-cultural Study of Sibling Relations

Charles W. Nuckolls

In the epilogue to *Sibling Relationships: Their Nature and Significance across the Lifespan,* Brian Sutton-Smith concludes: "Let us first try to *explain* in general what is going on, rather than arrive at some fairly reliable covariances between this variable and that variable without much sense of what it all means" (Lamb & Sutton-Smith 1982: 336). The contributors to this volume agree. We start from an appreciation of the primacy of cultural meanings and social structures, and from the finding that these two phenomena vary. Our purpose is to understand these variations among cultures and their effects on other phenomena, including some of those on which, like birth order and sibling conflict, psychological research on sibling relations has traditionally focused. This book thus starts from where Sutton-Smith leaves off, that is, with the recognition that "what it all means" is not secondary to the study of sibling relations but fundamental to defining the questions we may usefully ask.

South Asia—consisting of the modern nation states of India, Pakistan, Bangladesh, Nepal, Bhutan, and Sri Lanka—provides a richly varied set of cultural contexts in which to examine sibling roles. These contexts differ significantly from those in the United States and Britain, where the majority of sibling studies have been undertaken. By "cultural contexts" I refer to both the different family settings in which sibling relations develop and express themselves and to the relevant meaning systems that shape and constrain the development of sibling relations. How do different household and family structures affect the development of sibling relations? Do different models of personhood lead to different models of siblingship? How do siblings respond to the expectation that they should relate harmoniously to each other? Addressing such questions is ambitious, but it is consistent with the direction that Lamb and Sutton-Smith (1982: 1) argue sibling studies should be moving, that is, away from examining global covariances and toward a greater focus on constitutive processes, including increased attention to cultural meaning and development across the life span.

One of the most striking differences between South Asian and Western social thought is that the latter views the development of individuals into fully autonomous beings as natural. While the free and autonomous individual exists in South Asia, it is only in highly unusual states—either pathologically, as an aberration, or spiritually, as a form of enlightenment or release. In South Asia, the individual is not distinguished from the status she or he occupies; obligations and rights are apportioned by role; and no intrinsic worth is attributed to people as people (Shweder 1990: 151). Shweder calls this a "sociocentric" definition of the person, as opposed to the Western "egocentric" definition. Various consequences follow from a sociocentric perspective. For one thing, this type of socialization typically creates people with high dependency needs: What Western psychologists might describe as *folie à famille,* a pathological enmeshment of family members, is in South Asia a desirable developmental outcome. South Asian practices foster a sense of "we-ness" characterized by affective exchange and empathic sensitivity. The result is an adult interdependence that is so strongly felt that even the loosening of the family bond, not to mention its actual disruption, is cause for considerable anxiety.

The sociocentric "familial self" (Roland 1988) is created and reinforced through family structures and activity settings that are very different from their Euro-American counterparts. The point of view presented in this volume is that one must first understand these structures and settings before one can proceed to interpret sibling relations, interactions, and behavior. Consider just a few of the most obvious features of South Asian family structures and activity settings that differ from those in the Euro-American world.

First, the hierarchically organized extended family is common throughout South Asia, where it is the norm for brothers to live with each other and with their parents in multigenerational households. The ideal of fraternal solidarity is the rationale for the extended family which then requires common residence and common social and economic activities. Hierarchy is determined by sex (males over females) and by age (old over young). Second, wives may be recruited at some distance, as in the north, or may come from among the family's own relations, as in south India, where the most desirable spouses are the children of parental cross-siblings. Third, children of adult brothers, whom we would call "cousins," call each other "brother" and "sister," and are treated as such by their parents. Older children, not parents, are their younger siblings primary caretakers for most of the day, and as children grow up, they are accustomed to look on each other as lifelong participants in each other's lives.

The structural and developmental consequences of life in the South Asian extended family are readily seen in siblingship. Siblings are crucial to adult maintenance and support. Brothers often live in the same extended household, sharing work and resources and closely involved in each other's affairs. Brothers and sisters often share strong economic ties. But even when they do not, they may have the right to call on each other for mutual support and assistance at any time. Thus, to understand household economies and domestic units of production, as well as the larger corporate entities these may constitute, sibling relations must be considered in the context of South Asia family structure and development.

Second, siblingship and marriage patterns are closely linked. In south India, for example, cross-cousin marriages are often preferred, and so brothers and sisters must look to each other for their children's future marriage partners. Cross-siblings must therefore carefully monitor and adjust to each other's needs. Since this sometimes fails, especially at the point when marriages are being planned, the relationship between siblings often becomes the primary locus of conflict and community attention.

Third, older siblings take care of younger siblings, partly usurping a role that in the West is usually assigned to parents. This means that children learn nurturance and caregiving much earlier and more intensively, and that such learning has implications for future adult relationships, both within and outside siblingship.

Fourth, mythic siblings pervade South Asian epics and legends, including the most famous of these, the *Ramayana* and the *Mahabharata.* Stories serve as mythical charters, providing models of and for sibling relations, and often constitute the focus of commentary and debate in everyday life. The contrast to Western, and especially Christian, mythology is striking: Where the Christian account emphasizes between-generational structures (e.g., "the father" and "the son") through a linear series of "begats," South Asian stories stress within-generational dynamics centered on the sibling relationship. The meaning of mythic archetypes, and their significance for sibling roles, must be examined in any analysis of South Asian sibling roles.

Fifth, siblings figure prominently in the way South Asians conceptualize and discuss their own and other's mental processes, behavior, and relationships. American ethnopsychology, by contrast, tends to stress the relationship between a child and his parents, and so, in cases of incomplete or dysfunctional development, a therapeutic transformation of this primary between-generational structure is held to be necessary (e.g., Mahler, Pine, & Bergman 1975). If siblings, not parents, are the primary caretakers in South Asia, then some part of the process that Americans typically attribute to the parent–child relationship must be located in the sibling relationship instead. A sister, not the mother, might be the male child's primary object choice, just as a brother, not the father, might be the rival of as well as the model for his other siblings. One can only begin to imagine what Freud's construction of psychosexual development would look like if the sibling and not the parent–child relationship were the theoretical starting point.

This list summarizes only a few of the many important ways in which South Asian siblingship is different from the western concept of siblingship. The point I wish to make here, and to emphasize, is that existing models of the siblingship do not necessarily help us understand such differences. This will be clearer in the next section, in which I situate the study of South Asian siblingship in three literatures—the psychological, the anthropological, and the Orientalist.

Sibling Relations and Human Development

Developmental psychologists traditionally study changes in the life course in terms of situations, interactions, and abilities. The most important of these is "ability," which is most often defined cognitively and pertains to how humans develop the capacity to think abstractly, behave autonomously, and create imaginatively. The focus of research has usually been the situations and interactions that psychologists consider most relevant to the development of these abilities. The situation most often studied has been early childhood, and the interaction most researched has been the one between mother and child.

"Rivalry" between siblings was assumed to be the most important aspect of sibling relationships. As early as the 1920s, for example, Adler (1924) showed that birth order and sibling rivalry were related. A first child was assumed to possess and then be forced to relinquish exclusive rights to the mother's nurturance. Younger siblings, we were told, must compete for maternal attention amongst themselves and with their elder counterparts. And intense sibling jealousy, combined with the growing urgency of competition for scarce resources, forces children to develop the intellectual and interpersonal abilities they will need as adults. Sibling rivalry, in this view, was not just an aspect of development, but the workplace and proving ground for the necessary adult capacity to compete. Even recent studies that no longer concentrate exclusively on rivalry still stress the development of the capacity to compete and negotiate. Exactly why competition should be considered inevitable or desirable is not clear. But it is surely no accident that most studies were conducted in Western societies where capitalist competition is the assumed natural basis for social existence.

The study of sibling rivalry was the dominant research focus in sibling studies for decades (see Levy 1937; Ross 1930; Smally 1930; Spock 1957). While continuing to dominate the popular imagination, in more recent development research rivalry has been replaced by other concerns. One important focus is the effect of the sibling's sex on the sex-role characteristics, interests, and abilities of other siblings. Sutton-Smith and Rosenberg (1970), for example, hypothesized that each sex increases the importance of its own sex-role traits in siblings, so that girl siblings heighten affiliation and conformity in younger siblings (because these are seen as feminine traits) and boy siblings heighten achievement in younger siblings (because these are seen as masculine traits.) These researchers found that in two-child families the boys with brothers had higher masculinity scores, and the girls with sisters had higher femininity scores. In families with three or more children, the results were not quite as straightforward. For cognitive abilities, Koch (1954) found that siblings with brothers were superior to siblings with sisters on verbal meaning and quantitative tests. Sutton-Smith and Rosenberg (1970), however, discovered the reverse effect, finding that female subjects with girl siblings were higher on cognitive abilities than female subjects with male siblings. Other studies showed that birth-order spacing was a crucial variable. In their work, Sutton-Smith and Rosenberg (1970) discovered that males' scores rose as the distance between siblings increased, and females' scores decreased with sibling distance. Koch and others (e.g., Brim 1958; Koch 1957) examined the effects of sibling sex status on interactional style, concluding that such effects can be detected in how often and to what extent boys and girls engage in prosocial behavior.

Contemporary studies of siblings have shifted away from a concern with various global differences, such as birth order and sex status, toward concern with the interactions between young siblings (e.g., Abramovitch, Corter, & Lando 1979; Abramovitch, Corter, & Pepler 1980; Abramovitch, Pepler, & Corter 1982; Lamb 1978). These studies seek to reveal how differences among siblings become manifest in everyday interactions. The importance of such behaviors is in setting the stage for future social development. In terms of methodology, direct observation in the home and school and on the playground has replaced the laboratory and survey methods of earlier research. Interactional studies focus on who initiates fights, what kinds of helping behavior occur, and the presence or absence of imitation. Results appear in the form of rates per hour for each type of behavior.

Abramovitch and her colleagues (1982) found that children with siblings may learn to deal with a full range of behavior, from prosocial to aggressive, whereas children without siblings may be less accustomed to dealing with aggressive behavior from others. Sibling interactions are thus prototypical of interactional styles (fighting, cooperating, etc.) that may become elaborated later in life. Some of these studies contradict earlier findings. For example, Abramovitch and her colleagues found that although sibling interactive styles were very important, sibling differences—in terms of age, sex, and power status—were not strongly predictive of what that style would be.

The most interesting studies are those of Dunn and her colleagues (Dunn 1985, 1988; Dunn & Kendrick 1980, 1982a, 1982b). Dunn does not deny the relevance of accepted variables (age, sex, etc.), but she attempts to show that they are significant for siblings because of their *meanings*. What sense does it make, she argues, to tally up and compare "behaviors" as observed instances of hitting or carrying unless the meaning of these actions can be known for those who participate in them? "The quality of the relationship between siblings will of course be profoundly affected by the extent to which each child perceives and understands others' feelings and intentions" (Dunn & Kendrick 1982a: 100). Dunn argues that the development of abilities is important, but the most important of these abilities are not necessarily cognitive, but emotional and interpersonal. How does the child learn to assimilate the perspective of the other, an ability that depends upon a clear sense of the other as separate from the self? How does the child learn to conceive the situation of another as distinct in character and significance from his or her own? Dunn argues for the importance of the sibling relationship in the development of these abilities, taking for granted, of course, that such abilities are universal and of equal importance everywhere.

"My proposal," Dunn writes, "is that situations of conflict and threatened self-interest are encounters in which the child's growing understanding of the social world is not only revealed by fostered" (1988: 82). She assumes that brothers and sisters compete for limited resources and develop social skills (such as perspective-taking) through the negotiation of competing interests. Yet Dunn's argument emphasizes naturally occurring contexts and meaningful interactions, thus making her work more compelling to an anthroplogist than most developmental studies. Yet the presumption of conflict and the assumed necessity of autonomy is culturally specific, recalling the presumption of sibling rivalry in earlier studies. Cross-cultural developmental work, such as that of Kakar (1981, 1990) in India and Markus and Kitayama (1991) in Japan, casts doubt on the above assumptions. What would psychologists predict in circumstances where sibling competition does not exist or where the value of autonomy is significantly downplayed or even, as in India, viewed as pathologically aberrant? The contributors to this volume seek to answer questions such as this.

It may be useful to summarize the major paradigms that dominate the psychological study of sibling relations. They include:

1. The Status-Power Paradigm (e.g., Sutton-Smith & Rosenberg 1970), with its emphasis on competition for parental favors. This approach focuses on birth order and its effect on sibling rivalry, competitiveness, and adult achievement. The measures used are global assessments derived from experimental observations or survey reports. The goal is to explain the development of adult skills and behaviors.
2. The Interactional Paradigm (e.g., Abramovitch et al., 1982), with its emphasis on concrete observation and quantification of interactive behaviors. This approach retains the emphasis of the Status-Power Paradigm on covarying factors, such as age and sex, but plots them against observable behaviors, such as instances of fighting and helping in nonlaboratory settings. Competition among siblings is assumed. Behaviors are defined implicitly as universal indexes of relational attributes. The goal is to understand the development of adult capacities.
3. The Intersubjective Paradigm (e.g., Dunn & Kendrick, 1982a, 1982b), with its emphasis on perception of self and other, and on the development of skills, such as sharing. This approach emphasizes the development of understanding as an intersubjective process. Competition and cooperation among siblings are assumed to play a crucial and universal role. The development of adult capacities remains an important goal, but these are not limited to the cognitive realm but also include the emotional and the interpersonal.

It should be apparent that sibling research conducted along the lines of all three paradigms concentrates on a limited and culturally specific set of themes. These include status and hierarchy; competition and achievement; conformity and dependency; intelligence and ability. Weisner advocates an expanded focus that is sensitive to cross-cultural differences:

> Now siblings are indeed rivalrous; they often compete fiercely with each other, and age and ordinal position are important for understanding sibling relationships. But these are far from the only important topics. A cross-cultural view suggests a number of aspects seldom considered. (Weisner 1982: 305)

Weisner (1982) argues that phenomena that seem to be universal, such as sibling rivalry, are really outcomes of the ecological context in which families live. In societies where siblings must take care of each other, a stronger emphasis on cooperation and caretaking is found compared to in most Western societies where children assume comparatively fewer such roles. this challenges one of the central tenets of traditional western siblings research, for in the absence of competition and conflict, it is not clear how necessary adult capacities can develop.

Moreover, siblings in many cultures share social obligations throughout their lives. These obligations are not optional and fleeting, as in the United States (Schneider 1980), but obvious and expected role attributes that last for a lifetime (and even beyond, in some cultures). In south India, brothers and sisters practice cross-cousin marriage, that is, arranged marriages between their children. In north India, the explanation of illness and the prediction of future events in traditional medicine must take into account the lives and interests of siblings, so deeply connected are the two. Other important obligations include life crisis and rite of passage ceremonies, mutual support in time of need, formation of political alliances, and the creation of business relationships. These obligations challenge other important Western presuppositions: that development means *child* development and that adult siblings do not play important roles in each other's lives after childhood ends.

The finding that siblings remain closely connected does more than belie the claim that sibling relations (conflictual or cooperative) prepare the way for fully autonomous adult functioning, for "efficacy and control," as Dunn (1988: 176) and others suggest. It challenges the assumption that an autonomous ego is everywhere and for everyone a desirable and worthwhile developmental goal. What are the alternatives? Markus and Kitayama found that the Japanese self is fluid and inclusive, that "others are included within the boundaries of the self" (1991: 61). Ito claims that the Hawaiian self is "highly interpersonal" and based on "the reflexive relationship of Self and Other and on the dynamic bonds of emotional exchange and reciprocity" (1985: 301). Roland describes the Indian self as being "far more relational and situational" (1988: 205). (See also Kakar 1981.) These examples make the point clear that as conceptions of the self vary cross-culturally, so, probably, do conceptions of human development, with possibly significant consequences for sibling relations. In light of this knowledge, we must question the assumed universality of "the urgency of self-assertion" and "driving self-concern" (Dunn 1988: 176).

However, anthropological research on siblings is exceedingly sparse. The little that exists strongly suggests that cross-cultural differences, like those mentioned above, deeply influence many aspects of human development. For example, Weisner and Gallimore (1977) have shown that children of a culture that practices sibling caretaking show a more diffuse affective style and a diffuse pattern of attachment compared to cultures in which children are cared for by adults. Caretaking responsibilities by siblings produce increased social responsibility, increased nurturance, earlier and stronger sex-role identification, and a more task-specific division of labor. "Sib care appears to decrease orientation and involvement with adults, and increases orientation toward a multiage, multisex group of peers and playmates" (Weisner 1982: 311). Of particular interest is the finding that under such circumstances children do not develop the same "negotiated rationalizations" (Weisner's term) that Dunn notes among Western children. There is a less elaborate rehearsal of rules, reasons, rationales, and arguments, and most important, there is less overt conflict—less fighting, less quarreling, less competition. What happens to the development of adult skills such as autonomy, competitiveness, and perspective-taking—skills that many developmental researchers deem vital—when the circumstances thought necessary to their development do not arise?

These are serious issues. Would the field of sibling research even exist as we know it without taking for granted the assumed necessity of developmental autonomy, conflict and cooperation, and sex and birth-order effects? We are left with Sutton-Smith's (1982) question: What is the *meaning* of siblingship? Anthropology's contribution to the study of sibling relations resides in the answers it can provide to this question.

One of the problems with making anthropology relevant to research on siblings is that, up to this point, only one kind of anthropology has been seen as directly relevant to developmental psychology. This is the anthropology of John and Beatrice Whiting and their colleagues at Harvard. The Whitings studied the following correlations: between a child's learning environment, as measured by reported child-training practices, and various projective systems (Whiting & Child 1953); between economy, viewed as ecological adaptation, and children's behavioral styles (Barry, Child, & Bacon 1959); and between household structure, mother–father–child sleeping arrangements, and the development of sexual identity (J. Whiting 1964). The list of research topics follows from a basic theoretical assumption. Cultures are adaptational structures that respond to environmental variations, with concomitant effects on the divison of labor, economy, settlement pattern, social structure, and patterns of child raising and child behavior.

In describing their orientation, the Whitings refer to William Graham Sumner's statement, "Men begin with acts, not with thoughts. Every moment brings necessities which must be satisfied at once. Need was the first experience, and it was followed at once by a blundering effort to satisfy it" (1906; quoted in J. Whiting & B. Whiting 1978: 41). The materialist and evolutionary orientation of the Whitings' approach places primary emphasis on environmental adaptations as processes that shape and constrain cultural forms. That is why observable behavior is so often the focus of their research. Sibling relations and roles, like most of culture, are the outcome of trial-and-error processes that people pursue in order to meet their needs and get the job done.

It should be evident why the Whitings and their associates are so often invoked by developmental psychologists. They share basic assumptions. One of these is the emphasis on constraints and capacities: People have needs; needs vary according to different constraints; structures evolve as organized capacities to meet those needs. As noted above, for developmental psychologists, needs are usually assumed to be universal or very nearly so, including the need to be autonomous, the need to be intelligent, the need to be competitive. Therefore, the psychological study of sibling relations typically focuses on the processes that foster the development of the abilities to meet these needs. The anthropologists of the Whitings' school qualify this in only one fundamental regard, by stressing that needs and the development of abilities to meet them vary in different ecocultural environments. The recognition that cultural differences are important is a significant step forward and one that few psychologist have made. But what developmental psychologists are apt to find most congenial in the Whitings' approach is its reliance on a theory of adaptation. People do things because they have to in order to survive. Such behaviors make sense, whether the people doing them know it or not, and so the explanation for their behavior remains utilitarian. A kind of adaptationalsim, strongly ecological and with a materialist bent, is what makes developmental psychology and Whiting-style psychological anthropology natural allies.

Methodologically, too, there is convergence, since both the developmental psychological and the psychological anthropological studies of sibling relations are correlational. The investigator looks for inputs—adaptations to the environment or to the power and status relations of the nuclear family—and for outputs—pattered behaviors identifiable as ecoculturally or cognitive-developmentally motivated acts. Both the psychologists and the anthropologists whom psychologists cite speak the language of measurement. There is nothing wrong with that. But when only phenomena that *can* be measured, and thus correlated, are defined as data, the role of *meaning* as a phenomenon that itself shapes and constrains behavior gets lost (Schneider 1984). One is left with the behavior, and with whatever environmental influences (universal or cross-culturally variant) are assumed to shape it. While this approach has yielded important insights, it has relegated much of significance to the category of the derived and epiphenomenal, including the ideologies, conceptual systems, unconscious processes, and symbolic frameworks within which sibling relations are embedded.

Are behavioral and symbolic, psychological and anthropological, materialist and culturalist studies of siblings necessarily divergent? Of course not. Both types of approaches direct attention to important aspects of sibling relations. But an integrated approach to ideological and adaptational factors is needed. Weisner (Chapter 1, this volume), Shweder (1991), and Dunn (Afterword, this volume) each makes a case for this type of integration. The development of both cultural patterns and intracultural differences should be examined by reference to both material and symbolic conditions. That such an account has been difficult to come by is as much a result of academic territoriality as of anything else. The contributors to this volume believe that parochialism can be overcome.

Sibling Studies in Social and Cultural Anthropology

Anthropologists have not given much attention to sibling relations. This seems odd, given that anthropologists are well known for their studies of kinship systems. There are three reasons for this. The first is that anthropologists (like most people in the western world) assume that "real" siblings are uterine siblings and that others represent terminological extensions from the uterine categories. People to whom basic kinship categories are extended are called "classificatory," as if they are somehow less real or significant compared to true biologically related kin. Prejudice in favor of Western category structures seriously distorts social reality for those whose kinship categories do not make these distinctions (Schneider 1984).

The second reason anthropologists have ignored sibling relations is that in "primitive" societies, corporate groups whose members refer to each other using sibling terms are assumed to be organized in terms of descent. Kinship studies have long displayed an overt fascination with descent systems, because of their assumed centrality as the creator and maintainer of social solidarity, especially in societies that seem to lack other mechanisms of social control, such as government institutions. Structural-functionalists attributed importance to different kinds of social relations in a kind of hierarchy defined by their functional significance in maintaining descent solidarity. In a patrilineal society, for example, characterized by the extension of the term brother to all those males related to each other in a single generation as descendants of a common ancestor, siblingship was assumed to be important only as a marker of group membership. Otherwise, when measured on the scale of functional significance, it was seen as irrelevant.

Even though descent-centered kinship analyses are no longer the rule, studies of South Asian sibling relations continued until very recently to concentrate on patterns of succession and inheritance, residence and authority, as structures contingent on patterns of descent (e.g., Gough 1956; Kapadia 1966; Shah 1974; Von Ehrenfels 1974). Studies of the Hindu joint family, for example, still focus on the relationship between brothers as it reflects patterns of authority and residency within the extended family, and on how disruption of the fraternal bond affects lineage structure and patterns of alliance. More attention has been given to links between generations than within generations, except insofar as they have a direct bearing on succession. Only recently have there been signs of a change, as in Bennett's (1983) study of brothers and sisters in Nepal.

The nature of sibling relations in white middle-class America provides a third reason sibling relations do not stand out for anthropologists. Because Americans do not put much emphasis on sibling relationships, they tacitly assume that no one does. It is the marital and the parent–child bonds, not the relationship between siblings, which are normatively important in America. While recent work by Dunn, Bank, and Cicirelli now challenges this view (see Bank & Kahn 1982; Cicirelli 1982; Dun 1985), the popular conception remains that, for Americans at least, siblings are just not very important to each other.

Compared to other cultures, the American indifference to sibling relationships is nothing less than extraordinary. South Asian villagers, who frequently inquire about the siblings of their visitors, typically express shock when confronted with answers like "I don't know" or "I haven't seen my brother/sister for years." For Americans in general—and for American anthropologists in particular—sibling relations just do not show up on their social radar. They may be there, but their significance is not easily acknowledged or appreciated.

In a slowly developing but noticeable trend, anthropologists studying other world areas have begun to turn their attention to siblings. The contributors to a recent collection on siblingship in lowland South America found that the relationship between siblings provides the conceptual framework for all social space, from the individual community to the wider formation of descent groupings at all levels (Kensinger 1985). According to Shapiro, "rituals, myths, and the general body of cultural knowledge relating to sib and phratic organization reveal that vertical, or temporal, reckoning is less concerned with the genealogical ordering of successive generations than with connecting living sibling groups to the ancestral sibling sets with which society originated" (1985: 4). Similar findings are reported from Oceania, where, according to Marshall (1983), siblings relations are "analytically primary" over all others, including the parent–child, nuclear family tie. Indeed, Weisner goes so far as to suggest that in some Pacific Island cultures, sibling relationships are "a metaphor for how the entire culture should be organized, what cultural ideals are worth pursuing, and the ways in which one's self and one's community should be reproduced" (Weisner 1989: 17).

That anthropologists of South America and Oceania only recently turned their attention to siblingship is attributable, at least in part, to the preoccupation among anthropologists with rules of descent, and also, among South Americanists, to the looming presence of Levi-Strauss, whose work on South American kinship strongly emphasized generational and marriage structures. Nevertheless, anthropologists of South America and Oceania have done much to look beyond the descent-centered studies of the past. Significantly, they have found that sibling relations are important at every level of social organization, perhaps (some have argued) constituting "the core symbols" and "conceptual model" of social relations in these societies (see Kelly 1985: 42; Marshall 1983: 10–13).

That anthropology can make us question our basic assumptions has led us to radical reformulations in areas from the structures of kinship to the epistemology of knowledge. Our work in this volume has followed a similar progression. We have learned that sibling relations in South Asia are important. Our own cultural framework, however, gets in the way, and so we have had to develop ways both to see past it and, more constructively, to use it as a research tool. The results are classically anthropological: First, they help us to understand something new, and thus add in some way to the accumulated knowledge about different cultures; and second, they help us to develop new ways of understanding ourselves as culture-bearing individuals.

Orientalism and the Study of Sibling Relations

The anthropology of South Asia consists of issues common to anthropology, and of other, more narrowly circumscribed issues, that long ago became signature attributes of the anthropology of South Asia. The latter includes the enduring influence of Indian Orientalism that is at least partly reducible to the "great tradition" of Sanskrit texts that for two centuries provided the principal lens through which scholars viewed South Asian cultures. In earlier work, ancient texts were used as maps or blueprints (Basham 1954). Social realities that did not match were either ignored or dismissed as elaborations, departures, or corruptions of textual archetypes.

The effect of Indian Orientalism on the study of South Asian siblingship has been mixed. On the one hand, studies of India's textual traditions have called attention to the famous accounts of brothers and sisters. The first and most important impression of India for many scholars comes through reading about the Pandava brothers in the *Mahabharata* or of Rama and Laksmana in the *Ramayana,* two of India's most revered and most widely known classical epics. In many ethnographies, references are found to villagers who compare themselves to these figures as representatives of a normative ideal: Good brothers, it is said, should be like Rama and Laksmana. On the other hand, there have been few attempts to develop a picture of sibling relations as they occur in real communities, or to examine to what extent mythic models mediate the lived experience of real siblings. More often, siblingship is subsumed within symbolic systems elicited from textual sources. This has produced important insights, yet the exigent qualities of sibling relations as they are experienced and understood by real people remain obscure.

Plan of This Volume

Perhaps it will be objected that to consider sibling relations by themselves is to commit, as Kolenda (Chapter 5) has put it, "an anthropological sin." Is it not inappropriate to take out of context a topic that properly belongs to the discussion of South Asian kinship systems and conceptual structures? None of the contributors believes that sibling relations can be discussed outside their relevant contexts. What Schneider said in his commentary on another book applies just as much to this one: "The contributors to this book attempt to treat siblingship not as a well established, clear-cut, universal category, but rather as a question to be put to each culture to be answered in that culture's own terms" (1981: 392).

The degree to which we focus on sibling relations, and the manner in which we do so, are issues determined largely by context. In this volume, there is considerable diversity in the contexts we deem most relevant: marriage organization, patterns of socialization, economic maximization, social strategies and conflict resolution, and ethnopsychology. Theoretical positions and methodological strategies also differ, from purely structural accounts to fine-grained psychocultural case studies. Common to all, however, is the finding that siblings are important.

The main part of this volume is organized in two parts. The first part "Siblings, Social Structures, and Patterns of Socialization," containing chapters by Seymour, Beals and Eason, Kolenda, and de Munck, focuses on the organization of sibling relations in childhood and adulthood. The second part, "Siblings in Myth, Religion, and Ethnopsychology," containing chapters by Derné, Nuckolls, and Pugh, focuses on the ambiguities of sibling relations and their realization and representation in diverse cultural registers, including mythology, astrology, and life history. An afterword by Dunn, which reviews this volume's contribution to the developmental literature, follows. Some readers may discern in this organization a grouping of the chapters into sociocultural and psychocultural segments, the first devoted to matters traditionally termed "social organization and socialization" the second to matters traditionally termed "personality and culture." To some extent this is true. Yet there is much overlap, due in part to our agreement that both approaches need each other. Where we contributors differ most is in the kind of research context we have chosen to study.

To introduce more fully the approaches we take to the study of sibling relations in South Asia, consider the implications of choosing different research contexts.

If we construct the relevant context as socialization, then sibling relations are important in the process of development, especially in places like South Asia, where older siblings, rather than parents, function as primary caretakers. Seymour's longitudinal study of childhood interaction and socialization in a rapidly changing Indian city

(Chapter 3) starts from the work of Lamb and Sutton-Smith (1982) and Dunn and Kendrick (1982a). Seymour finds that siblings in India can be affectionate, rivalrous, playful, nurturing—just as they can be in the West. But there is a difference. Due to the very different sociocultural contexts in which South Asian siblings develop and the very different adult roles they must assume, the balance of behaviors is not the same. The cultural ideal of long-term fraternal solidarity is encouraged, while rivalry between siblings is frowned upon and viewed as aberrant. As Seymour points out, this does not mean that one mode of interaction exists and the other does not, but that cultural norms and socialization practices enhance one and mute the other. Seymour traces variations in these norms and practices as they relate to the development of fraternal, cross-sex, and sororal relationships. Both community status (judged in terms of caste rank and occupational background) and household structure (joint or nuclear) are highly influential. Because she has been working in the same location and among the same people for 25 years, Seymour (unlike most anthropologists) is able to assess the ways sibling relations are changing in response to the rapid urbanization and cosmopolitanization of the Indian city.

Beals and Eason (Chapter 4) start from a similar interest in comparative socialization practices. They ask about the norms that govern sibling interaction in Indian and North American families, and then, using observational data of sibling interactions coded for interaction type and duration, they compare relations between siblings in a south Indian village and a Canadian city. They find startling differences between North American and South Asian patterns. Fraternal relations in the two are virtually mirror images of each other since brothers in India fight and quarrel much less. The authors suggest that North American children might be compelled by their competitive society to *repress* a natural tendency toward harmony.

If we construct the relevant context as marriage organization, then sibling relations, because they vary systematically with marriage rules, reveal important variations among the societies of north, central, and south India. In north India, for example, marriage alliances are widely dispersed. The strong brother-sister relationship that prevails throughout the region accords with widespread concern for the welfare of married sisters who marry into different villages. While brothers remain geographically close, brothers and sisters in this region may see each other only occasionally. Sisters, who usually marry into different villages, may see each rarely or not at all. In central India, the marriage of related women (often sisters) to men of the same village and even the same family is common. Therefore, the bond between sisters is likely to be strong. Brothers are close, as in the north, but the brother–sister relationship is not especially important. By contrast, in south India, the children of brothers and sisters are expected to marry in a pattern anthropologists call "cross-cousin." In general, the partners in such cross-cousin marriages are from the same place and have lived in close proximity to each other from childhood on. This means that there is a special relationship between siblings whose children are normatively expected to marry. In general, the relationship between brothers is important, but that between sisters is not.

Kolenda believes that it is possible to predict from marriage rules and patterns of residency some of the norms that govern sibling relations in South Asia. In her contribution to this volume (Chapter 5), she approaches the study of sibling relations from this perspective, and provides an encompassing comparative framework for the interpretation of South Asian siblingship.

If we construct the relevant context as economic organization, then sibling relations emerge as strongly determinative of resource management and control. This is most evident in the property exchange that is, for South Asian families, the largest and most important they ever make: the dowry. The dowry can be understood as an investment in the future of a daughter-sister, one that is or is not realized depending on the outcome of the marriage that is made. In some places, dowries are large, sometimes amounting to the equivalent of several years' accumulated income, but in other places they are small or even nonexistent. The greater the dowry, the greater the brother's stake in his sister's family and the more likely their pattern of interaction will conform to the norms of reciprocity that, in some places, govern the cross-sibling bond. The lower the value of the dowry, the lower the brother's stake in his sister and the less likely their interaction would accord with such norms.

In his study of cross-sibling relations in a Sri Lankan Muslim community, de Munck (Chapter 6) shows that economic decisions centering on the dowry are crucial as determinants of cross-sibling interaction and involvement. His results support the view that marriage and siblingship are strongly connected as institutions, confirming what Weisner (1982) has described as an interesting correlation.

If we construct the relevant context as psychosocial, then sibling relations are important as contexts for emotional development and individual fulfillment. For example, where brothers are expected to remain close, tied together through the multiple bonds of joint-family life, how do they balance their individual needs against the needs of the fraternal group? Or, where brothers and sisters are obligated to render mutual support even after their marriages, how do individuals adjust to the competing demands of marital and cross-sibling obligations? In this study of fraternal relations in Benares (north India), Derné (Chapter 7) addresses the first dilemma. He asks to what extent the dominant north Indian ideology of fraternal solidarity is affected by potentially competing ideologies of hierarchy and equality. He focuses on how brothers negotiate the problems that arise in this context, showing that in many instances brothers are frustrated and ambivalent in their relationships with each other.

Nuckolls (Chapter 8) examines the second dilemma and finds that brothers and sisters in a south Indian fishing village struggle against normative demands to fulfill strongly felt dependency needs for each other. This results in an ambivalence for which goddess myths provide a partial resolution. Stories about the origin of the goddesses—in which mythic sisters are transformed into goddesses and brothers into devotees—provide resolutions by acknowledging such needs and satisfying them in a culturally legitimate register. Strong emotions can be resolved through the transactive language of worship in a context outside the ambivalence-generating domain of the normative sibling relationship.

If we construct the relevant context as ethnopsychological, then here, too, sibling relations emerge as important determinants of experience. Hindu astrology is an ethnospychological system in which the exigencies of everyday sibling relations are plotted onto the horoscopically constructed map of individual and family development. Magic also makes sibling relations relevant, since it is often through siblings that magical effects are transmitted and felt. Therefore, astrologers, diviners, and other magicoreligious specialists pay special attention to sibling relations as crucial determinants of success anf failure. Pugh (Chapter 9), in her study of brothers in the city of Benares, examines sibling relations from this perspective providing an interesting point of comparison and a contrast to Derné's study of the same north Indian community.

The contributors to this volume interpret sibling relations in different contexts, which each contribution defines as most relevant to his or her study. What some might view as wide theoretical divergence, however, we see as yet another indication that no matter from which theoretical angle the subject is viewed, sibling relations inevitably emerge as vitally important to the understanding of social life and individual development in South Asia.

In addition to all of the culturally specific factors just mentioned, there are reasons why siblings anywhere—no matter what their position structurally—need greater analytic attention. Siblings spend a great deal of time together, at least during the period of greatest dependency, and thus during critical developmental stages. In South Asia, the importance of this is recognized; siblings (especially those of the same sex) are assumed to be more like each other than different. In the West, the opposite holds true. Americans typically deny that they are like their siblings. Does that mean that the South Asians are seeing something that we overlook? Or could it mean, by virtue of our individualist ideology, that we undo a tendency to similarity among siblings that would otherwise seem inevitable?

These are mere speculations of course. The significance of siblings to the understanding of South Asian cultures does not depend on our answers to such questions. In the end, what makes siblings in South Asia important is quite simply the fact that South Asians tell us that they are. As anthropologists (or psychologists) we have an obligation to listen to what our informants (or subjects) keep telling us.

References

Abramovitch, R., Corter, C., & Lando, B. (1979). "Sibling Interaction in the Home." *Child Development* 50: 997–1003.

Abramovitch, R., Corter, C., & Pepler, D. (1980). "Observation of Mixed-Sex Sibling Dyads." *Child Development* 51: 1268–71.

Abramovitch, R., Pepler, D., & Corter, C. (1982). Patterns of Sibling Interaction among Preschool-age Children. In M. E. Lamb & B. Sutton-Smith (Eds.), *Sibling Relationships: Their Nature and Significance across the Lifespan* (pp. 87–123). Hillsdale, NJ: Erlbaum.

Adler, A. (1924). *The Practice and Theory of Individual Psychology.* New York: Harcourt, Brace.

Bank, S., & Kahn, M. (1982). Intense Sibling Loyalties. In M. E. Lamb & B. Sutton-Smith (Eds.), *Sibling Relations: Their Nature and Significance across the Lifespan* (pp. 251–67). Hillsdale, NJ: Erlbaum.

Barry, H., III, Child, I., & Bacon, M. (1959). "Relation of Child Training to Subsistence Economy." *American Anthropologist* 61: 51–63.

Basham, A. (1954). *The Wonder That Was India.* London: Fontana.

Basso, E. (1985). Comment on *Siblingship in Lowland South America.* In K. Kensinger (Ed.), *The Sibling Relation in Lowland South America* (pp. 46–9). Working Papers on South American Indians, no. 7. Bennington, VT: Bennington College.

Bennett, L. (1983). *Dangerous Wives and Sacred Sisters.* New York: Columbia University Press.

Brim, O. (1958). "Family Structure and Sex Role Learning by Children." *Sociometry* 21: 1–16.

Chernela, J. (1985). The Sibling Relationship among the Uanano of the Northwest Amazon: The Case of Nicho. In K. Kensinger (Ed.), *The Sibling Relation in Lowland South America* (pp. 33–41). Working Papers on South American Indians, no. 7. Bennington, VT: Bennington College.

Cicirelli, V. (1982). Sibling Influence throughout the Lifespan. In M. E. Lamb & B. Sutton-Smith (Eds.), *Sibling Relationships: Their Nature and Significance across the Lifespan* (pp. 267–84). Hillsdale, NJ: Erlbaum.

Dunn, J. (1985). *Sisters and Brothers.* Cambridge, MA: Harvard University Press.

Dunn, J. (1988). *The Beginnings of Social Understanding.* Oxford: Blackwell.

Dunn, J., & Kendrick, C. (1980). "The Arrival of a Sibling: Changes in Patterns of Interactions between Mother and First-Born Child." *Journal of Child Psychology and Psychiatry* 21: 119–32.

Dunn, J., & Kendrick, C. (1982a). *Siblings: Love, Envy, and Understanding.* Cambridge, MA: Harvard University Press.

Dunn, J., & Kendrick, C. (1982b). Siblings and Their Mothers: Developing Relationships within the Family. In M. E. Lamb & B. Sutton-Smith (Eds.), *Sibling Relationships: Their Nature and Significance across the Lifespan* (pp. 39–61). Hillsdale, NJ: Erlbaum.

Feinberg, R. (1981). The Meaning of "Sibling" in Anuta. In M. Marshall (Ed.), *Siblingship in Oceania* (pp. 105–49). Ann Arbor: University of Michigan Press.

Goodale, J. (1981). Siblings as Spouses: The Reproduction and Replacement of Kaulong Society. In M. Marshall (Ed.), *Siblingship in Oceania* (pp. 225–302). Ann Arbor: University of Michigan Press.

Gough, E. (1956). "Brahman Kinship in a Tamil Village." *American Anthropologist* 58: 826–49.

Harkness, S., & Super, C. (1985). Child-Environment Interactions in the Socialization of Affect. In M. Lewis & C. Saarni (Eds.), *The Socialization of Emotions* (pp. 21–37). New York: Plenum Press.

Hecht, J. (1981). The Cultural Contexts of Siblingship in Pukapuka. In M. Marshall (Ed.), *Siblingship in Oceania* (pp. 53–79). Ann Arbor: University of Michigan Press.

Huntsman, J. (1981). Complementary and Similar Kinsmen in Tokelau. In M. Marshall (Ed.), *Siblingship in Oceania* (pp. 79–105). Ann Arbor: University of Michigan Press.

Ito, K. (1985). Affective Bonds: Hawaiian Interrelationships of Self. In G. White & J. Kirkpatrick (Eds.), *Person, Self, and Experience* (pp. 301–28). Berkeley: University of California Press.

Kakar, S. (1981). *The Inner World: A Psychoanalytic Inquiry into Childhood and Society in India* (2nd ed.). Delhi: Oxford University Press.

Kakar, S. (1990). *Intimate Relations: Exploring Indian Sexuality.* New Delhi: Viking.

Kapadia, K. (1966). *Marriage and Family in India.* Bombay: Oxford University Press.

Kelly, R. (1985). Sibling Relations in Lowland South America: A Commentary on Symposium Papers. In K. Kensinger (Ed.), *The Sibling Relation in Lowland South America* (pp. 41–6). Working Papers on South American Indians, no. 7. Bennington, VT: Bennington College.

Kensinger, K. (Ed.). (1985). *The Sibling Relation in Lowland South America.* Working Papers on South American Indians, no. 7. Bennington, VT: Bennington College.

Kirkpatrick, J. (1981). Meanings of Siblingship in Marquesan Society. In M. Marshall (Ed.), *Siblingship in Oceania* (pp. 17–53). Ann Arbor: University of Michigan Press.

Koch, J. (1954). "The Relation of Primary Mental Abilities in Five- and Six-Year-Olds to Sex of Child and Characteristics of His Sibling." *Child Development* 26: 13–40.

Koch, J. (1957). "The Relation in Young Children between Characteristics of Their Playmates and Certain Attributes of Their Siblings." *Child Development* 28: 175–201.

Lamb, M. E. (1978). "The Development of Sibling Relationships in Infancy: A Short-Termed Longitudinal Study." *Child Development* 49: 1189–96.

Lamb, M. E., & Sutton-Smith, B. (Eds.). (1982). *Sibling Relationships: Their Nature and Significance across the Lifespan.* Hillsdale, NJ: Erlbaum.

Lambert, B. (1981). Authority, Equality and Complementarity in Butaritari-Makin Sibling Relationship. In M. Marshall (Ed.), *Siblingship in Oceania* (pp. 149–201). Ann Arbor: University of Michigan Press.

Levy, D. (1937). "Studies in Sibling Rivalry." Research Monograph no. 2. American Orthopsychiatric Association.

Mahler, M. Pine, F., & Bergman, A. (1975). *The Psychological Birth of the Human Infant.* New York: Basic Books.

Markus, H., & Kitayama, S. (1991). "Culture and the Self: Implications for Cognition, Emotion, and Motivation." *Psychological Review* 98: 224–53.

Marshall, M. (Ed.). (1983). *Siblingship in Oceania.* Ann Arbor: University of Michigan Press.

McKinley, R. (1981). Cain and Abel on the Malay Peninsula. In M. Marshall (Ed.), *Siblingship in Oceania* (pp. 335–89). Ann Arbor: University of Michigan Press.

Ostor, A., Fruzetti, L., & Barnett, S. (Eds.). (1982). *Concepts of Person: Kinship, Caste, and Marriage in India.* Cambridge, MA: Harvard University Press.

Pollock, D. (1985). Looking for a Sister: Culina Siblingship and Affinity. In K. Kensinger (Ed.), *The Sibling Relation in Lowland South America* (pp. 8–16). Working Papers on South American Indians, no. 7. Bennington, VT: Bennington College.

Price, D. (1985). Nambiquara Brothers. In K. Kensinger (Ed.), *The Sibling Relation in Lowland South America* (pp. 16–20). Working Papers on South American Indians, no. 7. Bennington, VT: Bennington College.

Roland, A. (1988). *In Search of Self in India and Japan: Toward a Cross-cultural Psychology.* Princeton: Princeton University Press.

Ross, B. (1930). "Some Traits Associated with Sibling Jealousy in Problem Children." *Smith College Studies in Social Work* 1: 364–76.

Schneider, D. (1980). *American Kinship: A Cultural Account* (2nd ed.). Chicago: University of Chicago Press.

Schneider, D. (1983). Conclusions. In M. Marshall (Ed.), *Siblingship in Oceania* (pp. 389–404). Ann Arbor: University of Michigan Press.

Schneider, D. (1989). *Critique of the Study of Kinship.* Ann Arbor: University of Michigan Press.

Shah, A. (1974). *The Household Dimension of the Family in India.* Berkeley: University of California Press.

Shapiro, J. (1985). The Sibling Relationship in Lowland South America: General Considerations. In K. Kensinger (Ed.), *The Sibling Relation in Lowland South America* (pp. 1–8). Working Papers on South American Indians, no. 7. Bennington, VT: Bennington College.

Shweder, R. (1990). *Thinking through Cultures.* Cambridge, MA: Harvard University Press.

Smally, R. (1930). "The Influences of Differences in Age, Sex, and Intelligence in Determining Attitudes of Siblings towards Each Other." *Smith College Studies in Social Work* 1: 6–20.

Smith, D. (1983). Palauan Siblingship: A Study in Structural Complementarity. In M. Marshall (Ed.), *Siblingship in Oceania* (pp. 225–75). Ann Arbor: University of Michigan Press.

Spock, B. (1957). *Baby and Child Care.* New York: Cardinal Pocketbooks.

Sutton-Smith, B. (1982). Epilogue. In M. E. Lamb & B. Sutton-Smith (Eds.), *Sibling Relationships: Their Nature and Significance across the Lifespan* (pp. 383–87). Hillsdale, NJ: Erlbaum.

Sutton-Smith, B., & Rosenberg, B. (1970). *The Sibling.* New York: Holt, Rinehart & Winston.

van der Veen, K. (1971). *I Give Thee My Daughter: A Study of Marriage and Hierarchy among the Anavil Brahmans of South Gujarat.* Assen: Van Gorcum.

Weisner, T. (1982). Sibling Interdependence and Child Caretaking: A Cross-cultural View. In M. E. Lamb & B. Sutton-Smith (Eds.), *Sibling Relationships: Their Nature and Significance across the Lifespan* (pp. 305–29). Hillsdale, NJ: Erlbaum.

Weisner, T. (1989). Comparing Sibling Relationships Across Cultures. In P. Zukow (Ed.), *Sibling Interaction Across Cultures* (pp. 11–25). New York: Springer-Verlag.

Weisner, T., & Gallimore, R. (1977). "My Brother's Keeper: Child and Sibling Caretaking." *Current Anthropology* 18: 169–91.

Whiting, B. (Ed.). (1963). *Six Cultures: Studies of Child Rearing.* New York: Wiley.

Whiting, J. (1964). Effects of Climate on Certain Cultural Practices. In W. Goodenough (Ed.), *Explorations in Cultural Anthropology: Essays in Honor of George Peter Murdock* (pp. 511–45). New York: McGraw-Hill.

Whiting, J., & Child, I. (1953). *Child Training and Personality: A Cross-cultural Study*. New Haven: Yale University Press.

Whiting, J., & Whiting, B. (1978). A Strategy for Psychocultural Research. In G. Spindler & L. Spindler (Eds.), *The Making of Psychological Anthropology* (pp. 41–61). Berkeley: University of California Press.

PART ONE

SIBLINGS, SOCIAL STRUCTURES, AND PATTERNS OF SOCIALIZATION

Photo by Susan Seymour

CHAPTER 3

Sociocultural Contexts
Examining Sibling Roles in South Asia

Susan Seymour

South Asia provides a rich set of sociocultural contexts in which to examine sibling roles—contexts that are strikingly different from those in the United States, where most of the existing sibling studies have been undertaken. By "sociocultural contexts" I refer to both the different settings in which sibling ties first develop and are later expressed in adult roles and also to the relevant ideology guiding that development. What kinds of relationships, for example, do brothers in South Asia have, and how are these different from the relationships of sisters, or of brothers and sisters? What cultural expectations and structural factors help to guide the development of these different relationships? How successful are they when measured by their children's adult behavior? Trying to address such questions is ambitious but consistent with the direction that Lamb and Sutton-Smith (1982: 1) argue sibling studies should be and are moving, that is, away from examining just effects toward a greater focus on formative processes, including an increased concern with cultural diversity and with development across the life span.

Sibling studies usually begin with the family, the principal context in which siblings first interact and begin to learn culturally appropriate roles. Whereas studies of siblings in the United States usually assume a nuclear family setting, the ideal type family in South Asia is a patrilineally extended one. This one factor alone has many implications for sibling roles and relationships both in childhood and adulthood. First, drawing on some of the research presented in this volume, together with selections from the general ethnographic literature, I shall try to identify some of the more critical sociocultural contexts and associated ideals that affect the development of sibling roles in South Asia. I will then examine some of these factors within the specific setting of one Indian town, an area in which I have been doing fieldwork for the past 25 years.

The Patrilineal, Patrilocal Joint Family

As Kolenda (Chapter 5, this volume), rightly points out, "To write about sibling relationships . . . outside the entire kinship system . . . is to commit an anthropological sin: taking relationships out of context." Quite appropriately, Mandelbaum (1970), in his landmark synthesis of Indian ethnology, embeds his discussion of sibling ties in six chapters that describe kinship and family relations in India. He begins with the following description of the ideal patrilineal joint family: "The common ideal is that of filial and fraternal solidarity, which prescribes that brothers should remain together in the parental household after they marry, sharing equally in one purse and in common property, helping each other according to need and each giving according to his best abilities" (1970: 34). Citing the 12th-century Hindu text *Mitakshara*, Mandelbaum points out that Hindu law entitled all males at birth to an equal share in family property, and hence all brothers were coparceners. Sisters, by contrast, were entitled to maintenance by male kin but had no vested rights in family property (1970: 35).

The Priority of Fraternal Ties

This model of family structure and inheritance rights has many implications for sibling relationships in South Asia. First of all, long-term fraternal solidarity is assumed and is considered a symbol of family honor. Brothers are expected to grow up together, marry, and continue to reside harmoniously in the same extended household with their parents and their respective wives and children. Ideally, all of these family members constitute one social and economic unit in which everything is shared equally. The long-term nature of fraternal relationships is, therefore, quite different from soronal ones, or from brother–sister ones. Furthermore, the context of growing up is not just with one's siblings but also with one's patrilateral first cousins, who are generally referred to in Indian kinship terminologies as "brothers" and "sisters." Thus, one's potential sibling ties are extended well beyond those recognized in the predominant American kinship system. Finally, this family model implies that brothers, even as adults, should continue to reside with their parents. They are not autonomous individuals, nor should they be, and they may not acquire much authority within the family until the death of their father.

The same system that gives preeminence to brothers as the persons through whom descent is traced, who inherit property, and who should reside together, also places a special burden on them. Mandelbaum recognized this when he subtitled his discussion of fraternal ties "Partners and Sometimes Rivals" (1970: 63). He captured here the tension between the ideal of fraternal solidarity, on the one hand, and the day-to-day potential for conflict, on the other. And he identified one of the factors that can produce tension and conflict between brothers—namely, the hierarchical system that crosscuts the concept of fraternal equally (see Derné, Chapter 7, this volume). Older brothers have authority over younger brothers, and such authority is critical at the time of a father's death when the oldest brother assumes the role of household head.

It is this institutionalized tension between fraternal equality and hierarchy that both Pugh's and Derné's research help to illuminate. For example, in Pugh's ethnopsychological analysis of astrological texts (Chapter 9, this volume), the concepts of "love" and "cooperation," on the one hand, and "hostility" and "conflict," on the other, co-occur in the description of brothers. Similarly, Derné's interviews with upper-caste men in Benares (Chapter 7, this volume) provide rich and personal insights into the nature of joint-family living and fraternal cooperation, on the one hand, and the inevitability of conflict, on the other. Derné's informants support Mandelbaum's (1970) contention that paternal authority is crucial to the maintenance of fraternal harmony. When a father is alive and in charge, fraternal equality can flourish because all sons are equal before him. However, when the father dies, the age hierarchy becomes predominant as the oldest brother assumes authority over younger brothers and their wives and children. It is this potential conflict between feelings of fraternal equality and the reality of hierarchy, it is suggested, that often leads to the dissolution of the joint family.

Brother–Sister Ties

In Mandelbaum's model of the joint family, which is more characteristic of north India and Nepal than of south India and Sri Lanka, brother–sister relationships are described as "stable, durable, and affectionate" in contrast with fraternal ones (1970: 67). Because sisters marry out of their natal family and because by tradition they do not inherit property, their relationship with brothers is characterized as nonrivalrous. As adults, sisters and brothers do not have to cooperate on a daily basis, nor will they potentially quarrel over the division of property at the time of their father's death. Although ever since the Hindu Succession Act of 1956, Hindu women have had the legal right of inheritance, in practice they rarely assert this right because it would put them in a rivalrous position with their brothers (Jeffrey 1979: 56, 166; Mandelbaum 1988: 46; Sharma 1980: 47–59). As one village man put it:

> If a brother and sister are on good terms, then the sister will not take her share. She will tell her brother that she does not want her share of the inheritance. After all, if he eats, then she can eat (i.e., the sister will benefit by the brother's prosperity as he will then help her). (reported in Sharma 1980: 57)

In north India, where rules of village exogamy and patrilocality isolate married sisters from their natal kin (see Kolenda, Chapter 5, this volume), a brother is viewed as a woman's distant guardian and benefactor. He represents the warmth and security of childhood that existed before her marriage into a household of strangers, and only if the sibling relationship remains amicable will she be able to return home for visits or be taken in should trouble emerge in her marriage. Thus, sisters are dependent on their brothers for the maintenance of social and ritual ties with the natal kin—a dependence that reflects women's more vulnerable and, in general, lesser status in much of South Asia.

The inequality of brothers and sisters, already marked at birth by the greater celebration of sons than of daughters, is somewhat mitigated in north India and Nepal by the belief that sisters represent the patriline's most sacred gift, that is, the gift of a virgin daughter or *kanyadan* in marriage to another patriline (Bennett 1983; Fruzzetti 1982). Moreover, a sister is believed to bring her brother long life, a belief that is ritualized in the annual rites of *Bhai Tika*, or *Raksha Bandhan*, when sisters bless and ritually protect their brothers (Bennett 1983: 246–52; Goody 1990: 222–23). Reciprocally, brothers are supposed to give their sisters gifts. Generous gift-giving, especially to a married sister and her children, is a means of acquiring both personal merit and family honor (Mandelbaum 1988: 24).

This characterization of the brother–sister tie as unequal but relatively "stable, durable, and affectionate" (Mandelbaum 1970: 67) is less applicable to much of south India and Sri Lanka, where patrilineality is combined with cross-cousin marriage and women's rights to property. Here, where sisters do not marry so distantly and may have a direct share in the patrimony, the brother–sister tie carries more potential for conflict. De Munck (Chapter 6, this volume), in his analysis of brother-sister relations in a Sri Lankan village, makes reference to conflict and ambivalence despite villagers' public views that the brother-sister bond is "enduring, affectionate and complementary." He makes the point that, unlike in north India where brother-sister relationships are manifested predominantly in "symbolic and affective displays," in south India and Sri Lanka they have a significant economic component: Brothers and sisters may share property and even exchange children in marriage—investments that can both bind them more closely together and produce serious conflict.

In the Telugu fishing village described by Nuckolls (Chapter 8, this volume; see also Nuckolls 1991a, 1991b, 1991c, 1992), sisters are their brothers' favored partners in trading, and thus sisters are likely to be in competition with members of their brothers' families (especially their wives) for assistance and support. This struggle between a brother's economic relationship with his sister, on the one hand, and his socioeconomic ties with the members of his patrilineage, on the other, can lead to divisiveness within the joint family. Nevertheless, for villagers the ideal remains one of harmony—both between brothers and between sisters and brothers—even in the face of family dissolution. Myth, Nuckolls demonstrates, helps to resolve the culturally induced ambivalence that conflicting sibling obligations create, so that a pretense of family harmony and cooperation can be maintained.

While the ideal in South Asia is for brother-sister ties to be durable, harmonious, and affectionate, this ideal is more easily realized in the north where, after marriage, sisters are geographically distant from brothers and do not compete with them for a share in the family patrimony. In the south, by contrast, where ideally sisters marry close kinsmen, sisters are geographically less distant from their brothers. They participate economically with their brothers in their father's patrilineage. Relationships can thus become less harmonious and more rivalrous. In such contexts, mixed feelings of love, solidarity, and ambivalence emerge that sound similar to those reported for fraternal relationships in the north.

Ties of Sisterhood

Interestingly, sororal relationships have generally been overlooked in the literature on South Asia. In Mandelbaum's synthesis (1970), for example, all male and female relationships are discussed *except* for that of sister to sister. Suggestively, however, there is mention of sisters-in-law. And the triangular relationship of brother-sister-brother's wife is alluded to in several of the chapters of this volume.

The reason for this oversight is that in a patrilineal kinship system, there is no formal place for ties of sisterhood. From the perspective of the patrilineage, women either marry in or marry out. Thus, daughters of the patrilineage disperse at the time of marriage and maintain ties with their natal kin through brothers. Only in instances where sets of brothers marry sets of sisters (see Kolenda, Chapter 5, this volume) is there a structural context for long-term sororal ties. Most of the literature, therefore, focuses *not* on consanguineal ties of sisterhood but on affinal ties of sisterhood.

When a woman enters her husband's family at the time of marriage, she is provided with a whole new set of relationships, including ones that can be loosely designated "sororal" (i.e., husband's sisters and husband's brother's wives) and the one with her mother-in-law. These are the women with whom she must learn to cooperate from day to day. As Roy notes:

> With her older sisters-in-law, who have already reached positions of higher authority because of their age and seniority, she has a somewhat distant relationship. Ideally, the older sisters-in-law are like her own sisters. In practice, she feels tinges of jealousy toward some of them, particularly if one of them happens to be close to her husband or close to the mother-in-law. There is also a subtle competition involved among these women because of their different backgrounds and looks. . . . Her relationship with her younger sisters-in-law (husband's brother's wives who are close to her age, and the husband's unmarried sisters) is usually one of friendship and cordiality. But there may be some tension involved because of her relationship with the unmarried sisters of the husband, particularly if he is close to them. (Roy 1975: 103–4)

There is an age hierarchy among sisters-in-law that parallels that of brothers and can produce feelings both of solidarity and tension. These affinal ties of sisterhood are also affected by brother–sister ties. A husband's undue attention to his unmarried sisters may produce feelings of rivalry in his wife. And when he provides his married sisters with gifts, he may be accused of taking money away from his own wife and children. As Kolenda (Chapter 5, this volume) notes, a jealous wife can then make life miserable for her sister-in-law when she returns to her natal home: "the loving relationship between brother and sister may be made ambivalent by the brother's wife's less-than-welcoming ways toward her husband's married sister" (p. 123).

Thus, for structural reasons, the South Asian literature focuses on affinal ties of sisterhood and neglects consanguineal ones. In subsequent sections of this chapter, I shall try to correct this deficit some by describing relationships among sisters as I have observed them in one part of India.

The Socialization of Sibling Ties

> First let us try to *explain* in general what is going on, rather than arrive at some fairly reliable covariances between this variable and that variable without much sense of what it all means. What are the day-by-day events that are different for brothers and for sisters with brothers or sisters? What do grandparents, aunts, and uncles do; what do they say? . . . How do kinship systems . . . have an impact on the immediate relationships of siblings? How are sex roles as defined by such groups . . . operative in affecting the day to day interactions of siblings? (Lamb & Sutton-Smith 1982: 386)

Having identified some of the broad sociocultural contexts relevant to the construction and operation of sibling roles in South Asia, in this section I want to examine more closely specific contexts of socialization and certain socialization practices that may be instrumental to the development of such roles.

For the most part, I shall be extrapolating from my own socialization research in India that, when undertaken, was not designed specifically to address the development of sibling relations. Nonetheless, the nature of that research is consistent with the spirit of Sutton-Smith's statement quoted above in which he calls for more intensive participant-observation that is sensitive to daily routines, the presence of extended kin, differences in gender roles, and so on.

The Research Setting and Methodology

Bhubaneswar is the capital of Orissa, a state in eastern India. Until 1946, when it was selected as the site for a new planned city of administration, it was a small temple town renowned for its ancient Jain and Buddhist caves and hundreds of medieval Hindu temples. It had a population of about 10,000 people who resided in neighborhoods organized by caste and dominated by a hierarchy of Brahmin priests, who were the principal owners of the surrounding rice fields. During the 1950s, a new capital city (known as the "New Capital") was built next door to the old temple town (the "Old Town"), and a set of civil servants arrived to run the state government. A new, secular hierarchy was now adjacent to an old, religious one; schools from the kindergarten to the postgraduate level were established; a boom in construction and transportation attracted other migrants to the city; and Bhubaneswar's population jumped from 10,000 to over 50,000 by the early 1960s. The population is now over 450,000.

In 1961, Cora DuBois selected Bhubaneswar as a site to examine the forces of sociocultural change in India. A long-term, interdisciplinary study of the impact of the New Capital on the Old Town and surrounding villages—known as the Harvard Bhubaneswar Project—was initiated (Seymour 1980a). My part in that collaborative project was to make a 2-year (1965–67) comparative study of family organization and child-rearing practices in the Old Town and New Capital (Seymour 1980b). Subsequently, I have returned to Bhubaneswar a number of times, most recently in 1989, and I have been able to follow the lives of most of the children from my original sample of families.

Along the lines of the Six Culture Study (Whiting 1963), I selected a sample of 24 households in which to examine family organization and socialization practices, using the more informal technique of participant-observation, together with systematic timed observations of parent–child behavior. However, unlike the Khalapur, India, part of the Six Culture Study, which focused only on one caste group (Rajput), I wanted a sample of households that would be more representative of the sociocultural complexity of Bhubaneswar. Thus, 12 households from the Old Town and 12 from the New Capital were selected to represent the two systems of stratification operative in Bhubaneswar. The Old Town sample included four high-caste Brahmin households, four middle-level clean Shudra households, and four outcaste ("untouchable") households. In the New Capital the household head's income and status in the civil service hierarchy were used as criteria to select a sample of families that represented a range from high-level government officers at the top to government-employed Sweepers at the bottom. These groups can loosely be designated "upper," "middle," and "lower" status.

In addition to representing a range of castes and classes in Bhubaneswar, households were also selected to represent a range in size, structure, and organization. In the Old Town, most households were either lineally or collaterally joint and ranged in size from 6 to 24 members (with a mean size of 12.7). Most adults had little or no formal education. Upper and middle-caste fathers averaged 5.1 years of schooling, and mothers only 1.4 years. Lower-caste mothers and fathers were uneducated. Among the upper- and middle-level castes, households were sexually segregated, with married women in purdah. Thus, men in these households did all the shopping and most pursued traditional caste occupations in the Old Town. Observing purdah was not possible for lower-caste families, however, where women, like men, had to work outside the home in order for the family to eke out a living.

In the New Capital, by contrast, most households were nuclear in structure because government officials had had to leave extended kin behind when they were assigned to the New Capital. However, nuclear households were frequently "supplemented" with visiting relatives, many of whom came for extended periods of time. For example, several households had father's nieces or nephews residing with them so that these children could attend schools in the New Capital, while others had aging grandparents for prolonged visits. One household was matrilaterally joint: A married woman, her husband, and children resided with her mother, father, and unmarried sister rather than with her husband's family. This unusual arrangement enabled her to attend graduate school in the New Capital and have her mother help with child care. Households in the New Capital were generally smaller than in the Old Town, ranging in size from 5 to 12 members (with a mean size of 7.4). The educational level of New Capital parents was much higher than that of Old Town ones: Upper- and middle-status fathers averaged 16.7 years of schooling and their wives 8.9 years. Again, lower-status parents were generally uneducated. Finally, in the New Capital, rules of sexual segregation and purdah were not strictly followed, although adult women did not generally leave the immediate neighborhood unaccompanied by male relatives.

The 24 households that I selected for study thus represented the more "traditional" and the more "modern" parts of Bhubaneswar. The Old Town families were all long-term residents of the temple town, many of whom resided in joint households and all of whom lived in tightly clustered houses in kin- and caste-based neighborhoods. Children thus grew up surrounded by relatives and close caste associates. Furthermore, traditional caste occupations were practiced by the majority of families, and most parents and grandparents had had little exposure to Western-style schooling. By contrast, New Capital families were all *new* residents of Bhubaneswar, living in recently created neighborhoods and houses to which they had been assigned because of their status in the civil service hierarchy. Accordingly, they did not reside in kin- and caste-based neighborhoods but were surrounded by families who were initially strangers to them. For most, their occupations were not traditional caste-based ones but ones that were achieved by right of Western-style schooling, competitive exams, experience, and expertise. These factors and others, such as the presence or absence of such modern amenities as electricity, piped water, and public transportation, produced strikingly different life-styles on each side of town.

There was a total of 144 children in the 24 households I studied, 103 of whom were under the age of 10. These younger children were the focus of my research. I spent the first 6 months of my initial 2-year stay in Bhubaneswar contacting families, selecting a sample, and getting them used to my presence as a participant-observer, for example, allowing me to sit in inner courtyards of their homes watching the daily routine of women bathing, cooking, and tending to children without my interrupting that routine. I used Oriya, the dominant language of the state of Orissa, as the principal mode of communication with children and adults. All children learned to address me, and continue to address me, as "auntie" (mother's sister or father's sister). When families were sufficiently used to my presence, and household members simply greeted me when I arrived and continued with their usual activities, I began to formally record timed sequences of caretaker–child interactions. I took samples from four different periods of the day when household routines were reasonably similar from family to family: (1) early morning, when family members rose, bathed, snacked, and prepared for the day and mothers bathed and fed school-age children and prepared a meal for the working men of the household; (2) late morning, when unemployed men and women and preschool children were home alone; (3) late afternoon, when school children returned home, had snacks, and did homework and women prepared the evening meal; and (4) evening, when children ate and went to sleep. In each family, therefore, 16 hours per household of formally recorded behavior protocols complemented many hours of informal participant-observation. These protocols were later coded and analyzed, using techniques adapted from the Six Culture Study.

I mention in some detail my research methodology because it is critical to the theoretical perspective taken in the socialization materials to be presented below. It assumes that children learn patterns of interpersonal behavior in the settings that they frequent and that the cast of characters in those settings is critical. The settings children frequent are in turn related to the culturally determined activities, based on age and gender, that adults and children engage in, that is, the usual division of labor, daily household routine, school attendance, and so on (cf. Whiting & Edwards 1988: 4).

Socialization for Interdependence and Sibling Solidarity

Young siblings fight with one another. They provoke and irritate one another with devastating lack of inhibition. They amuse and excite one

> another and engage in uproarious games together. They comfort and care for one another. (Dunn & Kendrick 1982: 84)

As Dunn and Kendrick point out in the their book, *Siblings: Love, Envy, and Understanding* (1982: 84–7), there has been a tendency in sibling development research to focus on jealousy and rivalry, a tendency that may be the result, they suggest, of focusing so much on the mother–child relationship within the context of the nuclear family. This focus "has meant that the relationship between child and sibling has been seen *only* vis-à-vis the mother–child relationship: that is, in terms of a response to displacement and competition for mother's affection (Dunn & Kendrick 1982: 87). In recent years, Dunn and Kendrick have tried to move beyond this bias by examining other characteristics of sibling relationships, such as affection, understanding, and communication (e.g., Dunn 1985; Dunn & Plomin 1990). Bryant (1982) and Weisner (1982) have both written about siblings as caretakers, and Cicirelli (1982) has stressed both rivalry and sibling helping behvior.

Whereas sibling rivalry is taken for granted in the United States, in the South Asian socialization literature there is a tendency to stress the *nonrivalrous* nature of sibling relations. In the Six Culture Study, for example, Minturn and Hitchcock (1963: 343) assert that in Khalapur, "sibling rivalry is conspicuous by its absence." And Beals and Eason (Chapter 4, this volume) find little agonistic behavior between siblings in the village of Gopalpur in south India. "There were no examples of pulling, pushing, biting, or pulling hair, and no exchanges of verbal abuse between siblings, all behaviors that were observed in Mississauga" (p. 81).

My research in Bhubaneswar suggests that sibling rivalry is *not* absent but that certain socialization practices, structural factors, and cultural values help to mute it. Among the latter is the value placed on familial interdependence and sibling solidarity. For example, rather than viewing the arrival of a new child as a unique individual to be nourished and treasured—thus potentially pitting that individual child against other individual children in the family for attention—there is a tendency to view a baby as just one more member of the household who requires certain kinds of care but who should not be lavished with attention. In fact, in more traditional households, there is a taboo on focusing any special attention on a young child for fear that it will attract the evil eye. Thus, kinsmen and visitors never make such remarks as, "Oh, what a beautiful baby." And a young child's first words and first steps go unnoticed and uncommemorated. Instead, the tendency is to treat the child as one more member of the extended household who should be socialized by everyone and who should, in turn, learn to cooperate with everyone.

The value placed on familial interdependence and sibling solidarity gets expressed in a number of ways, for example, in the emphasis placed on learning kinship terms, in sleeping and eating patterns, and in prolonged nurturance and familial decision-making. One way that children in Bhubaneswar, both in nuclear and joint households, learn the significance of extended kin is that, from infancy on, they are taught what are by American standards a complex set of kin terms. Learning appropriate terms of address is part of the first verbal instruction that young children receive. Mothers and other caretakers repeat over and over to infants and toddlers the terms for different family members:

> For half an hour grandmother, Sita (father's older sister), Gopal (father's younger brother), and Rabi (1½-year-old boy) sat in the front room of the Misras's house. Grandmother and Gopal took turns holding Rabi. They, together with Sita, told Rabi to greet me. They repeated the command over and over again, also asking Rabi who I was. Rabi finally looked at Sita, then me, and said *nani* (father's older sister.) Everyone laughed. (Rabi had addressed me in an appropriate fashion, presumably making an association between me and his aunt—we were of similar age—which pleased everyone.) Then Rabi began reciting the terms for "father" and for "father's younger brother" to everyone's delight. (excerpt from fieldnotes 1975)

Early on children learn that there are many important kinsmen whom they must know how to address, and that they can extend these terms to nonfamily members as they did with me. Later they learn that the nature of relationships with father's extended kin is different from that of mother's kin (e.g., that only patrilateral first cousins are "brothers" and "sisters"), that gender and age are significant factors, and that different categories of kin bring with them different sets of obligations.

An early sense of interdependence is also reinforced by group sleeping and eating patterns. In all Bhubaneswar homes that I studied, children from infancy to adulthood slept together with others. Even as infants, they did not have separate spaces, such as cribs or cradles, in which to sleep. Rather, they slept on floor mats or wooden platforms together with their mothers and siblings. Mothers and children characteristically slept together, separate from fathers, although sometimes older children slept with a father, grandparent, or some other relative. For example, Rabi, mentioned above, slept with his grandmother for an extended period after his younger brother was born. Having his grandmother to himself and not having to share his mother at bedtime may have helped to reduce Rabi's feelings of sibling rivalry. What is most significant, however, is that children are never left alone at bedtime and that siblings grow up sharing intimate spaces and experiencing much physical contact with one another.

Children in Bhubaneswar also eat together, separate from adults. Whereas with adults, gender is the factor that structures dining, for children gender segregation is generally not implemented. At mealtimes children line up to be served, usually in a squatting position on the floor, and then eat in unison. In some families, siblings sit in very close physical proximity to one another in order to eat out of the same bowls. This regular dining together, separate from adults, is another way in which close sibling ties are manifested and reinforced.

The practice of multiple caretaking is a further technique by which interdependence is stressed and sibling rivalry reduced. In Old Town joint households, children grow up with a variety of potential caretakers in addition to their parents—grandmothers, aunts, and older siblings and cousins. But even in New Capital nuclear households, there are usually other potential caretakers, such as visiting relatives or servants. The degree to which persons other than a child's mother participate in child care is illustrated in Table 3.1, where the percentages of all recorded nurturant acts directed to children under 10 years old by different categories of caretakers are presented. In the Old Town 47% and in the New Capital 42% of nurturant acts were performed by persons other than mothers, with the range of other persons being greater in the Old Town than in the New Capital. This means that children are less focused on their mothers for caretaking, a phenomenon that may help to reduce what Dunn and Kendrick (1982) refer to as "competition for the mother's affection." Multiple caretaking is one of the hypotheses that Minturn and Hitchcock (1963) also proposed for the lack of sibling rivalry that they observed in Khalapur.

The following excerpt from an observation at Rabi's household, an Old Town upper-status joint family, is an example of what is meant by multiple caretaking.

> Sita (father's older sister) left the room and returned carrying Kuni (Rabi's 1-month-old brother.) Two neighbor girls (16 and 18 years old) came in and sat down. Sita lay Kuni on his back on the wooden platform on which she was seated. Kuni urinated and began to cry. Sita ignored him. One of the neighbor girls picked him up and held him a moment. Then she passed him to the other

TABLE 3.1. Percentage of Nurturant Acts Performed by Mothers vs. Surrogate Mothers

Mother/surrogate mother	Old Town ($n = 100$)	New Capital ($n = 55$)
Mother	53	58
Father	5	11
Grandmother	10	12
Older sibling, female	17	5
Older sibling, male	4	3
Mother's sister	1	2
Father's sister	4	0
Father's brother's wife	2	0
Neighbor or servant	4	9
TOTAL	100	100

neighbor girl. They took turns bouncing him on their laps. Kuni's mother came in, took Kuni and held him for several minutes. Then she handed him back to one of the neighbor girls and left the room. Grandmother then came in with Rabi, who was half asleep. She told him to greet me, which he did. She smiled and took him out of the room. Several minutes later she returned with him and asked him where his brother was. Rabi pointed to Kuni. Grandmother then picked up Rabi and carried him out of the room. (excerpt from fieldnotes 1966)

"Older siblings," a category that includes first cousins in joint households, constitute a significant proportion of caretakers, 21% in the Old Town and 8% in the New Capital (see Table 3.1.) Siblings may be rivalrous, but as Weisner (1982) has so cogently argued, in much of the non-Western world they also actively nurture one another. Such behavior again helps to build a sense of interdependence and solidarity among siblings that is only recently being recognized in Western research. In Bhubaneswar, especially in lower-status households where mothers have to work outside the home, children often make major contributions to the family work load, and from the age of 6 on may be put in charge of younger siblings (Seymour 1988). While there is a preference to assign this task to girls, boys also participate in child care. In fact, in several families where the only older siblings were boys, they became the principal "other" caretakers.

Below is an example of sibling caretaking from an Old Town lower-status joint household. In such households most children are not sent to school because they are needed to help out at home. This excerpt illustrates the intimate way in which adults and children cooperate in such families. At a young age, girls are responsibly participating in the family work load without having to be directed by adults, and they are also serving as role models for younger siblings.

> Asa's (10-year-old girl) and Musa's (Asa's 10-year-old female cousin) mothers were drying rice paddy on mats in the courtyard. Asa and Musa were cooking on separate hearths. Asa held Rusi (10-month-old brother) with her left arm and cooked with her right arm. The girls were roasting nuts in the fires. Later Asa set Rusi down on one of the mats in the courtyard, giving him a nut to play with. Rusi sat chewing the nut. Then Asa picked Rusi up and carried him inside her parents' room. She set him on the floor and gave him a tin can to play with. Asa then helped her mother, who was dividing up some tea and snacks. The can Rusi was playing with rolled away from him, and he began to fuss. Asa picked him up and carried him out of the room. A little later Nakima (6-year-old female cousin) asked to hold Rusi. Asa handed him to her and she held him precariously for a few minutes. Then Rasi (Rusi's 6-year-old brother) took him from Nakima and held him. (excerpt from fieldnotes 1967)

In lower-status households in Bhubaneswar, familial interdependence and sibling solidarity grow out of shared work. From age 6 on, every family member participates in the operation of the household and contributes to its well-being. By contrast, in middle- and upper-status households, most children from the age of 5 or 6 attend school and cannot contribute to the same degree to household chores and child care. In fact, in these households, the nurturing of children by adults and older siblings is more prolonged then in lower-status household where children are expected to be fairly self-reliant from about 3 years onward (Seymour 1976.)

In lower-status Old Town households, up until the age of 10, children are frequently still bathed, dressed, and hand-fed by mothers and other caretakers. This is, however, a phenomenon of extended households, where there are a variety of caretakers available. Prolonging a child's physical dependence on others is another way of creating a sense of interdependence in a society that does not value independence and where one is never expected to go off and live on one's own. In fact, many critical decisions in a person's life—such as how long one goes to school, what field one concentrates in, what occupation one pursues, and whom one marries—will at best be joint decisions; they may simply be parental decisions.

Having identified a number of ways in which familial interdependence and sibling solidarity—highly valued constellations of behavior in South Asia—are enhanced in Bhubaneswar homes, it is appropriate to address other behaviors mentioned in the Dunn and Kendrick passage at the beginning of this section. "Fight," "provoke," and "irritate" are listed *before* "comfort" and "care." While it is appropriate to reverse the order for Bhubaneswar families, it is not that these other behaviors are absent. There may be a low level of sibling rivalry if it is measured by expressions of overt hostility toward a new baby, but there are other signs of tension between siblings and between mothers and young children. In Bhubaneswar, however, the direct competition between children over a parent's attention is restricted largely to small New Capital families where children do not have a variety of adults and older siblings to attend to them. In such circumstances, which are relatively rare, one begins to see signs of "classic" sibling rivalry. The following is an example from an upper-status nuclear New Capital household:

> Gita (1½-year-old girl) was carried into the sitting room by her uncle (father's younger brother.) He handed Gita to her mother. Her mother held her for a few minutes on her lap. Then Gita wanted to go to her father. Her mother helped support her while she walked the few feet to her father's chair. Her father held out his hands and took her. Bapu (Gita's 3-year-old brother) now ran to his mother and buried his head in her lap. Then he looked up laughing and again buried his head in her lap. Now Gita wanted to return to her mother. She motioned to her father that she wanted to get down from his lap. He set her down and against her mother. Now Bapu ran to his father and climbed onto his lap. Gita let herself drop to the floor and rolled over crying. She had seen Bapu go to her father. Mother (directed to me) said, "Both children want to be with their father." For the next 15 minutes the children ran back and forth, exchanging places with their parents. (excerpt from fieldnotes 1966)

I never saw this kind of competition between young children over a parent in Old Town joint families. On the other hand, there was a fair amount of "negative affect" expressed in Old Town homes, for example, efforts to get a caretaker's attention by assaulting or trying to assault her, by seeking to annoy her or disrupt her activities by crying, making monotonously repeated demands, or destroying property (Seymour 1983). Such behaviors constituted a much higher proportion of children's social behvior in joint and supplemented nuclear households (10% and 11%, respectively) than in nuclear households (6%) where there was a greater concentration of mother–child interaction.

Large extended households in Bhubaneswar, which provide children with a range of potential caretakers and which reduce overt sibling rivalry, may nonetheless produce other kinds of frustrations for children. In these large households, children regularly resort to disruptive behavior in order to get attention.

Disruptive behavior, when it occurred, tended to be focused on mothers but might occasionally be directed to older siblings who were in a caretaking role. More commonly, however, agonistic behavior among siblings took the forms mentioned by Dunn and Kendrick: action meant to provoke and irritate or to amuse and excite another. While my socialization research was focused more on caretaking than play behavior, the behavior protocols do include numerous instances of siblings pushing, shoving, and quarreling with one another.

> Ten children (siblings and cousins of the same joint household) were on the rooftop playing. Mitu (11-year-old boy), Prosant (7-year-old boy), and Namita (4-year-old girl) began chasing one another. They kept running to the edge of the roof to look over. Sita (16-year-old girl) and Nina (18-year-old girl) scolded them, but the children ignored them. Mitu and Prosant grew more and more excited in chasing one another, paying less attention as they got to the edge of the roof. Finally, Nina grabbed hold of Prosant and pulled him down so that he was sitting next to her. Mitu came over to Prosant and hit him. Prosant hit back. Then a battle was underway, with blows back and forth between the two boys. Once Sita tried to interfere. Mamata (9-year-old girl) imitated Sita but got hit by the boys in return. She retaliated by hitting them. Then the boys jumped up, and the chase was underway again. (excerpt from fieldnotes 1967)

This observation, which comes from an Old Town upper-status household, illustrates all of the behaviors mentioned above by Dunn and Kendrick. First, a set of siblings is amusing and exciting one another by chasing one another around a rooftop. The play turns into provocative behavior when one boy hits the other. It momentarily escalates into "fighting" (mutual hitting) and then returns to playful chasing. Meanwhile, the older siblings present adopt a caretaking role and try to keep the activity of their younger siblings under control. Play, mixed with occasional provocative and aggressive behavior, runs through the behavior protocols from all families, regardless of Old Town/New Capital residence, household status, or household structure. And most of the time it is ignored by adults, who allow children to work out their own relationships with one another.

Allowing children to socialize one another may be intrinsic to the development of hierarchical sibling relationships in South Asia. Older children are frequently in charge of younger children or are trying to monitor the play of younger children, and younger children often use their age and size to dominate one another. Such dominance hierarchies, according to Whiting and Edwards (1988: 212–19), are characteristic of children's behavior worldwide. The question, then, is how the potentially hierarchical relationships developed in childhood fit the cultural ideals of adult sibling roles. With respect to fraternal ties, they probably work quite well. Brothers close in age are playmates, but they also learn that older brothers may dominate (both aggressively and nurturantly) younger brothers and that parents will not interfere. Such age-stratified cooperation is what will be required for brothers in adult life.

For brothers and sisters the situation is more complex. Those close in age may be playmates in early childhood, but in later childhood and adolescence gender differences intervene. Girls become increasingly restricted to the house, whereas their brothers can wander some distance from home. An early egalitarian relationship between girls and boys changes as girls are increasingly groomed for marriage and life in a husband's household. Where there are greater age differences between brother and sister, however, ordinal position becomes critical. Older sisters are often in dominant caretaking relationships vis-à-vis younger brothers, regardless of cultural ideals about gender. In adulthood, such a relationship may be reversed: If there is no older brother, a younger brother will become his sister's benefactor after her marriage.

Sisters, like brothers, can have both close, egalitarian relationships and more distant, hierarchical relationships. Depending on age difference and ordinal position, they may be principally caretakers of one another or they may be intimate friends. But for both sisters and brothers, ordinal position is always marked; for example, the terms "first brother/sister," "second brother/sister," "third brother/sister" and so on, are commonly used, both as terms of address and as terms of reference, in Bhubaneswar families. When the age of marriage for girls was 14 or 15, as it had been for the mothers and grandmothers in my sample, close sororal relationships were abruptly ended at a relatively early age. After marriage, sisters might rarely meet. However, now that many girls are attending school, the age of marriage has been delayed until anywhere from 18 to 30 years, allowing for more prolonged sororal ties to develop—a new phenomenon in this part of India.

In general, socialization research in Bhubaneswar attests to the formation during early childhood of strong sibling bonds and a keen sense of familial interdependence. Training for sibling solidarity may be more effective in joint households, where there is potentially more sibling caretaking and less sibling rivalry than in nuclear households and where numerous adult role models are available. In nuclear households with many children, however, there is also extensive socialization of one another. And in poor lower-status families, regardless of household structure, sibling solidarity is built by means of early economic cooperation. What makes sibling ties in South Asia strikingly different from those in the West is the cultural expectation that they will continue into adulthood. Ideally, brothers will continue to reside together and, ideally, they will stay in close contact with their married sisters. Thus, with the exception of sororal ties, long-term sibling relationships are formally built into the structure of society.

The Stability of Sibling Ties: 25 Years Later

For the past 25 years, I have stayed in close contact with all but one of the families in my original Bhubaneswar sample. Therefore, I can provide data on the stability of sibling relationships over time. In the Old Town, all but one joint household has remained joint and all but 2 of the 42 boys in my sample continue to reside in their natal household.

The one family that has ceased to be joint consisted in 1965–67 of a man, his mother and grandmother, his wife, and unmarried son, and an older married son with the latter's wife and children. The older son has an advanced degree and is now employed in the New Capital, whereas the younger son has only a minimal education and is pursuing his father's caste occupation. Some years ago—perhaps due to the discrepancy in education between the brothers and to mother-in-law-daughter-in-law tensions—the educated son built a new house on family property, not far away from the natal household, and moved his wife and children there. Subsequently, his mother, grandmother, and great-grandmother have all died. His father, now a widower, at first remained in the old house with his younger son but has now moved in with his older son, whose responsibility it is to look after him. Thus, while the household is no longer formally joint, joint-family values of cooperation and mutual caretaking have been retained.

Of the 42 sons who have remained in their father's households, a number are not pursuing traditional caste occupations. They have been able to find other kinds of jobs in either the Old Town or the New Capital which allow them, nonetheless, to reside at home. Of the 2 sons who have left their father's household, one is a young man who

has become head of his father's sister's household. In the absence of any sons, he was adopted by his aunt and uncle and has assumed responsibility for that family since his uncle's death. In the other case, the eldest of 4 sons in a family quarreled with his father and moved out with his wife and children into separate quarters in the Old Town. His father remains angry and bereft despite the fact that his other sons and grandchildren reside with him.

Girls from the Old Town sample are more scattered. Some have been married within the Bhubaneswar area and are in close contact with their natal kin, while others have married some distance away and rarely visit. In one family, however, two nephews (the sons of two sisters) have been sent to live with their Bhubaneswar maternal uncle in order to attend college there, thus activating the ties between brother and sister. In two other instances, daughters with unhappy marriages have returned to their natal home. In one case, the young woman's brother is now head of the household and has assumed responsibility for his sister and her two children.

These Old Town joint families, it should be noted, cut across caste lines. Mandelbaum (1970) and others have suggested that there is less incentive for members of lower castes to remain together in joint household because they hold little or no property in common. Nonetheless, lower-caste joint families in Bhubaneswar have remained as stable as middle- and upper-caste ones. By pooling what meager resources they have and by sharing child care, these families have adapted reasonably well to the increasingly urbanized environment of Bhubaneswar. Two Washerman caste brothers, for example, cooperated and sent their youngest brother through college. That brother now has a government job in the New Capital and can contribute more substantially to the joint family. The oldest of the three brothers has four sons, all of whom lived at home until recently, when the oldest one, who has a government job, was assigned government quarters in the New Capital. Because he and his wife are both employed, however, they bring their baby to his father's house to be taken care of during the day. Thus, while this son now resides separately, he continues to participate intimately in the joint family.

In the New Capital, most households have continued to be nuclear or supplemented nuclear in structure, but they now contain adult unmarried children. Among the upper- and middle-status families, all sons and daughters have completed college, and many have continued in school for more advanced degrees. For daughters, this means that their time at home is far longer than in the past. For sons, a prolonged education often involves a departure from Bhubaneswar to pursue graduate work elsewhere, something that daughters are rarely allowed to do. Thus, only 5 of 19 boys in my original sample were resident in Bhubaneswar in 1989, whereas a high proportion of the girls was still there. Employment also takes these highly educated, professionally oriented young men out of Bhubaneswar. Growing up in nuclear households where there are usually fewer siblings than in joint households, combined with the pursuit of advanced degrees and professional work requiring physical mobility, may result in weaker ties among New Capital brothers than among Old Town ones. Most may never reside together as adults. However, in at least one New Capital family that was formerly nuclear, a father has built a home large enough to hold all three of his married sons and their wives and children. While currently only one son, who is locally employed, lives there with his parents, the expectation is that one day all three brothers will be together again.

It is too early to make any long-term predictions about the kinds of patterns that will develop among New Capital brothers. What is clear, though, is that sons are staying in regular communication with members of their families, and that whenever it is necessary, at least one returns home. For example, there seems to be an understanding among siblings that at least one brother should be available to live with and care for aging parents. In several families, one brother has been groomed for this task, leaving the others free to pursue their careers elsewhere. Thus, while adult brothers may not reside together, they remain cognizant of their familial responsibilities, which include assisting in arranging marriages for their sisters.

Brother–sister ties in New Capital families are affected by the same kinds of factors as fraternal ones. What is substantively different for this generation, however, is that brothers and sisters have received nearly comparable educations. This, combined with delayed marriage and the employment of sisters, has enabled many brothers and sisters to develop closer and more egalitarian relationships than was previously possible.

As Kolenda (Chapter 5, this volume) predicts, sororal ties have also been strengthened by the same set of factors. Since New Capital daughters are typically not marrying until at least the age of 24 and even as late as 30, sisters now have a prolonged period together in their parents' household as children and as young adults. They tend to provide a supportive atmosphere for the development of one another's educational and career ambitions in a context where women have never before been able to pursue such goals. In one family, for example, with seven highly educated but until recently unmarried daughters, such mutual support has been critical. When not in school or working, sisters generally tend to spend their time together at home;

there is no dating in Bhubaneswar, and unmarried women are not free to go out in public for recreational purposes. The only disruptive factor in New Capital sororal relationships is the pressure to marry and to marry in order of birth. Since marriage implies dowry, it places sisters in a certain amount of competition with one another with respect to parental resources and with respect to potential husbands. For example, intense resentment between sisters arose in one household when an older sister was passed over by a groom in favor of her next younger sibling.

There is also evidence from the New Capital that after marriage sisters continue to have close ties with one another. If they reside within the Bhubaneswar area, they visit one another frequently, while those who are more distant visit whenever possible. In fact, sister–sister households may be an emerging phenomenon. In one instance, a married sister and her younger divorced sister share a house together with the older sister's children. The husband of the older sister is employed outside Bhubaneswar and returns weekends as often as possible. In this case both sisters are employed and contribute to the maintenance of the household. In another case, two sisters do not actually reside together but visit on a daily basis. Both employed, the older sister is married while the younger one is separated from her husband and lives with one of her two children. The older sister, who worries about her separated younger sister living without another adult, has encouraged her retired parents to return from their natal village to spend extended periods of time with the separated sister. Another factor that draws these two sisters close together is their sense of responsibility, in the absence of a brother, for their aging parents.

Conclusion

Siblings in South Asia exhibit the same range of behaviors that have been identified by researchers in the United States. They can be affectionate, rivalrous, playful, nurturing, and so on. However, due to the strikingly different sociocultural contexts in which South Asian siblings develop and the very different adult roles they must assume, the balance of behaviors is quite different. For example, the cultural ideal of long-term fraternal solidarity is nurtured whereas sibling rivalry is culturally downplayed. Behaviorally, this does not mean that one exists and the other does not, but that various structural and socialization factors help to enhance one and mute the other. Growing up in large joint households, with a variety of caretakers that include older siblings, helps to decenter the mother–child relationship, to reduce sibling rivalry, and to build sibling solidarity. Growing up in poor households and having to contribute to the welfare of the family from an early age seems to have similar effects. Furthermore, living under the authority of one's father as an adult can also enhance fraternal solidarity and discourage sibling rivalry.

Sibling roles are more clearly delineated in South Asia than they are in the West. The patrilineal, partilocal joint family creates a context in which siblings as adults are expected to assume certain specific roles with respect to each other. Sets of brothers should live together and cooperate. Sisters should leave at the time of marriage. Brothers should look out for the welfare of married sisters. And sisters, once married, have no built-in relationship to each other. This cultural system makes the relationship of brothers intrinsically different from that of brothers and sisters, or of sisters. Moreover, it builds on ordinal position as well as on gender to create sibling hierarchies that are often established in childhood, when siblings socialize one another, and that become critical in adulthood, for brothers in particular. For sisters, ordinal position is mostly important at the time of marriage. Once married, though, women in their roles of wives, daughters-in-law, and sisters-in-law assume the hierarchical position of their husbands. As this volume makes clear, however, regional variations in kinship patterns, marriage practices, and inheritance rights can create some significant degree of variability in this model of sibling roles.

Finally, longitudinal research in a rapidly changing town like Bhubaneswar, with its diverse population, offers other kinds of insights into sibling roles and relationships in South Asia. On the one hand, it suggests that despite extensive educational and occupational change, the joint family has remained quite stable. Most of those who grew up in joint families continue to reside in them and to carry out traditional fraternal and fraternal–sororal roles. On the other hand, certain kinds of change are evident. Prolonged education, delayed marriage, and the employment of women have created a context in which some brothers and sisters are more nearly equal and in which sororal relationships can flourish. New educational and occupational opportunities have also led to the geographic dispersal of some young men, the long-term consequences of which remain unclear. And rapidly changing and urbanizing conditions are allowing some young men and women to experiment with family forms different from those in which they grew up and, hence, with different sibling roles.

References

Bennett, L. (1983). *Dangerous Wives and Sacred Sisters: Social and Symbolic Roles of High-Caste Women in Nepal.* New York: Columbia University Press.

Bryant, B. K. (1982). Sibling Relationships in Middle Childhood. In M. E. Lamb & B. Sutton-Smith (Eds.), *Sibling Relationships: Their Nature and Significance across the Lifespan* (pp. 87–121). Hillsdale, NJ: Erlbaum.

Cicirelli, V. G. (1982). Sibling Influence throughout the Lifespan. In M. E. Lamb & B. Sutton-Smith (Eds.), *Sibling Relationships: Their Nature and Significance across the Lifespan* (pp. 267–84). Hillsdale, NJ: Erlbaum.

Dunn, J. (1985). *Sisters and Brothers.* Cambridge, MA: Harvard University Press.

Dunn, J., & Kendrick, C. (1982). *Siblings: Love, Envy, and Understanding.* Cambridge, MA: Harvard University Press.

Dunn, J., & Plomin, R. (1990). *Separate Lives: Why Siblings Are So Different.* New York: Basic Books.

Fruzzetti, L. M. (1982). *The Gift of a Virgin: Women, Marriage, and Ritual in a Bengali Society.* New Brunswick, NJ: Rutgers University Press.

Goody, J. (1990). *The Oriental, the Ancient and the Primitive: Systems of Marriage and the Family in the Pre-Industrial Societies of Eurasia.* Cambridge: Cambridge University Press.

Jeffrey, P. (1979). *Frogs in a Well: Indian Women in Purdah.* London: Zed Press.

Lamb, M. E., & Sutton-Smith, B. (Eds.). (1982). *Sibling Relationships: Their Nature and Significance across the Lifespan.* Hillsdale, NJ: Erlbaum.

Mandelbaum, D. G. (1970). *Society in India: Vol. 1. Continuity and Change.* Berkeley: University of California Press.

Mandelbaum, D. G. (1988). *Women's Seclusion and Men's Honor: Sex Roles in North India, Bangladesh, and Pakistan.* Tucson: University of Arizona Press.

Minturn, L., & Hitchcock, J. T. (1963). The Rajputs of Khalapur, India. In B. Whiting (Ed.), *Six Cultures: Studies of Child Rearing* (pp. 203–361). New York: Wiley.

Nuckolls, C. (1991a). "Culture and Causal Thinking: Prediction and Diagnosis in a South Indian Fishing Village." *Ethos* 17: 3–51.

Nuckolls, C. (1991b). "Becoming a Possession-Medium in South India: A Psychocultural Account." *Medical Anthropology Quarterly* 5: 63–77.

Nuckolls, C. (1991c). "Deciding How to Decide: Possession-Mediumship in South India." *Medical Anthropology* 13: 57–82.

Nuckolls, C. (1992). "Divergent Ontologies of Suffering in South Asia." *Ethnology* 31: 57–74.

Roy, M. (1972). *Bengali Women.* Chicago: University of Chicago Press.

Seymour, S. (1976). "Caste/Class and Child-Rearing in a Changing Indian Town." *American Ethnologist* 3: 783–96.

Seymour, S. (Ed.). (1980a). *The Transformation of a Sacred Town: Bhubaneswar, India.* Boulder, CO: Westview Press.

Seymour, S. (1980b). Patterns of Childrearing in a Changing Indian Town. In S. Seymour (Ed.), *The Transformation of a Sacred Town: Bhubaneswar, India* (pp. 121–54). Boulder: Westview Press.

Seymour, S. (1983). "Household Structure and Status and Expressions of Affect in India." *Ethos* 11: 263–77.

Seymour, S. (1988). "Expressions of Responsibility among Indian Children: Some Precursors of Adult Status and Sex Roles." *Ethos* 16: 355–70.

Sharma, U. (1980). *Women, Work, and Property in North-West India.* London: Tavistock.

Weisner, T. (1982). Sibling Interdependence and Child Caretaking: A cross-cultural View. In M. E. Lamb & B. Sutton-Smith (Eds.), *Sibling Relationships: Their Nature and Significance across the Lifespan* (pp. 305–27). Hillsdale, NJ: Erlbaum.

Whiting, B. B. (1963). *Six Cultures: Studies of Child Rearing.* New York: Wiley.

Whiting, B. B., & Edwards, C. (1988). *Children of Different Worlds: The Formation of Social Behavior.* Cambridge, MA: Harvard University Press.

Photo by Alan R. Beals

CHAPTER 4

Siblings in North America and South Asia

Alan R. Beals
Mary Anne Eason

Concerned about the impact of parochialism on linguistics and social science generally, Bloomfield wrote, "The ancient Greeks studied no language but their own; they took it for granted that the structure of their language embodied the universal forms of human thought or, perhaps, of the cosmic order" (1933: 5). When modern linguists began to compare a variety of languages across cultures, the existence of universals undreamt of by the Greeks became apparent (Greenberg 1966; Greenberg, Ferguson, & Moravcsik 1978). Now, some 60 years after Bloomfield, a few psychologists and anthropologists are beginning to suspect that the patterns of domestic relationship observed or reported in Euro-American society may not be much more universal than the structure of the Greek language.

As part of his cross-cultural study of social structure, Murdock (1949) concluded that the nuclear family was universal and presented the results of chi-square tests to support his view. Publishing in the same year, Lévi-Strauss (1949), perhaps wiser in the ways of the male animal, argued that the basic unit of kinship was the mother and her children. Years later, in what might be taken to be a summation of progress in the cross-cultural study of families and domestic groupings, Hammel (1984) communicated confusion (expressed by a string of asterisks in his title) concerning the universality of the domestic group itself. Even so, something like the nuclear family can be found almost anyplace. The problem is that it exists in relationship to a variety of other kinds of families and domestic arrangements, and the rules and expectations as to how people should behave toward each other within the nuclear family or within other kinds of family structures are quite variable as well.

The contrasts that we report between South Asia and North America raise, but do not answer, a variety of questions about the possible universal features of sibling relationships. We wonder, for example, if it is natural for young siblings to quarrel frequently while older siblings get along, as many do in North America, or if it is natural for young siblings to get along virtually without quarreling while older siblings quarrel, as many do in South Asia. Given such differences in behavior, questions must be raised about which sorts of behavior are to be regarded as natural and unnatural. From a psychoanalytic point of view, it could be argued that siblings in South Asia repress their natural tendencies toward conflict in early life, but repress their natural tendencies toward cooperation in later life. North American siblings, by contrast, appear to repress their cooperative tendencies in early life and repress their conflict tendencies in later life. This mirror image quality of sibling relationships in the two regions raises further doubts about the value of approaches to sibling behavior that are based largely upon North American concepts of "normalcy," while viewing other kinds of behavior as "abnormal."

What we "know" about siblings stems almost entirely from research and clinical experience carried out in Euro-American cultural settings, and this knowledge is deeply influenced by these settings. About twenty years ago, Sutton-Smith and Rosenberg (1970) reviewed sibling research and found it to be unsatisfactory. More recently, Sutton-Smith wrote:

> Imagine, for example, if instead of those thousands of relatively worthless studies, we now had available thousands of case studies of siblings in context. Imagine, less probably, that they were longitudinal, and involved great amounts of taped (perhaps even video recorded) material across carefully sampled life situations. (Sutton-Smith 1982: 386–87)

Indeed, for many years sibling research has been based upon simple statistics and even simpler research designs. The failure to develop a more critical research stance may well stem from the researchers' deep personal experience of sibling relationships.

Cicirelli (1982: 227) reports that in the United States, 90% of children have siblings. He found that 88% of young adults and almost equal numbers of elderly individuals have a living sibling. Because all of us have siblings or know people who do, it is easy for us to discount data that conflict with our preconceptions and ignore the impact of siblings upon such things as the growth and maturation of the individual. Even though relationships between siblings might be said to be "problematical" in the sense that siblings are not always completely happy with their relationships, it appears that sibling relationships in our culture are regarded as fixed and invariant. In the folk wisdom, it is just another of those biological legacies that cannot be changed (Schneider 1980, 1984).

Studies of domestic relationships in general have been restricted to a handful of cultures. Research has often proceeded through the calculation of averages and other normal curve statistics based upon relatively homogeneous populations. All this leads to a relatively simplistic picture of normal sibling relationships, culminating in newspaper headlines such as "older brothers are smarter" or "younger sisters are docile." At least until recently, much information concerning siblings was derived from structured and/or therapeutic interviews of various sorts. For much of the rest, a continuing preoccupation with Western themes of child development and adult achievement is apparent. As Weisner comments:

> Some peculiar preoccupations characterize sibling research in the United States and Western Europe. Western views of siblings are limited—one might even say scientifically ethnocentric—because the preoccupations of Western sibling research are by and large the preoccupations of Western society: achievement, status and hierarchy, conformity and dependency, intelligence, rivalry and competition. Now siblings are indeed rivalrous; they often compete fiercely with each other, and age and ordinal position are important for understanding sibling relationships. But these are far from the only important topics. (Weisner 1982: 305)

Much of the certainty and simplicity that attended earlier work on sibling relationships has dropped away, perhaps partly in response to criticisms leveled by Rosenberg and Sutton-Smith or arising out of the cross-cultural studies carried out by Weisner (1977) and others (Zukow 1989). Investigators have recently begun to look at new variables ranging considerably beyond the familiar ground of fraternal rivalry. The work of Dunn (e.g., Dunn & Kendrick 1982) is especially apposite in this regard.

Overall, research concerning familial and domestic group relationships has broken away from the confines of the idealized Euro-American nuclear family consisting of one father, one mother, one sister, and one brother, each playing out roles that might have been scripted by a Greek dramatist. Family structure, family size, birth order, birth spacing, and sex have been shown to be important determinants of sibling behavior. Independent cultural, natural, and environmental variables are beginning to be considered, but in a fairly unsystematic way. Overall, we must stress the probability that several important determinants of family behavior have yet to be identified. In the following section, we will argue for the need for serious study of the ideology of sibling relationships, surely another major determinant of sibling behavior.

On the Status of Observations versus Ideology

In this section we describe sibling behavior as observed in two distinct settings: (1) the south Indian village of Gopalpur in Karnatak State, based on observations carried out by Beals and his coworkers[1] in the 1960s and (2) the Canadian city of Mississauga, a middle-class community in Ontario, based on observations carried out by Abramovitch, Corter, and Lando (1979) in the 1970s.

Many of the differences in sibling behavior observed in these two settings appear to stem from contrasting cultural standards concerning the appropriate behavior of siblings. Although there are sharp differences in behavior in the two places, there are also many behaviors that are similar. For example, sibling rivalry, understood as conflict between brothers, is a major concern in both societies. In South Asia, sibling rivalry in its most extreme form is depicted as leading to a disastrous war fully comparable to World War III in its genocidal impact. In North America, sibling rivalry appears to be considered inevitable and even desirable, and siblings are described as launching violent pinching, hitting, hair-pulling attacks on each other with a frequency appalling to a South Asian. This universality of conflict between siblings, hardly matched outside the divorce court, is thrown into question by the fact that sibling rivalry occurs under different circumstances and has different characteristics in the two regions. Perhaps, it is not so much fraternal sibling rivalry that is universal but concern about it.

Before moving on to discussion of the actual observations, we will provide a sketch of what seem to be the prevailing cultural ideologies concerning siblings characteristic of North America and South Asia.

We feel that a discussion of ideology needs to precede discussion of actual behavior because ideology determines what people do and how they respond to specific behaviors. From the research perspective, ideology stands between the observer and the observed and poses problems for the interpretation of behavior. Ideology must be understood, at least in some degree, before observations can be intelligently discussed or perhaps even thought about. It is, after all, our own beliefs posing as knowledge which pose the most formidable obstacle to our seeing of that which takes place before our eyes.

In North American ideology, some degree of conflict among siblings is considered inevitable. Yet there is a range of opinions as to the value of such conflict. Some believe that it is essential to normal personality development; others see it as something that needs to be stopped or controlled. Siblings, especially brothers, are not supposed to hate each other, but there is acceptance that they frequently do. Harmony among siblings is sometimes seen as highly desirable, if perhaps unattainable. In South Asia, conflict among siblings seems to be universally regarded as avoidable and dangerous. Even if North American ideology is taken to be ambivalent concerning the question of conflict among siblings, it differs strikingly from South Asian ideology in which conflict among siblings is considered disastrous and intolerable.

Systematic studies of South Asian and North American folk ideologies concerning siblings appear to be nonexistent. Mainstream scholarship tells us virtually nothing about what siblings are supposed to be like, what they are supposed to do to each other, or what they are supposed to think about each other. We have not encountered any studies that describe ideal patterns, scripts, scenarios, or models presumed to guide individuals in their decision-making and behavior with regard to sibling relationships.

In the absence of detailed studies, we will confine ourselves to a brief review of written materials that seem to us to represent prevailing regional ideals for sibling relationships. Especially for North America, it is difficult to establish the nature of the folk wisdom concerning siblings, for there seems to be no general or very strong concensus concerning the ways in which siblings are supposed to behave toward each other. Writers often display ambivalent attitudes toward such things as sibling rivalry and sibling caretaking. For South Asia, the ideology of sibling relationships is much more explicit, and there seems to be little disagreement or ambivalence concerning proper relationships among siblings.

The Cultural Construction of Ideal Siblings

In South Asia, a search for definitive materials concerning the ideology of sibling relationships leads inevitably to the *Mahabharata*. As the most widely known literary and mythological text in Karnatak State and throughout South Asia, the *Mahabharata* and works derived from it provide a detailed account of the relationships among the Pandava brothers and their patrilateral first cousins (classificatory brothers). As the longest epic poem ever written, the *Mahabharata,* together with a second epic poem, the *Ramayana,* are believed to provide the historical and scriptural bases for Hindu society and perhaps for human society in general. The authority of the *Mahabharata* is, then, unquestioned. As recently as the 1960s, it was the only text used in traditional south Indian religious schools.

For North America, we interviewed a number of friends and colleagues concerning the possibility of similar authoritative texts. Although at first stumped by the question, they eventually produced the names of a variety of novels and television programs, all of which lacked the broad audience or the scriptural or official authority of the *Mahabharata.* The story of Cain and Abel was deemed lacking in detail. With some trepidation, we finally settled upon a review article published in the popular journal, *Psychology Today.* Lacking a *Mahabharata,* it is to such a source that ordinary, or at any rate, middle-class North Americans might turn in search of authoritative instruction concerning the proper relationships among siblings. Although the intent of *Psychology Today* is to present authoritative summaries of recent scientific discoveries, changes in emphasis and decisions as to what is worth reporting bring it considerably closer to folk knowledge than the research materials that it quotes.

An article in the June 1981 issue of *Psychology Today* by Adams describes sibling rivalry as a natural and desirable state of affairs, a constructive force in the social development of the child. The article suggests that without sibling conflict—especially rivalry—children may fail to develop independence or a strong personality. If parents interfere by suppressing expressions of sibling rivalry, siblings may come to avoid each other in later life. Finally, feelings of rivalry among rivalrous siblings often persist into adult life. The article's view of sibling relationships seems consistent with a larger society that encourages controlled and regulated contest in many social situations.

In a somewhat different vein, the article presents a selective summary of a study of siblings carried out by Bank and Kahn and the results of an interview with Bank. These authors have a particular interest in what they call "fervent sibling loyalty." According to Bank, this involves "an irrational and somewhat blind process of putting one's sibling first and foremost" (quoted in Adams 1981: 34). In some cases, as reported for two brothers, Bank is quoted as saying there are such "fantasies" as desiring to purchase a home jointly where their wives and children would blend with them into a big, happy household. Such a household is a commonplace and highly desirable situation in South Asia and in many other parts of the world. In the article, such attachment is attributed by Bank to a "family collapse" when the children were growing up. Deprived of all other support, siblings cling desperately to each other. A deep bond between siblings will not develop if parents are "real good parents." Bank stops short of referring to such siblings as "only neurotic," and says, "I don't want to put down the absolute altruism we've seen in these very loyal siblings" (quoted in Adams 1981: 38). Finally, Bank relates sibling loyalty to chimpanzee siblings, who care for each other when the mother dies. For North America, then, it appears that close attachment among siblings is, at worst, a dangerous neurosis and, at best, the result of a genetic survival from our simian past.

It should be noted, again, that the materials cited above were taken from a popular journal in order to describe popular ideology concerning siblings. Thus, the quotations from Bank seem not to be from his written work and do not always accurately convey the substance of his written work. Be that as it may, it seems reasonable to believe that *Psychology Today* represents popular ideology somewhat better than a more narrowly focused work of research.

For South Asia, the *Mahabharata* presents an ideal of fraternal relations quite different from that in *Psychology Today*. The Pandava brothers, ideal culture heroes, are fervently loyal to the point that they are able to share a single wife without sexual jealousy or rivalry. In a south Indian drama based on the *Mahabharata*, Arjuna, the second brother, spends a period in embarrassed and voluntary exile after he accidentally blunders into the tent where the older brother is enjoying conjugal relations with their joint wife. In much of South Asia, the implied injunction to share a single wife is considered to have a largely symbolic content; in northwest India and in several marginal regions, wife sharing among brothers and fraternal polyandry are not unknown.

The oldest of the Pandava brothers exercises authority over his juniors; disobedience or conflict with the older brother is rare and occurs only in the form of verbal protest. For example, the younger brothers protested vociferously when the older brother lost their joint wife and their kingdom in a gambling game, but they were unable to contest their brother's claim that the action was necessary and virtuous. In their youth, the Pandava brothers maintained close relationships with their patrilineal cousins and foster brothers, the Kauravas. When the Kauravas began to engage in such rivalrous actions as attempting to burn them alive or, later, to cheat them out of wife and kingdom, the Pandavas, compelled by their older brother, peacefully agreed to an imbecilic solution to the conflict. In the end, when the rival armies of the Pandavas and Kauravas family assembled on the

field of battle, God Krishna himself had to use all of his powers of persuasion to convince Arjuna, the second and brightest of the five brothers, that war between the "cousin-brothers" was necessary and right.

The contrast between *Psychology Today* and the *Mahabharata* indicates that some North American and some South Asian textual stances present radically different ideologies concerning the nature of sibling relationships. These differences foreshadow actual differences portrayed in studies based upon observations of sibling behavior. In both regions, sibling rivalry, explained primarily in terms of conflict between brothers, appears to be the most important aspect of sibling relationships. In South Asia the result of sibling rivalry is depicted as unmitigated disaster (the entire race of Kshatriyas is exterminated in the war between the "cousin-brothers"), and fervent sibling loyalty, regarded with suspicion in *Psychology Today*, is presented as the ideal. Both ideologies are patriarchal in the feminist sense of the term; relationships between brothers and sisters or between sisters are hardly mentioned.

Siblings as Children

Observations of sibling interactions carried out in Mississauga, Ontario, and in Gopalpur, Karnatak State, support in a general way the contrasts noted above.

North American Children

In Mississauga, Abramovitch and her colleagues (1979) observed 34 pairs of same-sex siblings in their homes for two 1-hour periods each. The younger siblings were about 20 months old, and the older siblings were 1 to 4 years older. The children were observed to engage in "assertive physical contact," which included "hitting, pushing, pulling, shoving, kicking, biting, pinching and pulling hair" (Abramovitch et al. 1979: 1000). The siblings fought over objects, ordered each other about in a threatening manner, insulted each other, made threats, and tattled. These behaviors were labeled "agonistic." In contrast "prosocial" behaviors included cooperating, sharing, smiling, and praising. The observed children initiated a different action almost every minute. Older male siblings engaged in assertive physical contact with their younger brothers approximately 9 times each hour, while older female siblings did the same to younger sisters approximately 3 times each hour. Total negative, "agonistic," behaviors took place approximately 27 times each hour on the part of older male siblings and around 20 times each hour for older female siblings. Friendly or prosocial behaviors took place considerably less often: Older male siblings were nice to their younger brothers about 13 times each hour, while female siblings were nice to their younger sisters about 28 times each hour. Younger siblings responded to attack primarily by displaying submissive behavior, male younger siblings displaying agonistic behavior only about 5 times each hour, while submitting about 14 times.

South Asian Children

Each observation in Gopalpur lasted between 30 and 45 minutes, and 98 observations were made in all. Thirty-one of the observations involved interaction between siblings or patrilateral cousins of both the same and opposite sex. As noted previously, patrilateral cousins often share the same joint-family domicile, are raised together, and refer to each other as "brother" and "sister." At the outset, South Indians define "sibling" differently from North Americans. Children in Gopalpur make no distinctions between siblings and coresident cousins, although such distinctions may be quite important when they get older.

Although Abramovitch and her colleagues did describe the family situation of the sibling pairs they observed, we may infer that it was a fairly typical North American family situation, in which the observer is invited into the house by the children's parents and conducts observations within private areas of the house. In Gopalpur, people do not live in their houses in the same way that North Americans live in theirs, especially those North Americans who live in cold climates. Gopalpur houses are large, but they are dark. People sleep inside their houses in cold weather and during the heat of the day in hot weather. Cooking and bathing are carried out in kitchen rooms. Grain is stored in other rooms, and cattle spend the night tethered just inside the front door. The house is not considered a fully private place, and, during the daytime when the door is open, friends and neighbors generally walk right in. Children and adult men spend relatively little time inside the house. Families rarely eat meals together, and there is little socializing between husband and wife. Both men and women work long and hard, having little time to dedicate to child care.

Most family life is carried out in the village street or on the veranda in front of the house. In a way, the open spaces of the village might be described as a large communal livingroom shared with neighbors who are generally addressed by household kinship terms appropriate to nonmarriageable relatives such as "brother," "sister," "mother," "father," "son," or "daughter." When husband and wife are away from the house or busy inside, as they usually are, child-care duties are assigned to older children, preferably females. As soon as they are able to do so, older children are expected to pick up the baby and carry it around outside. In Mississauga, the primary caretaker for young children is generally the mother. In Gopalpur, the mother is the primary caretaker for her oldest child if no one else is available. The oldest child of either sex is generally the primary caretaker for the younger children, but female caretakers are used whenever possible. When young caretakers pick up the baby to take it outside, they are generally warned not to leave the baby on platforms from which it might fall and not to allow it to be trampled by cattle. Outside, adults generally ignore groups of children who play quietly, usually imitating such adults activities as plowing, grinding grain, or cooking, while the adults make rope, gossip, or grind grain. Any substantial disturbance will immediately draw the attention of mothers, grandfathers, or other nearby adults. To some extent, then, the supervision of child caretakers is the diffuse responsibility of the entire community.

The ideal type of family organization in Gopalpur is a large joint family composed of parents (if living), and their sons, son's wives, and children. The kinship terminology in use is a Dravidian cross-cousin terminology, in which terms used to describe nuclear family members are applied to all persons thought to be related along lines of patrilineal descent to the speaker (Ego), roughly half the population. A separate set of "in-law" terms is applied to the other half of the population. Speakers of Kannada, the language of Karnatak State, can specify "own" brother or "own" sister if they desire to distinguish their own relatives from classificatory relatives, but the general practice is not to do so. We do not know at what age children are able to distinguish their own siblings from their patrilateral cousins or from other village children in general. Before female children reach puberty, usually between the ages of 9 and 16, marriages are arranged for them. Because residence after marriage is almost invariably in the household of the husband or his family, it follows that many marriages involve the movement of the female sibling to a different village, usually between 4 and 12 miles away. Marriages to one's own mother's brother's daughter, father's sister's daughter, or sister's daughter are favored, but most marriages are to more distant relatives referred to by the same "in-law" terms used for the ideal close relatives.

Observations

The observer attempted to write down all of the Gopalpur children's activities. The materials were not coded in any way. Analysis of the observations, which was carried out by Eason, involved breaking down each observation into a series of activities. The following sections provide defining examples of each of these activities.

Hitting

Siblings usually hit each other with sticks. Sometimes the reason for the hitting is not apparent to the observer. Often the hitting is an attempt to discipline or to bring undesirable behavior to a halt. At times siblings are hit in retaliation for previous hits or as a consequence of refusal to follow instructions given by the other sibling. Males were hit more often than females, usually by an older sibling. All of the siblings who hit their sisters were younger. In Gopalpur, there were no examples of pulling, pushing, biting, or pulling hair, and no exchanges of verbal abuse between siblings, all behaviors that were observed in Mississauga.

Physical attacks were not serious and ended promptly. In the 31 observations, there were 2 incidents involving the exchange of physical violence and 2 incidents of nonviolent attack and violent retaliation. There were no cases where violence was on a scale that might be considered worthy of notice in most Euro-American settings. All 4 incidents involving exchanges of violence could equally have been classified as discipline administered in parental fashion. The 4 incidents of violence and retaliation are summarized below:

> Mallya (brother, 1.5 yrs) crawled over to Sitavva (sister, 6 yrs) and put his hand on hers. She pushed it away. Again he put his hand on hers and she pushed it away. He sat beside her looking at her hands. Then he hit her hand with a stick and held it. Sitavva hit him on the back, picked him up, and took him away.
>
> Hanumantha (brother, 2 yrs) went over to his sister Manikamma (5 yrs) and put his hand in the winnowing fan as she winnowed. She put the fan down and hit him on the back. Hanumantha ran into the house and came back with a stick, grabbed Manikamma's hair and hit her on the back three or four times. Manikamma shouted for her mother, and she came and took the stick from Hanumantha.
>
> Bhimsha (brother, 3 yrs) had made a house by digging a hole in the sand. Narsya (brother, 2 yrs) began to pound the sand with a stick. Bhimsha saw this and hit Narsya on the head with his hand.

> Ramlinga (brother, 3 yrs) was looking at a toy ox his father had on his lap. Devendra (brother, 7 yrs) came out with another toy ox and showed it to his father. His father told him to bring one to Ramlinga, but he didn't. Devendra was repairing the ox when Ramlinga walked up behind him and hit him on the back. Devendra moved away. Ramlinga tried to hit him again, but his father shouted at him not to hit his brother. Ramlinga looked at his father and laughed. His father smiled and called him over.

Ignoring

Abramovitch and her colleagues (1979) observed cases in which an action made by one sibling was ignored by another, but they did not use these materials in computing their results. In our calculations, we included lack of response under the heading of agonistic behavior in order to insure that no incidents involving possible sibling rivalry were overlooked. Ignoring behavior in Gopalpur is usually in response to a request or statement made by the other sibling. For example, one sibling may want the attention of another who is busy playing and does not want to be disturbed. Some typical incidents follow:

> Ramlinga (brother, 3 yrs) sat on a palm frond as Devendra (brother, 7 yrs) dragged him up and down the street. They stopped for 10 minutes and then Devendra asked Ramlinga to drag him. Ramlinga didn't and ran away with a neighbor girl.
>
> Manikamma (sister, 5 yrs) came out of the house with a doll. Hanumantha (brother, 2 yrs) held out his hand because he wanted her to give him the doll. She ignored him, so he asked his mother for the doll.
>
> Mallappa (brother, 1 yr) went to the cot where Mallamma (sister, 6 yrs) and another girl were sitting. He wanted up and began to cry in front of Mallamma. She ignored him, and Mallappa managed to climb onto the cot by himself. When the girls got up from the cot, Mallappa cried for Mallamma to help him down. She ignored Mallappa until she was instructed by an adult to help him.

Mothering

Mothering behavior, for the most part, involves some type of nurturing. An older sister or brother may feed, clean, comfort, or hold a younger sibling. One sibling may also watch out for another sibling's well-being. Of the types of behavior we have referred to as mothering, only comforting seems to have taken place among the children observed in Mississauga. Some examples follow:

> Buranuddin (brother, 4 yrs) goes inside his house and brings out a green mango to eat. His brother Chahussain (14 yrs) tells him not to eat the mango because he is suffering with fever.
>
> Sitavva (sister, 6 yrs) goes over to her brother Mallya (1.5 yrs) and looks at his backside after he has had a bowel movement. Mallya says something to her, and she takes a banyan leaf, cleans him off and throws it away. She puts sand on the spot where he had his bowel movement. He speaks to her and starts to play again. Sitavva takes another leaf, holds Mallya between her legs and wipes his hip. She takes another leaf and tries to wipe as he crawls forward. She follows him and wipes him off again. Then she goes back to where she was playing.
>
> Devamma (sister, 5 yrs) wipes the nose of her brother Bhimanna (2 yrs) in front of their house. Later, he begins to cry inside the house, and she leads him outside by the hand, where they sit on the veranda. He puts his arms on Devamma's shoulder, and she puts him on her lap. He stays there for a couple of minutes, then he gets up. Bhimanna pulls the hair of another girl (presumably not a sibling) on the veranda, and Devamma removes his hands from the girl's head. Bhimanna goes back inside the house.

These examples of what we have called "mothering" behavior represent most clearly the ideal pattern suggested by the *Mahabharata* in which the older sibling functions primarily as a parent and exhibits primarily parental behavior. Previously cited behavior involving hitting and ignoring is not clearly inconsistent with a model of sibling as parent because parents also may hit or ignore children. The problem of distinguishing between violence motivated by rivalry and violence motivated by love seems not to have been addressed in the literature concerning sibling relationships.

Requesting

Siblings in Gopalpur make requests of one another, though it appears that the younger ones do most of the requesting. Requests are usually for something tangible, for help, for one sibling to come to another, or for one sibling to play with another. For example:

> Buranuddin (brother, 4 yrs) goes into the cow shed and asks Chahussain (brother, 14 yrs) to come. Chahussain goes into the

shed and asks Buranuddin what he wants. Buranuddin says he wants the buffalo untied and given water. After they've finished, Buranuddin cries and asks Chahussain to cut up a mango and give it to him. Chahussain doesn't and Buranuddin continues to cry looking at the mango.

Basavaraj (father's brother's son, 6 yrs) is eating bread, and Mariappa (father's brother's son, 1 yr) asks him for some. Basavaraj doesn't give him any. Mariappa goes to Sabavva (daughter, 7 yrs) who is drinking water, cries and asks for some. Sabavva gives water to Basavaraj, but not to Mariappa.

Instructing

Instructions from one sibling to another often involve play. One child may instruct another as to what to do while playing. Sometimes one sibling will instruct another, usually younger, sibling as to where to go, what to say, what to do, or what not to do.

Devendra (brother, 7 yrs) told Ramlinga (brother, 3 yrs) to sit inside a basket and that he would get a rope to drag the basket. When Devendra couldn't drag the basket with Ramlinga in it, Devendra told Ramlinga to get out. Ramlinga said he wanted to drag the basket too, so Devendra told him that he would drag it halfway home, then Ramlinga could drag it the rest of the way. When they returned home, Devendra told Ramlinga to go in and get some bread for them to eat, which he did.

Bhimavva (sister, 4 yrs) was collecting seeds with a boy when her brother Tirkappa (10 yrs) came by and told her to come home with him. Bhimavva took her bowl and went with him.

Laksmamma (sister, 6 yrs) told Mariamma (sister, 3 yrs) to bring some small stones to her so they could cook. She brought her some stones, and Laksmamma made a cooking stove out of them. Then she told Mariamma to bring some water. Mariamma pretended to bring water and Laksmamma pretended to light the stove and cook. The girls continued to play, and their sister Hanumavva (13 yrs) joined them. Mariamma brought sticks to Hanumavva and told her to put the pounding handle inside the house or somebody would take it.

Promising

There were two observations in which an older sibling promised food to a younger sibling to appease the child.

> Narsamma (sister, 6 yrs) had some ground nuts in the front of her shirt. Lingappa (brother, 4 yrs) asked what she had in her shirt, and she said she had ground nuts. Lingappa asked for some, and Narsamma said she would give him some when they sat down to eat.

> Sidanna (father's brother's son, 4 yrs) and Buganna (son, 5 yrs) were eating nuts. When Sidanna finished his nuts, he went over and asked Buganna if he had finished his. Sidanna said that he brought some nuts, but that Buganna had brought more. Sidanna asked for some and when Buganna didn't give him any, he began to cry. Buganna said that he would give him some later and patted his back.

Threatening

There was one observation in which one sibling threatened to leave another in order to get what he wanted.

> Sidanna (father's brother's son, 4 yrs) was pounding a stone on the ground while Buganna (son, 5 yrs) sat next to him gathering sand. Buganna asked Sidanna to give him the stone so that he could pound it, but Sidanna didn't give it to him. Buganna said he would go to the Hanuman temple without him. Buganna didn't leave, and Sidanna said he would give him the stone, which he did.

In summary, the following behaviors were observed in Gopalpur: hitting, ignoring, mothering, requesting, instucting, promising, and threatening. There were no recorded instances of pushing, pulling, shoving, kicking, biting, pinching, pulling hair, insulting, scolding, or praising, behaviors that were observed with substantial frequency in Mississauga. Table 4.1 provides a summary of negative and positive behaviors found between siblings in Gopalpur.

In Mississauga, interactions between siblings took place approximately 57 times per hour of observation. In Gopalpur, as the low totals in Table 4.1 indicate, the observed rate of interaction falls well under 10 times per hour. Differences in methodology may explain some of these differences in interaction rates. For example, in Gopalpur, observations may have been less detailed and interactions with non-siblings were ignored. Other possible explanations for the slower pace among Gopalpur's children are: the heat; their not needing to compensate for long periods in disciplined environments such as school rooms; their not taking long daytime naps; their having few toys; their rarely

TABLE 4.1. Positive and Negative Sibling Interaction in Gopalpur, South India

	Negative behaviors		Positive behaviors		
	Hits	Ignores	Instructs	Mothers	Requests
			Older to younger		
B → B	2	2	7	5	1
B → S	0	0	2	0	0
S → B	3	3	3	5	0
S → S	0	0	3	4	1
			Younger to older		
B → B	1	2	2	0	5
B → S	2	0	1	0	3
S → B	0	0	1	0	0
S → S	1	1	2	0	1
TOTAL	9	8	21	14	11

engaging in competitive sports or other contests; malnutrition; chronic illness; and poor sleeping environments. Words like "jazzed up," "frantic," or "hyperactive" do not come to mind in thinking about Gopalpur children. On balance, we think there is an important difference in rates of activity between the two groups of children. If a single explanation is to be sought for this contrast, it might be found in the excitement and drama of urban life. People in villages like Gopalpur rarely die of stress-related diseases such as mental illness, drug abuse, violence, high blood pressure, or heart disease.

When they hit each other, children in Gopalpur, like adults, almost always use sticks of varying sizes. Because there is little or no direct retaliation that would constitute fighting, it is hard to tell in individual cases of retaliation whether the action carried out by an older child is conceived as disciplinary caretaking or as antagonistic fighting. With younger children, hitting may symbolize antagonism or may simply be a means of attracting attention. As in Mississauga, male children are more likely to be the recipients of violence than are female children. Younger children will hit older girls, but otherwise females are almost never struck, in sharp contrast to Mississauga. Older sisters hit their younger brothers slightly more often than do older brothers; they also give fewer instructions. The absence of hair pulling, shoving, retaliatory hitting, or biting, which are familiar events in Mississauga, also suggests a reduced expression of sibling rivalry. There was only one case that might have been labeled "tattling" in our data and that was an older sibling requesting assistance in controlling a very young sibling.

Overall, there is not a single incident in the observational data that unequivocally supports an interpretation of actual conflict between siblings. Because our sample was small, this does not support the conclusion that rivalrous sibling conflict is absent among Gopalpur's children, but it does suggest that it occurs much less often in Gopalpur than in Mississauga. If all negative acts are seen as indicative of sibling conflict, there were 17 negative acts and 46 positive acts in the Gopalpur material. In Mississauga, each hour on the average, there were 27 negative acts and 13 positive acts. This figure is somewhat skewed because the Mississauga data used here involves same-sex sibling pairs, and negative actions are less likely with mixed-sex sibling pairs. Even so, the size of the difference between Gopalpur and Mississauga remains large. Most of the negative acts in Mississauga suggested sibling conflict; most of the negative acts in Gopalpur could have been interpreted as caretaking. A cautious view of the contrast in incidence of overtly expressed sibling conflict is that the real difference may be somewhat smaller than the figures suggest. Even so, expressed sibling conflict in Mississauga is many times more frequent than in Gopalpur.

In terms of more casual observations, it is to be noted that children in Gopalpur usually do not display aggressive behavior. During 2½ years of fieldwork in Gopalpur, children were not seen playing war games, although they did wave stick swords and sing songs like warrior kings and deities appearing in dramatic performances. No children were seen throwing rocks, and no children were seen shouting at or fighting with each other. The absence of rock throwing is supported by the presence of small birds that fly in and out of houses without apparent fear of human beings.

Beyond the question of sibling conflict, the data presented in Table 4.1 suggest other important aspects of sibling relationships in Gopalpur. First, older boys almost never assume responsibility for younger sisters, the only recorded behaviors exchanged between them falling under the rather indecisive category of "instructs." It is tempting to view this near avoidance of younger sisters as related to the fact that the younger sister is more or less the same age as the older brother's future wife. As noted, older sisters caring for younger brothers give fewer instructions and slightly more blows than do older brothers with younger brothers, perhaps suggesting that the older sister is less secure in her authority than the older brother. Indications of a special relationship between brothers are that older brothers give more instructions to younger brothers than occur in any other sibling relationship and that mothering behavior occurs as frequently between brothers as it does between sisters and brothers. Again, younger brothers make more requests of older brothers than of older sisters while younger sisters rarely ask for anything.

In Karnatak State, the oldest of the Pandava brothers is referred to as "Dharmarayya," suggesting that he instructs his younger brothers in matters having to do with *dharma*, or right action. Consistent with this, the single most frequent activity observed in Gopalpur was instruction, and the most common form of instruction was in older brother instructing his younger brother. The next most frequent category, which we have called "mothering," consists of older children performing such "maternal" actions as feeding, dressing, and toileting for younger children. While brothers accept mothering from older sisters, the mothering of younger sisters by older brothers is rare. Some of the activities that we have described as "instructing," "mothering," and "requesting" may be included in the Mississauga data under the headings of "cooperating," "sharing," "smiling," or "praising," but it would seem that the differences in the headings themselves point to a radical contrast between unequal, parent-like, relationships in Gopalpur and more nearly egalitarian relationships in Mississauga.

Although some North American psychologists would interpret the absence or comparative absence of sibling conflict in Gopalpur as reflecting repression of a universal disposition or developmental tendency, an adequate and economic explanation of the observed data can be provided in contextual terms. In Gopalpur, the juvenile sibling belongs to the caretaker sibling in much the same way that a child belongs to a parent in North American culture. For the younger sibling, it is the caretaker sibling who dispenses punishment and reward. Because the relationship is unequal and parental, there is little to be gained from conflict over possessions or quarrels over status. From a strictly rational viewpoint the younger sibling wins nothing and loses much by expressing rivalry toward the older sibling. The caretaker sibling generally achieves his ends by telling the younger sibling what to do, and the younger sibling achieves his ends by asking nicely. Should there be a dispute, older third parties would instruct the younger sibling to obey the reasonable requests of the caretaker sibling. Conflictual behavior is not reinforced by word or deed.

Overall, the relationships among young siblings in Gopalpur closely resemble the phenomenon that Bank (in Bank & Kalm 1982: 34) describes as "frevent sibling loyalty." Some of the problems that psychologists relate to fervent loyalty do occur in Gopalpur. For example, there are a few adult younger siblings who seem unable to function in the absence of their dominating older sibling. Often younger brothers complain about being poorly equipped to manage a farm after the division of the property. Considering the caretaker role assumed by the older sibling, the parallel here might be with the North American overprotective mother. Most mothers in North America are not excessively overprotective, and neither are most caretaker siblings in Gopalpur. More common is the situation seen in the *Mahabharata* where siblings develop complementary specialized skills. Thus, among the hero brothers, Dharmarayya was saintly, Bhima was physically powerful, and Arjuna was clever. Although brothers of about the same age may be inseparable companions, the need to behave with formality toward an older brother will often cause brothers to develop different circles of informal friendship and thus avoid close identification with each other. On the whole, a comparison between South Asia and North America on the issues of fervent sibling loyalty and passionate sibling rivalry would seem to suggest that "anything in excess is bad," a sentiment frequently heard in South Asia.

Adult Siblings

In North America, as siblings move toward adulthood, opportunities for displays of sibling conflict are reduced. After moving out of the house, siblings may avoid each other or they may become close friends and associates. In either case, the continual exchange of hostilities tends to come to an end. Cicirelli (1982: 227) reports that almost all siblings, especially female siblings, feel close to each other in middle and old age. Among middle-aged adults only 2% reported experiencing feelings of rivalry. Apparently in North American culture, hostility or rivalry between siblings, while expected in childhood, practically disappears in later life. In South Asia, young siblings are not expected to quarrel or express rivalry, and, with the exception of relationships among some brothers, this is generally the case in later life.

In Gopalpur, where partly grown or adult women tend to move out of the village, female siblings frequently drift apart. If they marry men who live in the same village, they are often brought close together by an environment that is strange and sometimes hostile. Marriage rules permit marriage of two sisters to two brothers, and polygynous marriage to the same husband. Marriage to sisters is often preferred because "sisters won't quarrel." If women marry into nearby villages, and they usually do, their brothers often make a point of visiting them and encouraging them to visit Gopalpur. Since older sisters often marry mother's younger brothers, and since men are encouraged to marry mother's younger brother's daughter or older sister's daughter, the maintenance of close and friendly relationships among adult brothers and sisters is easily explained. In essence, they tend to become partners in the exchange of women and other familial network benefits between their two villages.

While sisters in Gopalpur are generally separated from their siblings when they reach marriageable age, brothers usually remain in the same household until all brothers are married or until the father dies. Sometimes brothers remain together longer. Under these circumstances brothers are expected to display respect and obedience first to the father, and later to the elder brother. Within the household, the most frequent and disruptive conflicts reported for Gopalpur and villages surrounding Gopalpur take place between husband and wife. Conflicts between mothers-in-law and daughters-in-law and between brothers are next most frequent and are reported with about equal frequency by village residents. Conflicts between the several wives of a single husband or among the wives of brothers were also fairly common but are usually reported as incidental to other conflicts. Conflicts between sisters or between brothers and sisters are never reported. It seems probable that the actual frequency of such conflicts are quite low (but see Nuckolls, Chapter 8, this volume). Expectations of good sisterly relationships are implicit in the recommendation that a second wife should ideally be a sister of the first wife.

Conflicts between mother-in-law and daughter-in-law and conflicts between husband and wife are not unrelated to conflicts between brothers since the escalation of either type of conflict will often force brothers to choose sides. Initially, the marriage of the oldest of a set of brothers reaffirms the solidary relationship between brother and sister. For those who obtain their brides from the sister's village, the sister's daughter or equivalent who enters the house is a kind of a gift from the older sister. Since the older sister, herself, may be married to mother's brother, the marriage may be a general reaffirmation of cross-sex sibling ties. The young girl who enters the household, often before reaching puberty, is placed under the direct control of her mother-in-law, who may also be her mother's mother and father's sister. Initially, the husband has very little to do with his wife or his mother's treatment of her. When the wife reaches puberty and begins to have regular sexual relationships with her husband, she often discovers her first supporter in her new household. With the birth of her first child, the daughter-in-law acquires a moral and religious obligation to her child, which equals and may eventually transcend her obligations to mother-in-law and husband.

As the husband's younger brothers acquire wives, who are somewhat less frequently sister's daughters or other close relatives, the first daughter-in-law acquires responsibility for organizing and controlling the labor of the new daughters-in-law. As her children and her responsibilities grow, she becomes more and more the equal of her mother-in-law. In many cases, especially where the first wife is a favorite niece or granddaughter, the mother-in-law gives ground graciously and with the death of her husband follows a pattern of semiretirement. In some cases, there is a power struggle between the mother-in-law and the senior daughter-in-law. Such a power struggle may begin on the first day of the marriage or it may develop over the years. In either case, it is about political control of the household and economic control of its material and labor resources. It is generated by an emerging equality between the mother-in-law and daughter-in-law, and it is fueled by the daughter-in-law's expectation that in the long run the son-husband must favor her over his mother. Of course, many husband and wife conflicts emerge over the failure of the husband to support his wife in her conflicts with his mother. Direct conflict between son and mother is unthinkable, or at least unreported.

As the younger brothers acquire wives and children of their own, they too acquire the moral and religious obligation to advance the interests of their wives and children. They rise steadily in status and importance. As husbands and fathers, they become progressively more equal to their father and older brother. The well-reported opposition between equality and hierarchy in Indian society (Dumont 1970; see also Derné, Chapter 7, this volume) strikes with special force here, for the brothers and the father are equal owners of the joint-family property. When one brother has more male children than the other brothers, the share of property to be inherited by the sons of the other brothers is automatically diminished. Very often one brother or another, perhaps under pressure from his wife if local ideology is to be credited, sees himself as working harder and profiting less than the other brothers.

As the brothers begin to quarrel among themselves or begin to feel their close relationship threatened by the hostility of their wives, they contemplate division of the joint family. When the family is divided, the brothers become politically independent of their parents and siblings, and very often the brothers become economic equals. Because a family farm corporation operated by a set of brothers enjoys important economies of scale, the division of the family can be a harsh economic blow. Younger brothers are often unfamiliar with business matters and may attribute their newly won poverty to unfair behavior on the part of the older brother. Enemies, who maintained a respectful distance when the brothers were united, may now take advantage of one of the more naive younger brothers and attempt to fuel the resentment.

The ideal joint family, which, like the Pandava family, consists of five adult brothers, is a force to be reckoned with in the village. Even though the family land-holdings may not be large in per capita terms, efficiencies of scale make the joint family comparatively wealthy. The five united sons provide an army that is dominant in village power struggles. Within the village, the large joint family, because it must increase its land-holdings to support five households in the place of one, tends to become a predatory organization that must feed its ever-increasing numbers by obtaining the lands and resources of other less successful families. Political opposition to its growing political and economic power is a strong factor in the maintenance of unity within the large joint family. Thus, five-brother families, although statistically rare, are frequently at the center of village factionalist disputes. In such cases, the absolute necessity for fraternal unity tends to postpone family division indefinitely. Because, like divorce in North America, family division tends to be expensive, it may be somewhat less common among the poor than among the rich. Certainly in Gopalpur, many families remain undivided even though (or perhaps because) several of their members work outside of the village. Short of these situations, brothers tend to plan for family division at the time of their father's or sometimes mother's death, and it often proceeds harmoniously with the brothers remaining friendly and cooperative.

Adult Conflict

Altogether, there are only seven reported cases of fraternal conflict among adult brothers in the recent history of Gopalpur. These cases include only quarrels or disagreements that became public and required intervention by village elders. In each of the cases, village elders were successful in bringing the conflict to a halt. Judging on the basis of other sorts of incidents, it is a virtual certainty that one or both of the quarreling brothers would have been forced to leave the village if they had not agreed to abide by the elders' decision.

Accounts of adult conflict in Gopalpur were collected by asking adults to dictate to an interviewer histories of any quarrels or fights that they knew about. There was no specific request that any particular type of fight or quarrel be described. Thus, accounts of sibling conflict were gathered in the process of collecting general accounts of village conflict. The present discussion of rivalry among adult siblings, all male, is based upon the eight accounts of quarrels among siblings provided by informants. These eight accounts, which cover a substantial period of time, are most probably all of the incidents that adults in Gopalpur remembered.

Almost all of the cases revolve around the development of some sort of perceived inequality in the treatment of adult siblings. At the simplest level, conflict may arise as a result of a perceived inequality in the labor contribution of the two siblings to the joint-family enterprise. For example:

> Big Bhimsha had a cold, so he stayed in the house rather than coming to work in the fields. His younger brother, Little Bhimsha hit him with a stick. Neighbors heard the angry quarrel, restrained the two brothers, and encouraged them to make up.

South Indians are generally unwilling to believe that quarrels between brothers can arise spontaneously, as in the above example. The general cause of conflict between brothers, perceived as naturally loyal to each other, is disturbance created by greedy, lazy, or badly behaved wives. In the following story, which is almost prototypical of the way conflict is thought to happen, the joint family, which consisted of four brothers, was divided into four nuclear families, and Narsamma, the cause of the trouble, was sent back to her parents (i.e., divorced):

> Narsamma, the wife of Biimanna's younger brother, Sanappa, said that she had a cold and was unable to work. She said to Biimanna's wife Manikamma, "Just this one day will you please do it?" She then went back to bed. Manikamma said, "Hey, do you think I am some kind of servant, I am not going to do anything. Today you have a chill and then a cough and then a headache. If you sleep for that sort of thing, then nobody will do anything." Narsamma said that she did not sleep everyday: "Today, just for this one day, I want to rest." "That's right, that's right," said Manikamma, "just this one day you slept, and every other day you just sat around; today, I am not going to bring food and give it to you." Then Sanappa, the younger brother came home and discovered that Manikamma had not fed his wife, Narsamma. He got very angry and gave Manikamma two hard blows. She cried out and accused him of trying to kill her. At this point, Bimanna came home and hit his brother with a stick.

Tension may also arise in joint families when wives treat the different brothers unequally. In one case, the older brother's wife scolded and mistreated the younger brother's family because she felt that they were having too many children. There was no overt quarrel, but the older brother and his wife left the village to work in a factory. The following case covers dissatisfaction among women and the problem of perceived inequality in the distribution of jointly held property.

> The oldest of three brothers, Yankappa, worked hard in the fields and came home hungry. He washed himself and sat down to eat. Maremma, the wife of his younger brother, Bhima, did not give him any food. Yankappa was very hungry, because of that he became angry and hit Maremma. She sat crying. Bhima, the younger brother, came from the fields, and the first thing he heard was the noise of crying. He asked Maremma what it was about, and she said that Yankappa had beaten her severely. Bhima got angry with his older brother and asked him why he had beaten Maremma. Yankappa, with anger coming from his empty stomach, said, "Why are you asking, I can hit her whenever I want to." Bhima got angry and hit Yankappa; then both brothers wrestled. At this point the village elders came and made peace, and everyone went to bed hungry.
>
> The next morning, Yankappa said, "I am not going to stay here anymore, I want my share and to live apart." The village elders assembled again and "spoke wisdom" to Yankappa. He said, "My younger brother just listens to his wife and hits me; don't tell me what's right, I won't listen to anyone, I really want my share." The elders told him not to divide the family, "You are still a young man, wait a few days and eat [i.e., wait until you have the skills and capital required for independent farming]." Yankappa didn't like those words. Finally Bhima said to him, "Yankappa don't say that you want to divide. There will be no fault if someday you want to divide. At that time, the next day in the morning go out to the fields with a rope, and we will make the division." Then Yankappa said, "If we divide the field into two parts, who will make the first choice?" Bhima said that Yankappa could make the first choice. Yankappa then insisted on an immediate division, taking the part of the field that had been well fertilized. Bhima was left with the infertile part of the field. Then they divided the house, and Bhimarayya let Yankappa make the first choice again.
>
> Everyone did their work and at harvest time. Bhima's wife, Maremma, said, "How come Yankappa's grain crop is well grown and yours is tiny?" Then Maremma quarreled with Bhima saying, "Why didn't you divide the property correctly? Why did you take the infertile field? I am not satisfied." These words fell on the ears of Yankappa's wife, Nagamma, and she asked her husband, "How come our field is full of grain and Maremma's field is scanty?"
>
> Because it couldn't be divided, the brothers had agreed to share a single cart. Yankappa took the cart to carry his ample harvest to

the house. When Bhima asked for the cart, Yankappa said he needed it and couldn't give it to Bhima. They both got ready to fight, but Bhima thought, I am a big man. He borrowed someone else's cart and did his work. Later, under pressure from the elders, the cart was sold and the profit divided equally.

During the hot season, Bhima was plowing in his fields. At that time, he dug up the stone that the elders had placed to mark the division of the field. He moved the stone forward into Yankappa's field. Yankappa noticed this and went to the village and called together the elders who had made the property division. He showed them the stone and said: "That day you divided our field and now my brother has moved the stone that you placed in the field. My brother is angry because my field grows a good crop and his doesn't." Finally, the elders made peace and sent the two brothers home.

In a second case where property division created problems, the two brothers divided their estate improperly while their parents were still living. This meant that the parents retained a share of the property. After the parents died, the older brother began cultivating his parents' field. The younger brother saw him plowing and came into the field and grabbed the plow. The older brother and his son then beat the younger brother unconscious with a stick. The elders made the older brother divide the field and awarded the younger brother four sacks of grain.

Even years after the family division, a suspicion of inequality can sour relationships between brothers. For example:

Many years ago Yankappa and Mahadevappa divided their fields, leaving two fields with one boundary. A tree grew on the boundary, and Yankappa watered and fertilized the tree. One day he asked his mother's brother and another man to cut down the tree. Mahadevappa ordered them to stop, saying that he was part owner of the tree. The workers went to Yankappa, and he told them that the tree was not shared property and ordered them to cut down the tree. When they started to cut down the tree, Mahadevappa and his younger brother came and started hitting them with sticks. People stopped the fighting and the village elders ordered both Yankappa and Mahadevappa to remain in their houses while the elders discussed the dispute. After two days of discussion the elders ruled that the tree belonged to Yankappa because he had cared for it.

The first and second cases above reflect the common situation in which the older brother simply assumes that he is entitled to a larger share than the younger brother. The case of the disputed tree illustrates the sensitivity that develops as brothers become economic competitors following the division of property. All three cases illustrate in various ways the emphasis placed upon *dharma,* or lawfulness, both in seeking one's rights and in doing the right thing.

Wives in the patriarchal joint family have a weak position because their brothers and other supporters frequently live far away. Nevertheless, just as subordinated younger brothers may seek their rights, so may wives, as the following complicated example illustrates.

> Four brothers lived in an undivided joint family along with their wives. The household ran well. The youngest brother's wife, Nagamma, was very young and so the marriage was not consummated. When Nagamma reached puberty, she discovered that her husband was impotent. She decided to run away but was afraid to do it alone. One of the other brothers, Hanumantha, beat his wife daily. One day when the two women were harvesting grain in the fields closest to their home villages, they put their baskets and tools down in the road and vanished. When the brothers finally found their wives, the youngest brother's wife refused to return to Gopalpur unless her husband proved he was man enough to come and get her. He never went to get her. Hanumantha had a long discussion with his uncles (presumably his wife's relatives) and was forced to promise to treat his wife properly, and his wife came back. After these incidents the brothers quarreled and divided their property. As a consequence of the poverty following the division of the family, the brothers had further physically violent disputes about the borrowing and lending of grain, which were settled by the village elders.

Questions concerning the righteousness of family division lead to bloody quarrels, and this may be why equal sharing is so strongly emphasized. Consider the following:

> Margappa, a younger brother, was working as an indentured servant in a neighbor's house. He managed to accumulate 30 rupees, which he left with some relatives. He and his brothers owed grain to these relatives. When Margappa asked for his money, the relatives said they would not give it to him because he owed them grain. There was a quarrel, and Margappa argued that the 30 rupees was his personal money, while the grain debt was owed by the family corporation. Then Margappa's older brother ordered him to come home and stop quarreling. Margappa remained unhappy and complained steadily to his older brothers. Finally, the elders came and explained that, as a joint family member, Margappa could not have separate earnings, and thus

> the money could be used to pay for the grain. As Margappa concluded, "After that I kept quiet; what could I do, it was my mistake."

The several cases above in which one brother is shown clearly to be in the wrong seem to permit fairly permanent resolution of the conflict. It is not so easy in the case of outright disloyalty and sabotage:

> The brothers Alyappa and Yellappa separated some years ago, and both did well. One day Alyappa's son, Alyanna, slandered the wife of Yellappa's younger brother, but denied doing so. Later, when Alyanna's marriage was being arranged, the family decided to avoid trouble by not inviting Yellappa and Mariappa, another brother, to the wedding. Yellappa told the relatives of the potential bride, who were visiting, that the marriage was a bad idea. The bride's relatives mentioned this encounter to their hosts. There was an angry quarrel. Peace was made, but "the brothers remain far apart."
>
> Guda Sab is the youngest of three brothers. His two older brothers, whom he loves dearly, have obtained excellent jobs in Bombay. The brothers send him marvelous T-shirts and other gifts from Bombay. Guda Sab wishes to go to Bombay, but his brothers want him to stay in Gopalpur and manage the family lands so they will have some place to go when they retire. Guda Sab sums up relationships between brothers as follows:
>
> "See here, older brother, younger brother, when they speak together that means that the younger brother says nothing. The older brother is really proud because when the father dies he becomes the head of the house. His words and his instructions control everyone. Sometimes if the younger brother makes a mistake, the older brother will hit him as punishment. Sometimes older brother and younger brother, between the two of them, there will be a quarrel. At times the brothers will become enemies. The cause of this anger and hatred between brothers is that one of their wives is greedy, and her husband listens to her words and an enmity grows. After this enmity has developed, one family becomes two families. Then, if one brother sees the face of the other brother, a quarrel may start. Quarrels may also start if one brother gets a bit of money or is doing well in life. To quote a proverb, 'At birth they are brothers, as grown men they are dividers.' Finally, older brother means father so you give your older brother the same respect that you give your father."

As of 1966, about 10 of the 100 households in Gopalpur consisted of two or more brothers. In every case, the father was still alive.

Normally, family division is considered acceptable after all of the brothers and sisters are securely married. The death of the father may also be the occasion for division. Substantial hostility may develop if one or more of the brothers attempts to divide the joint property early. On balance, there are more instances of brothers remaining friendly throughout their lifetimes than there are of brothers who no longer speak to each other. It is difficult to provide evidence of latent sibling conflict among otherwise harmonious sets of brothers, but adult younger brothers, as suggested in Guda Sab's above summation, do sometimes grumble and complain to close friends about their brothers' conduct. There is also some tendency for adult brothers to avoid each other and to have separate circles of friends. Thus, there is some rather equivocal evidence in favor of the existence of repressed hostile tendencies toward siblings in adulthood. If fraternal feelings of hostility are a psychosocial universal, the repression of such hostility must be interpreted as taking place most frequently in childhood in South Asia and in adulthood in North America.

Adult siblings in North America may remain apart, or they may become increasingly close as the years go by. It is noteworthy that, for the most part, they have no particular obligations to each other. Adult siblings in North America are considered to be equal and independent; they need not eat together, visit each other, or engage in economic activities together. Structurally, such siblings would seem to have no particular reason to engage in conflict as there is no prize for which both are competing. The comparative absence of conflict among North American adult siblings is perfectly consistent with their situation in life.

With regard to sisters, and to brothers and sisters, the situation is quite similar in south India. Such siblings may be thrown together by fate or by mutual self-interest in exchanging brides, and if so, they seem to get along. By contrast, male siblings in South Asia must share in the management of the joint-family estate. In particular, they must ensure that any division of that estate is carried out with the greatest circumspection. The management of complex joint-family estates involves economic decision-making. It also involves care and feeding of the often numerous members of the family. The economic and political value of the large joint family is such that an entire civilization mobilizes its greatest epic, the *Mahabharata*, in aid of preventing conflict between male siblings. Over the history of the family, as children grow and wives make increasing demands, the pressures upon brothers to divide the family grow increasingly strong. Ultimately families do divide, and often there is conflict between male siblings. As the above cited accounts illustrate, the village elders maintain a powerful presence designed to prevent violent interaction between brothers. Even so, there is conflict, but perhaps much less than might be expected given the many disruptive forces working against the perpetuation of the joint family.

Conclusion

In Europe and North America there has been a fair amount of research on siblings. Elsewhere there has been very little. Historically, research on siblings follows popular mythology in its emphasis upon negative and conflictual relationships and its near total neglect of such relationships between siblings as instructing, caretaking, and sharing. The data available for this chapter do not permit any definitive conclusions concerning sibling relationships in general, but they raise some fairly strong possibilities. To the extent that good data are available, it appears that sibling relationships in South Asia are markedly different from those in North America. Because little is known about variation in sibling relationships within North America or South Asia, it is not clear how far the contrasts noted in this paper can be generalized.

The prevailing North American and European view that there is some kind of biological or universal psychological basis for sibling conflict, or for other forms of sibling relationship, is not supported by our present data. Social structure, ideology, and the life cycle appear to provide an adequate explanation of the presence and absence of sibling conflict and other features of sibling relationships without calling upon any very complicated innate mechanisms. Cultural and social explanations of the contrast between South Asia and North America are strengthened by the fact that observed fraternal relationships in the two locations are superficially at least, mirror images of each other. Several earlier readers of this chapter, including one psychoanalyst, have commented upon the (to them) obvious fact that South Indians suffer from severe repression of their normal tendencies toward sibling rivalry. This is, of course, a possibility, but the data in this chapter provide equal support for the opposite conclusion that North American children are compelled, perhaps under the pressures of a competitive society, to repress their natural tendencies toward harmony. The question as to whether human beings are naturally conflictual or naturally harmonious brings us back once again to a Western dualism that places greater emphasis on conflict than on resolution. If the child and adult siblings of North America and South Asia are regarded as responding primarily to the world around them, rather than to obscure and contradictory biological drives, the presences and absences of sibling conflict, and of other forms of behavior, seem fairly easily explained.

The limited comparisons made here between *Psychology Today* and the *Mahabharata* and between Mississauga and Gopalpur are partly a reflection of the inadequacy of the existing literature concerning siblings. For Gopalpur, the relationships between ideal and actual sibling behavior are considerably closer than is usually the case when real and ideal behaviors are compared, perhaps because people in Gopalpur consciously utilize the *Mahabharata* as a model for sibling relationships. Under different conditions it can be expected that children elsewhere in India will turn out to be far more active and far more rivalrous than those of Gopalpur. Certainly, not all North American children are as violent as those described in Mississauga. Adult siblings seem to have rather different relationships than they had as children in both regions, but the data concerning adult siblings are even sketchier than that for children.

The evidence is strong that the children of India provide yet another lesson in the virtues of nonviolence and the malleability of the human condition. It is perhaps a cultural universal that relationships among close family members are considered a fundamental and immutable aspect of the human condition. Perhaps this is why anthropologists, despite their interest in kinship, have collected very little observational data concerning relationships among close kin. Cross-cultural variability was simply not expected. Again, the social significance of hostilities among brothers has focused such little research as there is, even with regard to psychological research concerning North American culture, on fraternal rivalry. Other aspects of family and kin siblings surely deserve more attention as a topic for cross-cultural research.

Note

1. Research in Gopalpur was carried out in 1956–60 and in 1966 with Alan R. Beals as the principal investigator through grants received from the National Science Foundation, The American Institute of Indian Studies, and Stanford University. The field observations of young children were carried out by Charles John and Constance Mayfield.

References

Abramovitch, R., Corter, C., & Lando, B. (1979). "Sibling Interaction in the Home. *Child Development* 50: 997–1003.

Bank, S. P., & Kahn, M. D. (1982). *The Sibling Bond.* New York: Basic Books.
Bloomfield, L. (1933). *Language.* New York: Henry Holt.
Cicirelli, V. G. (1982). "Sibling Influence throughout the Lifespan." In M. E. Lamb & B. Sutton-Smith (Eds.), *Sibling Relationships: Their Nature and Significance across the Lifespan* (pp. 267–84). Hillsdale, NJ: Erlbaum.
Dumont, L. (1970). *Homo Hierarchicus, an Essay on the Caste System* (M. Sainsbury, Trans.). Chicago: University of Chicago Press.
Dunn, J., & Kendrick, C. (1982). *Siblings: Love, Envy and Understanding.* Cambridge, MA: Harvard University Press.
Greenberg, J. H. (1966). *Language Universals, with Special Reference to Feature Hierarchies.* The Hague: Mouton.
Greenberg, J. H., Ferguson, C. A., & Moravcsik, E. A. (Eds.). (1978). *Universals of Human Language.* Stanford: Stanford University Press.
Hammel, E. A. (1984). On the **** of Studying Household Form and Function. In R. M. Netting, R. R. Wilk, & E. J. Arnould (Eds.), *Households: Comparative and Historical Studies of the Domestic Group.* Berkeley: University of California Press.
Lévi-Strauss, C. (1949). *Les Structures élémentaires de la parenté* [Elementary Structures of Kinship]. Paris: Presses Universitaires de France.
Murdock, G. P. (1949). *Social Structure.* New York: Macmillan.
Schneider, D. (1980). *American Kinship: A Cultural Account* (2nd ed). Englewood Cliffs, NJ: Prentice-Hall.
Schneider, D. (1984). *A Critique of the Study of Kinship.* Ann Arbor: University of Michigan Press.
Sutton-Smith, B. (1982). Epilogue: Framing the Problem. In M. E. Lamb & B. Sutton-Smith (Eds.), *Sibling Relationships: Their Nature and Significance across the Lifespan* (pp. 386–87). Hillsdale, NJ: Erlbaum.
Sutton-Smith, B., & Rosenberg, B. G. (1970). *The Sibling.* New York: Holt, Rinehart & Winston.
Weisner, T. S. (1982). Sibling Interdependence and Child Caretaking: A Cross-cultural View. In M. E. Lamb & B. Sutton-Smith (Eds.), *Sibling Relationships: Their Nature and Significance across the Lifespan* (pp. 305–327). Hillsdale, NJ: Erlbaum.
Weisner, T., & Gallimore, R. (1977). "My Brother's Keeper: Child and Sibling Caretaking." *Current Anthropology* 18: 169–91.
Zukow, P. (Ed.). (1984). *Sibling Interaction across Cultures: Theoretical and Methodological Issues.* New York: Springer-Verlag.

Photo by Pauline Kolenda

CHAPTER 5

Sibling Relations and Marriage Practices

A Comparison of North, Central, and South India

Pauline Kolenda

To write about sibling relationships without including other familial relationships, for instance those between parents and children, between grandparents and grandchildren, between in-laws—in other words, outside the entire kinship system—is to commit an anthropological sin: taking relationships out of context. Inevitably, other kinship relationships will be mentioned in this chapter. The main justification for looking at sibling relationships under a spotlight is their previous neglect by anthropologists. Much more has been written about the relationship between mother-in-law and daughter-in-law, father and son, and husband and wife in the Indian joint family. The most neglected sibling relationship in the literature on Indian kinship is that of sisters. The least neglected is probably that of brothers, especially the difficulties between brothers when they divide jointly inherited land. In-between is the brother–sister relationship.

Over the past 38 years, I have done ethnographic fieldwork in three different parts of rural India—in the north, in the village of Khalapur, situated in western Uttar Pradesh; in central India, in villages near the city of Jaipur, Rajasthan; and in the south, in Kanyakumari District, Tamil Nadu.[1] My consistent concern has been with caste and family among Hindus. In this chapter, I present briefly the cultural expectations for the brother–sister, brother–brother, and sister–sister relationships as they are alike and, especially, as they differ in the three regions. These culturally prescribed sibling relationships are those of adolescents and adults (rather than children), viewed in the context of similar and different kinship and marriage systems. As Weisner (1982: 324) has stated, "Most accounts of the cross-cultural diversity in the expression of sibling ties are closely linked to theories of descent and residence patterns around the world."

What is highlighted by a comparison between sibling relationships in three different regions of India is the relativity of these relationships to the marriage system followed. Each of the three regions has a different marriage system. In north India, marriage alliances are dispersed with a preference for maximizing ties, so that seldom do two sisters marry into the same village or family.[2] The strong brother–sister relationship fits well with the need for concern for the welfare of a married sister, living among strangers. Sisters seldom see each other after marriage, since they are usually married into different villages. Brothers, after marriage, either continue to live with their parents in a joint household, or live near each other, often working together in a joint-farming or artisan enterprise.

In central India, the marriage of related women to men of the same village and family is common, so that women have women relatives in their place of marriage. This makes the bonds between sisters unusually strong, especially when a pair or triad of sisters are married to a pair or triad of brothers. Joint families are prevalent in Rajasthan, and married brothers often continue to live together, or else, as in north India, are neighbors and work together and share a family pool of resources. The brother–sister relationship is not as idealized or as strong as in north India.

In south India, it is children of brother and sister who should marry. This means that there is a special closeness between the brother and sister whose children *do* marry, although there may be enmity between a sister and brother whose children were of the right age, but who did not marry. For the bride in a cross-cousin marriage, her mother-in-law may be her father's sister, or else her father-in-law may be her mother's brother; she does not move into a house of strangers at marriage. A brother may look after the land and gardens given as *stridanam* to a sister when she married; these may return to him later on when her daughter marries his son. Brothers may own land together jointly with their father, and may then divide it after their father's death. This can cause difficulties between brothers, as it can in north and central India. The relationship between sisters is not culturally emphasized, but sisters can maintain their relationships with each other, since travel for women is much freer for women in south India than in central or north India, where purdah limits a woman's freedom of movement.[3]

To begin, here are three kinship stories that characterize the three regions to be described and compared.

The Two Television Sets: A Story from North India

During the spring of 1984, my research assistants and I lived in Khalapur with a large joint family, one of the wealthiest and most educated of the village, owning about 120 acres of good sugarcane and wheat land. It was composed of 16 core members: the uneducated elderly parents (the mother in her 60s and the father in his 70s), their three educated married sons (one in his 40s, two in their 30s), and the sons' wives and children. Each son had exactly two sons and one daughter, one of whom was married, so there were eight unmarried children, ranging in age from 6 months to 15 years. Living with the family permanently, at least until her marriage, was a daughter's daughter, aged 16. By rule of patrilocal residence, this granddaughter was not residing in the "right" village; the "right" village was her father's village, at a considerable distance in a different district. She had lived with her maternal grandparents since the age of four, we were told. Possibly, her parents and grandparents agreed that the latter could better afford the expenses of her education. Living with the family while they attended the local high school were the second son's wife's brother and the third son's wife's brother's son.[4] While we were there, the grandfather's elderly married sister and the eldest son's married daughter, with her 6-month-old daughter, each visited for a number of weeks (see Figure 5.1).

The eldest of the three sons was the most educated, having both a BA and an MA degree; he was a teacher of English in the local high school. The two younger brothers both had completed 10th grade; both worked on the land, aided by a hired servant. They were very aware of the latest agricultural methods, true examples of rational farmers. The second son, who was the main manager of the family farm, once listed for me the dozens of different new wheat and sugarcane seeds he had tried over the years, each recommended by the local government agricultural officer. The family had a tractor, but also maintained cooperative relations with other farmers to work together on sowing and other tasks.

The division of labor was one in which the two younger brothers did all the work in the fields, while the eldest brother contributed his teacher's salary to the family income; he also was expected to negotiate with government distributors to get good seed and fertilizer or to obtain the products in a market in a nearby town. The three brothers

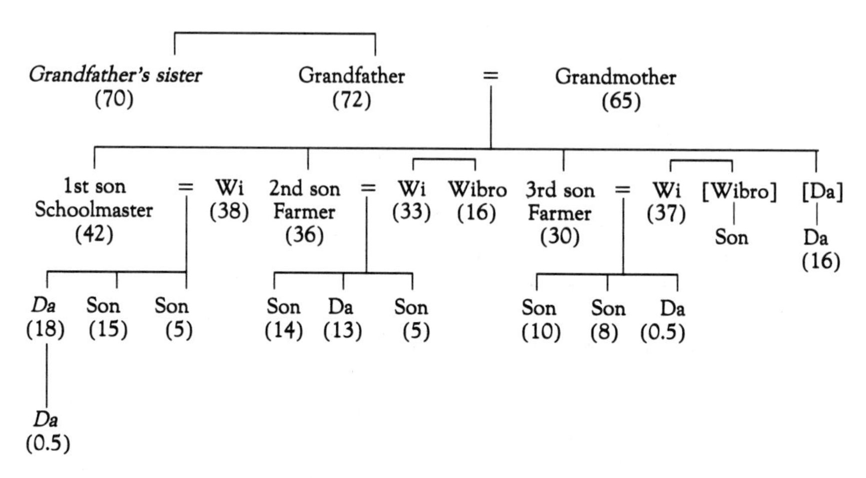

FIGURE 5.1. A Rajput joint family of Khalapur. Italics, visitor; [ ], absent; ( ), age of individual above, in years; Da, daughter; Bro, brother; Wi, wife.

were in agreement that all the children should be educated through high school, even the girls. Because they could foresee the small portions of land (at most, 20 acres) each of their six sons would eventually inherit, they had purposely limited the sizes of their families. Despite the rationality of the three sons, the integration of their joint family was fragile.

The second brother complained to me about what enormously hard work farming is. He hinted that the older schoolmaster brother should be making more effort to get them good seed and fertilizer. He did not complain about his good-natured younger brother.

The schoolmaster–eldest brother, indeed, may have neglected his agrarian duties, since he yearned to be free; he wanted to build a house in town where he could live a more sophisticated life, socializing with the educated elite, serving his guests tea out of china cups, as they sat on chairs around a polished table. It was he who had rented rooms to us; the cash we paid in rent was probably meant to help toward the cost of that town house.

What undoubtedly contributed to the two farmer-brothers' overwork, even though they had a full-time male field servant, was the fact that all eight boys (six sons plus the second son's wife's brother and the third son's wife's brother's son) attended school. Three of them (aged 5, 5, and 8) were too small to do heavy field work. The schoolmaster's eldest son was the oldest of the sons, but the schoolmaster would not allow him to do anything but study, since he wanted him both to pass his final year of high school and to get accepted into college. That left four boys big enough to help, a son of each of the two farmer-brothers, plus the two relatives of the farmer-brothers' wives, who lived with them while going to school. On school holidays, the farmer-brothers rounded up these four boys to help in the fields, while the daughter's daughter, also off from school, and the visiting elderly aunt carried huge baskets of bread and pots of curry out to the fields to feed the team of workers.

In a large joint family such as this one, siblings are not just full brothers and sisters but also cousins, for in north Indian Hindi kinship terminology, cousins are also called "brother" and "sister." Thus, 11 of the 12 children in this household could address each other as "brother" or "sister." One of the 3 boys attending high school was a mother's brother to these children, since he was an in-marrying wife's brother.

In general, the "brothers" and "sisters" seemed to get along. Only between the two little boys, both aged 5, parallel cousins to each other (their fathers were brothers), did there appear to be any bad feelings. These little fellows, constant companions, sometimes broke into arguments. Additionally, the head couple's daughter's daughter, the 16-year-old high school student who lived with her grandparents but whose home village was in another district, complained to us that the household chores she was required to do—we noticed that she was always up very early in the morning sweeping the courtyard—limited the time she had to study. Whether the other two boys (the second son's wife's brother and the third son's wife's brother's son), who were in high school, resented the schoolmaster's eldest son's freedom from chores, we do not know.

While the schoolmaster dreamed of living in town, it was his children who were causing the greatest expense to the joint family. His eldest child, a daughter, had been married a year before, at the age of 17, to an engineer. She lived with her husband in the city. This girl did not quite finish high school, since her wedding took place during the exam period of her 12th and final year. It was a joke around the house that she could not take her last year's exams and graduate because she got married instead. It was rumored that the joint family gave a *lakh* (100,000) of rupees (then roughly equivalent to $10,000) in cash to the groom's father as part of the wedding arrangement. Gifts such as a television set and motor scooter had also been given. The wedding had been attended by scores of guests, all of whom the bride's family fed luxuriously. This first daughter's wedding had strained the joint family's resources.

None of the other children of the three brothers was yet of marriageable age. The eldest was the schoolmaster's 15-year-old son. When he married probably depended upon whether he went to college. If he did, he would marry at a later age, but the joint family would have his college expenses to meet. It would probably be at least four years before either of the younger brother's children would be old enough to marry, but the brothers were already putting money into an interest-yielding bank account toward the second son's eldest daughter's wedding. She was 13 and in the 7th grade.

The strain between the brothers was symbolized by the two television sets in the large joint family women's quarters. The schoolmaster was unusual in having a private room on the roof of the women's quarters (originally built when the high school first opened in 1948 as a temporary residence for the principal and his family). Except for the two small boys of 5 who still slept with their mothers, all 9 of the other men and boys slept in the cattleyard, where the grandfather had built a fine men's clubhouse.

The schoolmaster kept his books and fine clothes in his room, where he also had a television set. He watched it alone unless he specifically invited others to see some special program. Even his wife and children were excluded from viewing the schoolmaster's television set. After his elder brother bought a set, the second brother bought one that was kept in his wife's room in the inner courtyard, where only women, girls, and unmarried boys were to be seen during the day.[5] That television was watched by the women and children.

It was the second brother who most resented his eldest brother—his teaching job to which he wore white shirts and fancy suits, his room on top of the women's quarters, and the high cost of his daughter's wedding, expenses the whole family had had to bear. The second brother could see looming ahead the costs of this brother's son's college education. While the schoolmaster-brother dreamed of a westernized city life, his next brother dreamed of getting his portion of the family land and living separately.

Not long before we knew them, this second brother had lost his temper (probably due to excessive drinking on Holi, the Hindu spring festival) and had marked off the outer courtyard of the women's quarters into fourths, saying that his father and the three brothers should each take an equal share of the women's quarters. His dramatic gesture and his anger frightened the women, who all got along harmoniously.

The second brother probably did not relish years of hard work ahead, the benefits of which his eldest brother would enjoy, as the eldest brother's family ate from the family harvests, made possible by the two farming brothers, while the joint family's savings were likely to go into the college education and marriage of the schoolmaster's eldest son. So far the brothers had not separated. Perhaps they will not do so as long as their elderly parents live. When the third and youngest brother told his father that he, too, might buy a television, the old man snorted, "Why don't you open a shop?" (meaning a television shop). The youngest son had not yet bought one when we left in mid-1984.[6]

The Untrained Daughter-in-Law: A Story from Central India

The Jat women were agog from the event one morning in the winter of 1966. It seemed that Kasturi, a handsome girl of about 13, had walked 14 miles home from her husband's village all alone, something an adolescent girl would ordinarily never do.

Her husband's brother and uncle had come to Maharajapur to take her back to her marital village some days before, and it had been very reluctantly that her father had allowed her to go with them. These men from her father-in-law's village had come twice and been refused. Kasturi had been married in her *shadi*, the first wedding ceremony, two years before, and the family was saving to celebrate the second wedding ceremony, the *maklava*, which usually takes place after the bride has reached menarche. But her husband's male relatives had come early, before the *maklava* had even been scheduled, asking that she be sent to help her mother-in-law right away. Let them skip the *maklava*, they had suggested, she was needed now.

There was, of course, the possibility that if her father refused a third time that the husband's people might stop coming, and when it was time for the *maklava*, they might refuse to come to it. Then what would they do? What man would offer a bride-price for a girl who was half-married already? So Kasturi's father had allowed her to go.

One reason Kasturi was needed was because her sister, who was married to Kasturi's husband's elder brother, the mother of four children, was coming back to visit her parents and natal family in Maharajapur. She brought her new baby and her toddler with her. While Kalavati, Kasturi's sister, was to be visiting at home, her mother-in-law would be left without sufficient help in cooking for her large joint family. Because her elder sister was coming home, Kasturi had to go to the village and house in which both sisters had husbands who were brothers. In this part of Rasjasthan, it is common for sets of sisters to marry sets of brothers.

All the women felt sorry for Kasturi, who complained that she had never been so badly treated. Her mother-in-law had expected her to churn the milk, to cut the fodder, to do many chores that she did not know how to do, chores that her mother had never required of her. Her older sister, Kalavati, sighed, "If only I had been there, I could have helped her and shown her what to do!" Now, the women felt that when Kasturi was sent back, she would not be allowed to visit home again for several years. That would be her punishment.

The Substitute Bride: A Story from South India

Again a scandal, with all the village of Arole marveling, shaking their heads, and laughing. That day in the summer of 1980, a big wedding was to take place among the Nadars, a lower-caste community of cultivators. Both bride and groom came from Arole itself, but they were not related. She was not a *murai penn*, a proper girl or proper bride, for her groom, because she was not his cross-cousin. Like most communities in Kanyakumari, proper mates were the children of brother and sister.

The groom had a high-school education and a job at the mill, and his father, a cultivator, did not want his son to marry any of his sister's daughters. They were uneducated. Nor did his wife's brothers have a suitable daughter. So he arranged a marriage for his son with an educated girl, one with eight years of education. The day of the wedding had come, a feast was ready, and the guests had arrived.

Then suddenly, the bride refused to go through with it. She refused to marry this groom. Her relatives could not prevail upon her. Educated girls have minds of their own. But all was ready! What to do?

A south Indian solution was found. The father caught the next bus into town, and he went to his married sister's house and asked for his sister's daughter in marriage. The sister and the girl herself readily agreed. The girl was decked in her best sari, and the wedding proceeded.

Universals in Indian Marriage and Siblingship

Before presentations of each of the regions, some background features universal to marriage and siblingship in India are listed. The term *universal* is used here in the sense of "that which is applicable to a large number of instances" rather than "the whole world at all times" (Fabian 1983: 3). Deviation from these Indian "universals" are more likely to occur among urban, educated, and middle- and upper-class people than among rural people.

First of all, weddings are a focus of Indian culture, ideally celebrated lavishly for days, even, in the past, for weeks, with many guests attending. Parents begin saving for a child's, especially a daughter's, wedding almost from the day of birth.[7] Indians are notorious for bankrupting their families or going deeply into debt in order to transact and celebrate weddings. Many of the cultural expectations with respect to attitudes and rights between siblings are written into various wedding rituals. For example, all over India, it is essential for a bride's or a groom's mother's brothers to attend the wedding, and it demeans the mother and child if the brothers fail to attend without an acceptable excuse.

Second, marriages are arranged by the bride and groom's elders; and third, they must be arranged between a couple from the same endogamous group (*jati*) or caste. Nowadays it is usually expected that a bride should be a few years younger than the groom and that he should be the taller and the better educated of the two. Besides trying to find a match of the right age, height, and education, the elders must be concerned about various rules of exogamy; a bride or groom cannot marry into his or her own patrisib, and there may be other stipulations as to who cannot be wed, even within the same *jati*. Elders seek a boy or girl from a "good family," with a reputation for honor and for enjoying a reasonable standard of living. They often stipulate that they seek a boy or girl from a large family and/or a sizeable lineage, so that their child, once married, will not find him- or herself without aid from marital relatives. As for the wedding itself, there are considerations of gift-exchange and dowry or bride-price, the dates for the events, the numbers of guests, and so on, which must be discussed and agreed upon.[8]

The elders must beware of deception and humiliation when seeking a mate for a girl or boy. It is particularly tempting to deceive bride-seekers or groom-seekers when a girl or boy has some handicap such as deafness, blindness, or lameness, and usually those who wish to pass off such a child as normal seek a mate residing in a distant place. An honest, well-off father is likely to offer a good dowry or bride-price to help compensate for such defects. Some successful men have gotten their start through such dowries and from continuing financial support from a grateful father-in-law. There is a certain shame to a family if it is known that the father, father's brother, or grandfather has made more than a few proposals to potential brides' or bridegrooms' elders and been refused. Then gossip begins that there must be something wrong with the girl or boy on whose behalf the elder has acted.

In rural areas where it is common for bride and groom to be young teen-agers who will not be receiving much education, neither bride nor groom sees the other or knows much about the other when they wed. As the age of marriage and number of years of education has gone up over the past 60 years, potential grooms and brides are increasingly requesting the opportunity to see the proposed partners before the engagement is fixed. Such viewing of the other, which may even include a brief conversation between the couple, is invariably in the presence of relatives from both sides. In communities where cross-cousins marry, a pair are likely to have known each other as children, but girls usually are kept away from boys their age and older once they reach puberty.

Self-selection of a mate through meeting members of the opposite sex at college, at work, through friends or relatives, or even more casually—eventuating in what is called a "love marriage"—is universally frowned upon; there is the implication that before wedding the bride and groom must have known each other *too* well.[9] Since a fair proportion of love marriages are also intercaste or interreligious marriages, they threaten the third universal feature of Indian marriage, that one must marry within one's own endogamous group, *jati,* and religion. Universally, intercaste and interreligion couples are socially ostracized by their families and *jati*s.

Fourth, one's behavior and success in social life, work, and studies reflect not just on oneself but on the good name of one's family and one's *jati,* especially the local *jati* chapter members, those who live together in the same villlage and neighborhood. Villagers are always talking about children who have given their families or *jati*s a good (or bad) name. Universally, the sure way for a girl to give her family a bad name is for her to indulge in a premarital flirtation or sexual relationship, or worse, to be thought to be promiscuous, or worst of all, to become pregnant. While an unmarried pregnant daughter should be ostracized, even killed, by some local norms, in fact she is more likely to be quickly married off to an elderly widower or bachelor who would otherwise have a great deal of trouble finding a young wife. A bad name is given to his family or *jati* by a boy who is known to be a thief, a gambler, or one who prefers to wander about and play rather than work.

Fifth, spinsterhood is almost unknown in India.[10] High-caste Hindu women are only allowed to marry once; such a prohibition holds among some lower castes as well, but generally middle- and lower-caste widows under age 40 are mated again, often to their dead husband's brother.[11] Men of all communities can marry repeatedly and, except among Christians, may have more than one wife at the same time.

Sixth, the purpose of marriage is to produce children; while a childless marriage occasionally endures, childlessness is the main cause for separation of a married couple. A husband may take his barren wife back to her parents or to her married brother's house and leave her there, never to return to her. This is a kind of de facto divorce, the most common kind to be found in rural India, where there are still few legal divorces.[12] Such a man usually takes another wife; in rural areas, bigamy for a man is not forbidden. Unless aged, a widower who can possibly afford it will almost always take another wife. In making village censuses, I have found such men with frequency, some of whom have had three or more wives and may thereby have had many children.

Rural Indian couples usually expect to have several children. There is no Indian cultural ideal for a two- or one-child family. Among the most enlightened rural people these days, people who appreciate the importance of family limitation, the ideal is two sons and one daughter.

Seventh, typically then, an Indian grows up in a family with two or more other siblings. Families with four, five, or six children are quite common. Table 5.1, which presents the sizes of sibling-sets among a 5% random sample of minimal patrilineages (*khandans*) in Khalapur, western Uttar Pradesh, illustrates this point.

In 1985, 45% of married women in the sample had 4 or more living children. Most of the 23 women who had no children were recently married and would probably have children in the future, and, of course, many of the other women were still in their child-bearing years

TABLE 5.1. Sizes of Sibling-Sets in a 5% Sample of Minimal Patrilineages (*Khandans*), Khalapur, Western Uttar Pradesh (1985)

Number of surviving children[a] ($n = 661$)	Number of married women ($n = 200$)	Percentage of married women
0	23	11.5
1	31	15.5
2	24	12.0
3	32	16.0
4	31	15.5
5	22	11.0
6	19	9.5
7	11	5.5
8	4	2.0
9	1	0.5
10	2	1.0

[a]308 girls and 353 boys; median = 3 children per married woman; mean = 3.31 children per married woman; mean = 3.73 children per existing sibling-set (excluding women with no children).

and would have more children, so these statistics suggest that in Khalapur, children grow up in sibling-sets of 3 or more. Indeed, these figures indicate that at least one-quarter of the children are in sibling-sets of 6 or more.

Table 5.2 lists the 35 different combinations of sons and daughters that these 200 married had.

TABLE 5.2. 200 Sibling-Sets Displayed by 35 Combinations of Sons and Daughters Belonging to 200 Married Women Found in a 5% Sample of inimal Patrilineages in Khalapur, Western Uttar Pradesh (1985)

Number of sons	Number of daughters	Number of occurrences	Rank of combination (top ½)
0	0	23	1
0	1	15	4.5
0	2	5	16
0	3	1	
0	4	1	
1	0	16	3
1	1	11	6
1	2	10	7
1	3	5	16
1	4	4	18
1	6	1	
2	0	8	12
2	1	18	2
2	2	15	4.5
2	3	8	12.5
2	4	4	18
2	5	1	
3	0	3	
3	1	8	12
3	2	6	16
3	3	7	13.5
3	4	3	
3	5	1	
3	6	1	
4	0	2	
4	1	4	
4	2	7	13.5
4	3	4	18
4	4	1	
5	0	1	
5	1	1	
5	2	2	
5	3	2	
5	5	1	
7	3	1	

While the most common combination was no sons and no daughters (23 occurrences), again because of the childlessness of the newly married, the second most common combination was the present cultural ideal of two sons and one daughter (18 occurrences). That there *is* some preference for sons is indicated in the total: out of the 661 children, 353 (53%) were sons and 308 (47%) were daughters.[13]

An eighth universal relates to the frequency of fairly large sibling-sets. It is quite common for older children to help care for their younger brothers and sisters. Everywhere in India, children of ages 5 to 10 can be seen carrying baby brothers and sisters. Strong affection for an older sister may stem from her surrogate-mother role, but boys usually help out with the child care, as well, and the responsibility that older children are taught to take for their younger siblings seems to preclude displays of overt jealousy toward them. Beals and Eason (Chapter 4, this volume) emphasize how sibling rivalry is less present in South Asia then in North America. Minturn noticed its absence among the children of the Rajputs of Khalapur (Minturn & Hithcock, 1966). By sibling rivalry, Minturn meant showing "hostility or resentment to a new baby" (Minturn and Hitchcock, 1966: 137). Older Rajput brothers and sisters do "shout at or even slap an erring child" (Minturn & Hitchcock 1966: 119), although "bullying . . . is strongly discouraged" (Minturn & Hitchcock 1966: 136).

Ninth, all over rural India, there is the expectation that an older brother should marry before his younger brothers, and an older sister before her younger sisters. There are various implications of this rule. If the elder daughter was given in marriage with a huge dowry, the community and she herself are both likely to expect that the younger daughter will be given with an equal dowry. There can sometimes be a long delay as the family tries to accumulate enough savings before the arrangement of the younger sibling's marriage. Often, the parents simply cannot afford to spend as much on the second or subsequent children's weddings as upon the first. Parents may feel they must get a large dowry when their sons marry in order to pay large dowries when their daughters marry, or if bride-price is given, the reverse holds. If a family has spent a great deal on the education of a son, they may expect a large dowry to defray their debts or make up for that expense. The reverse—high bride-price for educated brides—has not yet developed, but if such a girl's father is wealthy, he may choose a son-in-law who will accede to his father-in-law's wishes with respect to job and residence.

In some sibling-sets, the younger sister is considered to be more beautiful than her older sister, or a younger brother may be considered healthier, better looking, better educated, or having better prospects than his elder brother. In such cases the younger sibling may receive proposals before the elder is married. There are folk stories about how the beautiful daughter was allowed to be glimpsed by the groom's elders out seeking a bride, while the less beautiful daughter was actually given at the wedding. Parents almost always insist that the older be married off before the younger. As we shall see, in some parts of Rajasthan, the parents avoid these problems by marrying off two or more sons, or two or more daughters, at once.

There is an interdependence of fate among the siblings with respect to marriage. Birth order is a factor as it relates not only to the resources the parents have at the time a child is marriageable but also to the "desirability" of his or her older sibling's marriage contributing to a sibling's status when marrying. If an older brother or sister has indulged in either a "love marriage" or intercaste or interreligious marriage, this will affect a family's reputation within its caste community and almost certainly hurt the chances of marriage for the younger siblings. Once a family has allowed one such "undesirable" marriage, it may find itself having to accept others by default, because more conformist families within their endogamous group, their *jati*, will refuse to give a bride or groom to the family with the deviant son or daughter. People are likely to think, "If one daughter is 'bad,' then the other daughter may be bad, too." A "good" marriage, on the other hand, is likely to enhance the chances of the younger siblings to attract offers from the elders of other desirable mates, or to have the offers made on their behalf accepted. Thomas Weisner (1982: 323) has identified this phenomenon as "the norm throughout most of the cultures of the world: brothers and sisters are decisive participants in each other's fate concerning sexual access, marriage, or property."

Since the sororate is quite widely practiced, the younger sister, indeed, may repeat her sister's marriage to the very same man. With the levirate, a man may accept his older brother's widow.

Part of an elder's plan for a sibling-set may include a decision to let one son (practically never a daughter, unless she is crippled) remain unmarried. When there are three brothers, two may be married, and the third, well past a marriageable age, may have his food cooked for him by the wife of one of his brothers and may adopt one of his brother's sons as his heir. If one of his brothers dies prematurely and his community practices the levirate, he may, of course, receive his brother's widow as a wife.

The younger the rank of a sibling in a sibling-set, the more likely it will be that his or her marriage will be arranged not by the grandfather, father, or father's brother, but, because of the deaths or incapacity of the elder family members, by the eldest brother. The younger sibling in such a position may feel quite nervous because of the brother's lack of experience in such tricky matters as arranging marriages, and the younger sibling may also be doubtful about how seriously the elder brother will perform his duty. In villages, however, marriages are rarely arranged by a single elder without his taking the advice of others.

Tenth, another universal feature of larger sibling-sets in Indian families is that the father or grandfather often establishes a plan for a division of labor among male siblings, or a division of labor emerges among them. A common division of labor is: one or two brothers farm the land while the other brother, who has been educated longer, holds a job as a teacher or clerk. The better-educated brother is usually expected to contribute cash from his earnings for the weddings and other expenses of his nephews and nieces, or for other joint-family expenses, while he, in turn, gets grain, vegetables, milk, and *ghi* (clarified butter) from the family farm. Prevalent in north India more than in south India, the educated brother leaves his wife and children in the village to be looked after by his brothers while he works outside.[14]

Education is still very rare for daughters in rural families. But education for both boys and girls tends to delay marriage. Those few girls who go beyond four or five years of schooling are not married before or at puberty, as is typical for less-educated girls, but a few years later when they finish 8th, 10th, or 12th grade. These girls thus have a longer time to establish close relations with parents and siblings than girls who marry earlier. This is especially important for the relationships between sisters, who usually see little of each other after marriage unless they are married into the same household or village, as occurs among the Jaipur villagers discussed below. Sisters may attend school and study together and become girlfriends. An older daughter, still unmarried because she is attending middle school or high school, tends to take on more responsibility in the house. She may do much of the cooking and may be even more of a surrogate-mother to her siblings than if she had married when she came of age.[15]

The eleventh and last universal has to do with the terms "brother" and "sister," which refer not just to full brothers and sisters but to parallel cousins, the children of mother's sisters and father's brothers. In north Indian kinship terminology, these terms are used for all cousins (including mother's brother's and father's sister's children—that is, cross-cousins—as well as second and more distant cousins, both parallel and cross-), as well as for the other offspring of one's parents. To distinguish between a full brother and a cousin, the English term "cousin-brother" is often used; similarly, the term "cousin-sister" is

used. Since married brothers may live in the same household or, more likely, be neighbors, children may associate as much with their cousin-brothers and cousin-sisters as with their full brothers and sisters. In address, just the term "brother" or "sister" is used without the closeness of the relationship indicated. The pattern in Rajasthan in central India is similar.

In south India, one's parallel cousins, the children of father's brothers and mother's sisters, are called by terms for brother and sister, but not one's cross-cousins, the children of father's sisters or mother's brothers. While parallel cousins are brothers and sisters, cross-cousins are ideal as husbands and wives. It is customary all over India to extend kinship terms, especially those for brother and sister, to unrelated people within one's village and *jati*.

As detailed in this section, weddings are a cultural focus in India, indicated by their high expense in resources, kinship obligation, time, and interest. The arrangement of marriages by elders of the bride and groom is essential to the preservation of the Indian caste system, and the arrangement of marriages between very young brides and grooms is probably essential to the preservation of the Indian joint family: a young person allowed to choose a mate may not choose someone within his or her *jati*, and older brides and grooms are more likely to want to have some say in the choice of a mate and less likely to adjust docilely in a joint-family household. There are fewer joint families where there are older ages of marriage (Kolenda & Haddon, 1987; Kolenda, 1989). The requirement that the bride be virginal ensures the authority of elders who must protect the virgins in their families; the illiterate young woman has no honorable alternative to a marriage arranged by elders, and it is these very elders who may threaten to outcaste a wayward girl. Love between a man and woman is not considered a proper or good basis for marriage in India, and a healthy, normal young woman remaining unmarried is not an acceptable possibility either in most caste-communities.

Just as rigorous is the expectation that the married woman should produce children; there are few childless couples; a woman's failure to produce children is generally considered an acceptable reason for a man to take another wife, either keeping or separating from his first wife.

Rare also is a family with an "only child"; Indians usually grow up in families with one, two, or more siblings. There seems to be relatively little sibling rivalry in the Indian family, perhaps because of the strong emphasis on duty and obligation as opposed to individual freedom and individual gratification. Siblings enjoy or suffer an interdependence of fate, as the action of one, including actions relevant to marriage, affect the reputation of the entire family. One aspect of this

interdependence is the rule that an older child should marry before a younger one.

Siblingship is wide in India. One's brothers and sisters include one's parallel cousins, and in north India, all one's cousins; cousins of second and further degree in distance are still "brothers" and "sisters." Indeed, the children of friends often are called "brother" and "sister." Since the incest taboo between brother and sister is strongly adhered to, this "siblingizing" of others rules out a whole series of potential mates whom a boy or girl might meet and be attracted to—another prop to the arrangement of marriage by the elders.

The inevitability of marriage for women, the arrangement of marriage by elders within a caste, the elaborate celebration of the weddings of virginal brides, the high valuation on children and family, and the prevalence of large sibling-sets in India are universals found in all three of the regions presented in this chapter and, indeed, in most part of India.

Regional Comparisons in Sibling Relationships

For all three regions presented, it is rural Hindu villagers who are compared. The style of life of the three differ. Khalapur, in north India, is dominated by Rajputs, a martial caste who engage in patrilineal feuding and rivalries. They fancy themselves warriors and were cattle rustlers until the end of the 19th century. In the 1950s, they had agrestic servants who were untouchable Chamars, and they had, and still had in the 1980s, servants from other castes such as carpenters, barbers, washermen, sweepers, and potters. They also have private household Brahman priests. They are quite ready to defend themselves and their dependents and did so during the turbulent centuries before the 20th century.

Representing central India, in Rajasthan, the Maharajapur-Kishanpur Jat and Mina peasants were, until land reform in 1958, agrarian tenants. The Jats and Minas of Maharajapur were tenants of the Maharaja of Jaipur. Those of Kishanpur were tenants either of the *mahant* (supervisor) of the Kishan temple there or of one of the two *jagirdars* (vassals of the Maharaja) who had property there. The Minas also traditionally had been highway robbers and housebreakers, and, in the 1960s, they were still considered to be thieves, even though they had become tenant farmers in the late 1920s. The Jats allowed themselves to be "protected" by the Minas, giving them bags of grain after each harvest in payment for their "protection." If robberies occurred, the police came from the nearby town to arrest the Mina men; it was assumed that any theft must have been done by a Mina. They assumed that one of them was guilty, and they would keep all of them locked up until the name of the robber of the current incident was forthcoming.

Representing south India, in Tamil Nadu, the Vellala and Nadar cultivators of Kanyakumari had similarly employed mercenaries to protect them: the Thevars or Maravars. And like the Jats, the Vellalas and Nadars paid Thevars bags of grain for protecting them. Neither the Jats and Minas nor the Vellalas and Nadars were preoccupied with patrilineal feuds, as were the Rajputs of Khalapur. This was probably because the groups of central and south India did not consider themselves to be primarily warriors and because they had little land and only small local patrilineal groups, as compared to the large holdings and patrilineages of the Rajputs in the very large village of Khalapur.

North India: Khalapur, Western Uttar Pradesh State

Let us look first at the western Uttar Pradesh village. Khalapur is mostly Hindu; only about 10% of its huge population (in 1984, about 15,000) is Muslim. Like many other Hindus in north India, the 20-odd caste communities there practice village exogamy, as well as *jati* endogamy (marriage within the network of village chapters of a particular caste), patrilocality (the rule that after marriage a couple lives in the husband's village), and patrilineality (recognition of patrilines to which new sons must be continually added). In Khalapur, as in other villages in Uttar Pradesh (Gould 1960, 1961; Marriott 1959; Rowe 1960) and Delhi State (Lewis 1958), there is a tendency to maximize marriage ties by arranging marriages for daughters in different villages, and by not giving more than one daughter in each generation to a particular village. As Karve and other observers of north Indian Hindu life have noted, because of these ways of maximizing marriage ties, the bride almost always enters her husband's household as a stranger; she cannot expect to find there a father's sister, a sister, or a cousin-sister (Karve 1965: 125) (see note 2). Therefore, she not only does not know her husband but does not know any of his kinswomen.

Since brides, until recently, have been quite young, typically under the age of 16, this exile for a girl at such an early age was, and often still is, traumatic, often sung about in women's songs. The transition for a young bride is eased by the custom in Khalapur and elsewhere of having the first and most important wedding ceremonies when the girl has not yet reached puberty, while the second set of ceremonies take place a year or more later, after the girl has reached puberty. While the girl may go with her groom and his all-male party to her husband's village after the first set of ceremonies, she stays only with his womenfolk in the women's part of the house, and she may not see her husband at all. She returns home to her parental home after only a few days and remains with them until the second set of ceremonies a year or more later. The physical marriage usually is not consummated until after the second set of ceremonies when the girl has come of age. The first ceremonies establish the relationship between the two sets of kin and makes the marriage binding. The second ceremonies commence the actual cohabitation for the couple themselves.

Of course, a bride's adjustment to all the women of her husband's household is her greatest challenge; typically she sees her husband only briefly at night during her first years of marriage. However, in these early years, her life is made easier by her long visits to her parental home. In the years of marriage just after the *chala* (second ceremonies), the girl, often pregnant or with her first child, is in her parental home and village as much of the year as she is with her mother-in-law in her father-in-law's village (*sasural*). As years go by and she has more children and becomes more mature herself, and as her parents die off and her brother's wife becomes head of her once parental home, a woman returns to her home village less frequently and may only return for her brother's children's weddings. It is quite common for married sisters to return to help during their brother's children's weddings.

It is often held in north India that the affection between a brother and sister is great. The role of the brother as a sister's protector begins early, and at the time of a wedding, a new bride may be accompanied to her husband's house by none of her relatives except her small brother, old enough to be able to function on his own (between the ages of 6 and 12), but not old enough to be a sexual threat to the women of the groom's house. The role of the brother in north India is as the one who should check on the welfare of his sister. This is particularly true at three festival times of the year: (1) Bhaiya Dooj (Brother Second), right after the Festival of Lights (Diwali) in October or November, (2) Rakshabandhan, in March or April, when a sister ties a bracelet on her brother's wrist, and he gives her a gift, and (3) Tij, in August, when swings are strung from trees for women's enjoyment. On these three holidays, an adult brother should go with gifts to his married sister's marital village to see how she is faring. Often, he will escort her home at this time for a visit in her home village. His concern and gift-giving is not limited to his sister, but extends to her children. He, along with his father, should present jewelry to his sister's newborn child, and when each of her children marry, he must present special gifts in a special ceremony.

The culturally expected affection between a married sister and her brother is functional for the sister who is off among strangers. Women have often told me that they loved their brothers more than their husbands. It used to be quite common in Khalapur for women to have on their forearms above the wrist a tatoo showing a stick-figure boy and girl holding hands. If one asked, "Is that you and your husband?" the answer would be, "No, me and my brother. If I have that on my arm, I will have the same brother in my next life."

Facilitating this cultural expectation of love between brother and sister is the customary prohibition upon a daughter's inheriting a share in the joint-family land. Although daughters have a recent legal right to a share in inherited family land, Sharma's (1980: 39) statement, "A good sister does not claim the land which her brother might inherit," holds true still for rural north India. Sharma (1980: 57) suggests that maintaining a positive relationship with her brother in much more important and potentially beneficial to a married woman than would be land in her natal village that she would be dependent upon her brother, or some other male, to till for her. While landownership for women is common in Kanyakumari, as described below, it is rare in most parts of India.

In north India, a woman's brother is also, from her husband's point of view, a *sala* (wife's brother). The term *sala* has the connotation of "pimp" in English, and it is a curse word in Uttar Pradesh and the Punjab. The brother who is supposed to be a woman's protector, in giving her into marriage, is causing her to be injured by the sexual activities that marriage entails. This attitude toward the man giving a woman to a bridegroom is part of a wider honor-and-shame ideology, in which the honor of a family and of the men in that family are entwined with the virtue of its women. While honor requires that a sister be kept virginal and protected from predatory men, the brother who gives his sister in marriage has not only ceased to protect her but has delivered her up to be spoiled and harmed. The term *sala* connotes all of that (see Hershman 1981; Kolenda 1990).

In these parts of north India, far more than in south India, as will be seen below, a wedding is the establishment of an alliance between two distinctly different minimal patrilineages (*khandan*s) always located in two different villages. There is an inequality between these two sets of men, with the bride's men being inferior to the groom's. There is a ritual joking relationship between the inferior *sala* and the groom. During the wedding, there is much enactment, in both the ritual of etiquette and the ritual of joking, of the inequality between the two male wedding parties—the groom's men, who are guests, and the bride's men, who are the hosts (Kolenda 1990). Usually, by the end of the first set of wedding ceremonies, the *shadi* (the groom) and the *sala* have become friendly, but the etiquette of subordination forbids the *sala* from taking hospitality or from tarrying when he goes to his married sister's marital home to take her back to her natal home. If he accepts so much as a glass of water, he should pay for it. He should go and fetch her and bring her back. He may stay longer for a wedding, funeral, or birth ceremony, but at such, he is a guest, and it is only during such formal occasions that he may stay overnight in his married sister's marital village.

In Khalapur, a sister has cause for joy if her older brother marries, since the dowry given by the bride's people to the groom's at a brother's wedding may become the dowry given for this sister's wedding. Wedding gifts similarly may circulate from in-marrying wife to out-marrying sister.

However, one of the eternal triangles in north Indian kinship is that between a man, his wife, and his sister. The latter's jealousy is ritualized in a ceremony after the *shadi* when the groom and his party arrive home with the new bride, and the groom is greeted by his mother and the other women. His sister bars their way, and she does not let them enter the women's quarters until the bridegroom-brother gives his sister some jewelry or other valuable.[16]

Once a brother is married, and especially after their parents are dead, his married sister's visits to her natal village are partly by grace of his wife. Since a visiting married sister should be treated as a guest and not be asked to do arduous work while visiting, her presence increases the brother's wife's work. Additionally, it is customary for the married sister to take gifts, including food, back to her husband's house when she returns. Responsibility for the preparation of the food falls on the brother's wife. And money spent on gifts for married sisters take away from what might be spent on the brother's wife or upon his children. In other words, the loving relationship between brother and sister may be made ambivalent by the brother's wife's less-than-welcoming ways toward her husband's married sister. This is perhaps the process by which a woman's place of refuge, her parental home, becomes less and less available to her. By adapting herself to the ways of her mother-in-law and her husband's brothers' wives, and by bearing children, the married sister may feel less and less the need for such a refuge.

For the brother, there may be the problem of being fair not just to both wife and sister but to all his sisters. And once his daughters marry, he has gift-giving responsibilities to them that need to be coordinated with gift-giving responsibilities to his sisters (see Nuckolls, Chapter 8, this volume). The brother's obligations increase again when he becomes mother's brother to his sister's children, an affection-

ate, present-giving uncle. When Khalapur children run away from home, it is likely to be the mother's brother's village that is their destination.

In north India, the effect of the rules of village exogamy and patrilocality is that men of the same patrilineage continue to live together, and, indeed, a common Hindi term used for the local *jati*-chapter who live together is *biraderi,* brotherhood. The relationship between brothers is one of authority between the eldest and the younger in anticipation of the joint family these men may later belong to, the continuation of the family they enjoyed together before any brother was married. The kinship terminology does not reflect this authority difference, there being a single term *bhai* for both older and younger brothers; *bhai* is also used for all male cousins of varying degree and for friends and even casual acquaintances of one's own generation, for all men except for one's wife's brothers or one's brother's wife's brothers (the *salas*) (Dumont 1966: 99; Vatuk 1969: 175). Since there is sharp segregation between the sexes in Khalapur, women being secluded in women's quarters, men having their own clubhouses, a man lives very largely in a world of brothers, fathers, grandfathers, uncles, sons, and nephews, the men of his minimal patrilineage. Sometimes adjectives supplement the term *bhai,* and "big brother" and "little brother" are used, and sometimes the eldest brother is called *bhai sahib* to indicate special respect for him.

In the middle- and lower-ranking castes in Khalapur, and in north India more generally, widows are allowed to take a second mate (Singh 1947). The preferred mate may be the dead husband's younger brother. So a brother may inherit his dead brother's wife. In higher castes, like the Brahmans and Rajputs who proscribe remarriage for a widow, brothers may look after a dead brother's wife and children. And when a brother is away in the military and working far away, his brothers look after his wife and children.

The partitioning of the joint family in north India usually seems to involve bad feeling between the two or more families dividing a residence and/or land. After parents are dead, it is rare in Khalapur for married brothers to continue to share a single kitchen. Typically, the blame for the breakup of the two or more brothers' joint household is allotted to their wives. Villagers often observe that sisters-in-law cannot get along. Early in their relationship, they vie for the favor of their mother-in-law; later, they are likely to quarrel over children. The fact that it is increasingly difficult to manage cooking for a household, as there are more and more members, is overlooked in the public justification of the partition of the joint household. After the break-up, the brothers may continue to be somewhat soured on each other, but the sons of the two brothers are likely to be hostile. Cousin-brothers seem to bear grudges long after the division, even after their fathers' deaths.

This persisting hostility can be played out in the practice of the levirate among the untouchable Chuhra Sweepers of Khalapur (Kolenda 1987b). Among them, the underlying assumption seems to be that a woman has come in marriage to the men of a family, to a father and his sons, although she is sexual partner only to one of them, her husband. If her husband dies, she should then mate with her husband's brother. She is not considered to be compromised in any way if she does so. However, the dead husband may not be survived by a brother, or his brother or brothers may already be married. Frequently, it is suggested that a widow "sit with" her husband's cousin-brother (his father's brother's son)—"sit with" because only the first marriage is a true marriage. Once a woman has mated outside the father–sons unit into which she married, her new husband has the right to sell her. And this is not an empty threat; several of the Chuhris of Khalapur were bought wives. A woman who was sold not only had no say in a transaction planned primarily to profit the seller, but she was totally cut off from all her relatives, although eventually she might be able to reestablish relations.[17] Therefore, only 1 of the 12 Chuhra widows who had this choice (out of the 24 Chuhra widows whose marital careers I traced) (Kolenda 1982: 212–219) chose this option. A Chuhra widow's fears with respect to her husband's patrilateral parallel-cousin were well-taken, given the often intense hostility between cousin-brothers (Kolenda 1987b).

Among Hindus of north India, once sisters are married, they see each other when both visit their home at the same time, as when both are working at their brother's child's wedding, cooking for guests and helping in other ways. Married sisters are not allowed to visit each other in their marriage-villages, although this is not the case everywhere in the north (see Sharma 1980). They cannot even attend the weddings of each other's children or attend each other's funeral. They can only meet on their natal, parental home ground where they were girls together.

The great importance of siblingship in north India is also indicated by the taking of fictive brothers and sisters in the ceremonialized ties of *dharam-bhai*s and *dharam-bahan*s, brothers or sisters by duty and affection. Usually these are women friends of different caste who exchange gifts and food in a little ceremony and pledge to continue their friendship indefinitely, marking it by a periodic exchange of gifts. The assumption that the relationship is for life suggests a similar attitude about the relationship between blood-related sisters or brothers.

Central India: Jats and Minas of Jaipur District, Rajasthan State

In some parts of Rajasthan, and certainly among the Jats and Minas (important Rajasthani cultivating castess) living in Jaipur and Nagaur (Rosin 1978, 1987) Districts, many marriages (almost two thirds in the Jat-Mina villages of Maharajapur-Kishanpur) are in sibling-sets or collateral-sets (Kolenda 1978: 253; 1987a: 189–90). That is, sets of two or three brothers or cousin-brothers marry sets of two or three sisters or cousin-sisters—often in a wedding of two, three, or more couples at once. As in north India, there are two ceremonies, traditionally one before and one after the eldest bride has reached puberty. When sisters are married at the same time, the younger bride may be very young indeed, under the age of 10, since in Rajasthan brides are often under the age of 14 (Kolenda 1989: 87–91). The younger bride will usually not begin to reside with her husband and with her mother-in-law and elder sister (who is also her husband's brother's wife, her sister-in-law) until she has herself come of age, often several years after the *muklava*. In the story from Central India, Kasturi, in being sent to her mother-in-law before the *muklava*, was an exception to the general rule.

Although the Jats, Minas, and other caste-communities in Rajasthan are patrilineal, patrilocal, and practice village-exogamy, in this area a bride does not enter a household or community of strange women. Not only is there often a sister in the same household or nearby, but a father's married sister or cousin-sisters, or other women from her home village, may also have married into the same household, patrilineage, hamlet, or village. Therefore, a bride usually is not among total strangers. In the Jaipur village of Maharajapur-Kishanpur, almost three-quarters of daughters were married into villages in which there were other women married in from Maharajapur-Kishanpur (Kolenda 1978: 253: 1987a: 190).

Rajasthan is a premier place in India for joint-family living, and sibling- and collateral-set marriage seems to facilitate joint families by double-bonding them (Kolenda 1978, 1989). Not only are the component adult men brothers in relationship, but their wives are sisters to each other. The older sister who is also the sister-in-law may become the protector and guide to her younger sister/sister-in-law. Since girls may join their mother-in law at age 13 or 14, they may be quite untrained in household chores. The older sister may do the chores for her little sister and gradually train her in them.

Joint families among the villagers of Jaipur District endure beyond the death of the brothers' parents, and when breakup between the married brothers who have resided together takes place, there is not the bitterness that attends such break-up in Khalapur to the north. The brothers are more ready to see and say that break-up is necessary because, for instance, the elder brother now has too many children for the space they all share. And they do not blame their wives for the breakup. Since these peasants were until the late 1950s tenants of Jaipur royalty, clergy, or nobility, they could not build a new house without the landlord's permission, and there was no division of landownership to quarrel over. In Rajasthan, land is not the issue anyway, since there is plenty of land. What is needed is water, and until land reform, the wells were built by the landlords or with materials supplied by the landlord.

Joint families endure in this region because the irrigation system—driving bullocks down a ramp as they pull a leather pouch of water from the well—requires two men on the well. These men are usually father and son, or brothers (Kolenda 1978: 249; 1987a: 185). The irrigation system also requires a woman or older boy or two in the fields to guide the water into the patches of growing plants. Thus, while children are small, one wife stays at home and looks after the children while the other wife works in the fields guiding water, or else one tends the children and cooks while the other forages for fire wood and other forms of fuel.

A number of writers have observed that ecocultural factors influence the activity settings of siblings (Weisner 1989: 16) and of parents and children. Such factors include demographic ones, subsistence patterns, and the division of labor. The Rajasthani well team, based on the fraternal joint family, is an example of the interplay between the ecological adaptation made by these arid-zone farmers and their family structure.

The peasants themselves do not explain the purpose of sibling-set marriage as a way to bind the joint family so that it is an especially effective productive unit; they see it as a means of reducing costs of entertainment. If two wives have a single set of parents and siblings between them, there are half as many relatives to entertain at a wedding, birth or death feast. Whatever theoretical or practical explanations are offered, the Rajasthan family structure seems to promote family bonding. A sister can be expected to feel more affection for children who are not only her husband's nephews and nieces but also her own. If her sister/sister-in-law dies, she is more willing to nurse her dead sister's baby. That sisters/sisters-in-law do find their association agreeable is indicated by the number of instances in Maharajapur-Kishanpur of pairs of sisters who continue to live together as widows of brothers at a time when they no longer need to do so since each could presumably be supported by a married son.

This system of joint-family households seems to work far better than the system in Khalapur, in which sisters-in-laws are strangers to one another and hence rivals. The hierarchy among the women is clear when the younger sister-in-law is already used to being younger sister. The levirate here also seems to work well, women being more willing to join their dead husband's brother when he is married to her sister. The kind of child-rearing pattern found so widely in India, in which an older sister has been the caretaker of her younger brothers and sisters, may well mean that the younger sister/sister-in-law sees her older sister/sister-in-law as a caring mother-figure.

A survey of ethnographies from Rajasthan clearly indicates that middle- and lower-ranking castes and tribals generally give bride-price rather than dowry, or else little in the way of gifts is exchanged at marriage (Kolenda 1989). A Rajasthani married woman's brother, thus, is not obliged to bring his married sister gifts and to visit her in her marital village three times a year—at the Hindu holidays of Bhaiya Dooj, Tij, and Holi—as in Khalapur. The obligation of a brother to look after married sisters and, later, his daughters is not so strong in this area, where a man or his elders must pay a bride-price to get a bride. While in Maharajapur-Kishanpur, the giving of bride-price was not publicized, instances of it were known to us. The few young men who had completed 8th or 10th grade were in demand as bridegrooms and hence probably would not be required to give bride-price by hopeful fathers of brides, but, as yet, the giving of dowry among the Jats and Minas of Maharajapur-Kishanpur has not begun.

The contrast between north India (with the strong obligation on the part of a man toward his married sisters and the giving of dowry and then gifts throughout her marriage) and Rajasthan (with its weaker brother–sister bonds and bride-price) indicates the necessity of the culturally prescribed brotherly feeling to get the tasks of dowry-giving and gift-giving done. A brother in north India protects his married sisters in a solidly material way. In contrast, in the Jaipur region of Rajasthan, a new bride may receive the reassurance she needs in her husband's village from the other women from her home village, so her brother's periodic visits to check on his married sister are less necessary. The bond between brother and sister is not so strong as in north India, but the bond between sisters who are also brothers' wives or who reside in the same marital hamlet or village may be very strong.

So in the Jaipur region of Rajasthan, brothers are brothers all their lives because they reside in the same household, hamlet, or village, and so are sisters if they live in the same place of marriage.

South India: Vellalas, Nadars, Thevars, Acaris of Kanyakumari District, Tamilnadu State

In south India, the preferred marriage is between the children of brother and sister, that anthropologists call cross-cousin marriage. This means that for a couple in a cross-cousin marriage, a mother's brother is a father-in-law as well as an uncle, and a father's sister is a mother-in-law as well as an aunt. Presumably, the advantage for a bride in south India is that upon marriage, she does not enter a household of strangers, since either her mother-in-law is her father's sister or her father-in-law is her mother's brother. In either case, there should be affection already existing between them.

In the hamlets studied in Kanyakumari District, Tamil Nadu, live Vellalas, Thevars, Nadars, and Acaris. While the latter community's traditional occupations of carpenter and goldsmith are still followed, the first three are now almost entirely cultivators, although the Thevars were mercenary soldiers until the mid-19th century. Even in the 1960s, as mentioned above, they served as guards for Vellalas and other cultivators. Among these caste-communities, perhaps one third or more of marriages take place within the hamlet; unlike north and central Indian Hindus, there is no rule of village or hamlet exogamy. While all these caste-communities trace descent patrilineally and recognize patrilineal descent groups, the men of a single patriline do not necessarily continue to stay together in adulthood. Ready movement of a couple and their children from one hamlet to another is common, couples with children going wherever the means of livelihood seems most promising. Since women can own property, it is sometimes advantageous for a couple to live near her land, especially if the husband owns little or no land.

One of the difficulties of this system of cross-cousin marriage is the matching of the marital pair from among the possible cousins who could marry. I think of one young man who showed me the photographs of seven possible cross-cousins he could marry, since he could marry a daughter of either one of his mother's brothers or of one of his father's sisters. Since he actually married only one of these, his parents were left with somewhat strained relations with all their older brothers and sisters whose daughters were not chosen.

Another difficulty is the increasing preference for arranging a marriage with an outsider when one has a son or daughter who is well educated and likely to have a prestigeful and/or lucrative occupation. So a man with a son who is an engineer may not want that son to marry his sister's or wife's brother's daughter who has never gone to school. In such situations, a man may end up with angry sisters, his wife with angry brothers.

In Kanyakumari, it is not unusual for more than one sibling of one family to marry more than one sibling in another. As in Jaipur District, a pair of brothers may marry a pair of sisters. Unlike the places sampled above in north and central India, however, there is no prohibition on exchange-marriage in Kanyakumari, so a brother and sister may marry a sister and brother. This is another way for blood and marital ties to reinforce each other. Since intra-village marriage is allowed and since women are not kept in the kind of strict purdah of northern and central India, a mother can go and visit her married daughter in south India, whereas in northern and central India, she may not—marriage is not likely to be so traumatic.

There is a saying in the Kanyakumari area about divers for pearls, that a diver prefers to dive with his sister's husband or his wife's brother, rather than with his brother. The sentiment here is that brothers have no reason to want the other to survive, since one's death would give the other a larger share of their jointly inherited landed property. But a man does not want his sister's husband to die, lest he have to care for her, nor does he want his wife's brother to die, since the sister's brother is the source of support to the sister and, hence, to the couple.

This picture of affection between brothers-in-law must be modified by the fact that in Kanyakumari, non-Brahman caste women may own land, garden, houseplot, and houses. At marriage, a wealthy father tries to give his daughter a banana garden, a coconut garden, a paddy field, and a house. This is called *stridanam*, women's property. It is not dowry (called in Hindi *dahej*) in the north Indian sense, because it is *hers*, not transferred to her husband's elders, as in nothern India. A Kanyakumari husband, however, may not rest content with his wife's economic resources, land, or garden often tilled by her brother or father, and may pressure her to sign the property over to him or to sell the property for some purpose of the husband's. So women are often caught between the demands of a husband, who wants to use her property for his ends, and her brothers and father, who want her to retain it. A woman who manages to retain property may give it to her daughter when her daughter marries her brother's son—a way in which property given by a brother returns to him.

Actually, there is a great difference in the brother-in-law relationship between south India and north India. In south India, the brother is not seen as the one who is giving the bride in marriage, and sexual activity for a woman is not thought of as injury. Her destiny lies in the kinship rule that children of brother and sister should marry. A girl's proper bridegrooms (*murai mappillai*s) are well known to her and to her relatives from her childhood. Her mother's brother has a right to ask for her as a bride for his son when she is feted in her coming-of-age ceremony. She should marry her mother's brother's son, this ritual says. If the mother's brother does not ask for her—possibly he doesn't have a son of the right age, or possibly all his sons are already married—he should, nevertheless, attend her puberty rite. When the girl does marry, she and her husband must honor her mother's brother by getting his blessing before the wedding ritual. In south India, kinship "gives" the girl in marriage; in north India, her brother gives her in marriage, and in doing so makes himself the most cursed of men, a *sala.* (Differences in the conception of sexuality in north and south India are noted in Kolenda 1984, and a discussion of the *sala* appears in Kolenda 1990.)

There is a contrast between the role of the sister at her brother's wedding in north and south India. Whereas the groom's sisters resist their brother's return with the bride in north India, in the south, it is the groom's eldest sister who actually ties the *tali,* the wedding pendant, around the bride's neck, and it is the groom's older sisters who should pay the costs of making their brother's bride's *tali.* While in north India the sister must be bribed with a gift to let her brother and his bride come in, in south India the sister actually performs the symbolic act that makes the bride her brother's wife.

The patrilineage is a much less unified social unit in south India than in north India. In Kanyakumari, there is not the patrilineal feuding that there is in Khalapur. North India is a "hypergamous milieu" (Dumont, 1966: 94, 110): a married woman's brother is inferior to her husband and his patrilineal brothers, and in his married sister's marriage-village he should be only a brief guest. In south India, brothers-in-law—a man and his wife's brother or a man and his sister's husband—are much more likely to live near each other, and there are no barriers to asking a brother-in-law to help with a chore. In central India, as represented by the Jaipur villages described above, although brothers-in-law always live in different villages, their relationship is not unequal, and a brother-in-law may be called on for help, as when a family is digging or repairing a well, and more hands than usual are needed.

As for sisters, there is a good deal of sororal polygyny and practice of the sororate among the middle and lower castes of Kanyakumari. Woman marry at later ages in Kanyakumari than in north and central India, usually not until 17 or 18, and have their own separate households almost immediately upon marriage. Married sisters may well live in the same hamlet due to intrahamlet marriage, but with freer movement for women married sisters can visit each other by taking a bus from one hamlet to another.

Comparisons and Conclusions

The emphases in sibling relationships as I have been impressed with them center on marriage. So, in north India, the brother is above all the trustee of his married sister; he should keep in touch with her to see that she is being treated well; he should, if he can, bring her gifts and bring her home for visits. In central India, the double-bonding of the joint family through sets of brothers marrying sets of sisters is especially noteworthy. While in south India, the marriage or nonmarriage of the children of brother and sister may result in lifelong closeness between the families of a brother and a sister, or in lifelong enmity. Table 5.3 summarizes these comparisons.

To comment on Indian sibling relations in comparison to those reported for siblings studied in the United States, there are some similarities and differences. The American psychologist Victor Circirelli (1982: 276) states that some studies have found, "The relationship between brothers was the poorest when they were at different occupational levels." The occupational difference between the north Indian high school teacher and his farmer brothers seems to illustrate this generalization.

An issue of sibling rivalry in American families is commonly school achievement. Ross and Milgram (1982: 236) comment on the

TABLE 5.3. Summary of Similarities and Differences between Three Different Regions of India[a] with Respect to Sibling Relationships

	North	Central	South
Parents arrange marriages	+	+	+
Jati endogamy	+	+	+
Patrilineality	+	+	+
Patrilocality	+	+	P or M[b]
Wife visits home frequently	−	+	+
Maximize marriage ties	+	−	−
Bride knows other women	−	+	+
Bride knows husband before marriage	−	−	If cous:+
Two wedding ceremonies	+	+	−
Wedding traumatic for bride	+	−	−
Joint household	+	+	−
Characteristic form of marriage	With stranger	Brother set with sister set	With cross-cousin
Dowry/brideprice/stridanam	Dowry	Brideprice	Stridanam

[a]Represented by Khalapur Village, western Uttar Pradesh, Maharajapur-Kishanpur Villages, Jaipur District, Rajasthan, and Kanyakumari District Hindu Villages.
[b]P, patrilocal; M, matrilocal.

extreme pressure on the child in a family who is "to become the first who has ever obtained a college degree." As more children in India go to school, more such rivalry is likely to emerge. In the north Indian joint family, such pressure was already being exerted on the schoolmaster's eldest son.

While arguments between siblings are likely to arise in the United States at the time of the settling of their parents' estate, will, or property, such strain is highly institutionalized in the Indian joint family owning land together. It is the wise Indian father or eldest brother who tries to get the division of family land agreed upon by the various joint owners long in advance of its eldest member's death.

Cicirelli (1982: 281) in summarizing findings from American studies of siblings cites a study by Troll (1971) which concludes, "Sisters play a major role in preserving family relationships and providing emotional support to their siblings" during their entire lifespan. The possibility of sisters holding families together in India varies with the kinship system. As has been mentioned, virtually all Hindu women marry, so we must ask the question: Do married sisters hold families together? What we mean by family and what we mean by holding together will also vary regionally. So in the Jaipur area of Rajasthan where frequently sets of Jat and Mina sisters marry sets of brothers, sisters tend to hold together the fraternal joint family in which both women are married to the brothers. But in both this area and in western Uttar Pradesh where Khalapur is located, women are invariably married into villages other than their natal villages, a requirement of village exogamy, so sisters are not in a position to hold together their sibling-set composed of their brothers and sisters. The brothers should be in the natal village, and some of the sisters will be in other villages. All members of a sibling-set are likely to be together after marriage only when all gather for a parent's funeral or for a marriage of a brother's child in the home village.

Among the Kanyakumari caste communities, in south India, where there is a preference for cross-cousin marriage, the brother and sister whose children wed are likely to feel especially strongly bound together, but the frequent rivalry and jealousy connected with marriage arrangements also tend to undermind affection among adult siblings. Certainly the way in which adult married sisters solidify sibling relations differs greatly in India from such processes in the United States.

Cicirelli (1982: 268) has suggested, again primarily with American families in mind, that "the relationship between siblings is highly egalitarian, with the siblings of approximately equal power in the relationship. Each sibling feels free to say or do as he or she pleases in the relationship." Relationships among siblings in India are not supposed to be equal. In south Indian languages, one can not speak of just a sister or just a brother, but must speak of older sister and younger sister, older brother and younger brother. An older brother has authority over younger brothers and sisters. After adulthood, brothers are superior to sisters. These, at least, are norms that are general to India. Seldom does a person feel as much respect, however, for an older sibling as for a parent or grandparent.

These materials from India illustrate Thomas Weisner's point that in India, Africa, Polynesia, and other parts of the world obligations bind siblings throughout their lives (1982: 322).

Studies in the United States and elsewhere indicate that over 80% of American adults have living siblings and almost all maintain contact with siblings (Cicirelli 1982: 269, 271–72). A perusal of the results of American studies suggests that the sibling relationships among Americans are more voluntary and of less economic importance than those we have looked at in India, where brothers own land together and may farm together (illustrated by Khalapur, western Uttar Pradesh, and Maharajapur-Kishanpur, Rajasthan), where married sisters may be part of a combined agricultural enterprise (Rajasthan, central India), where a brother gives his daughter land as part of her dowry when she marries his sister's son, and where this land, in turn, becomes his daughter's daughter's dowry when that girl marries his son's son (her mother's brother's son) so that the land returns to the original patriline (Kanyakumari District, south India). Land given out as dowry in one generation may return in the following generation, if the right combination of cross-cousin marriages occur.

Ritual obligations are similarly more institutionalized in rural India: a brother must bring gifts to his sister after her marriage and when any of her children marry, a sister must tie the marriage pendant for her brother's wife in the south Indian wedding, and so on. Again American customs are more voluntary: a brother may be a groomsman and a sister may be a bridesmaid in an American wedding, adult siblings may or may not exchange Christmas gifts and so on. This difference of obligatory siblingship versus voluntary siblingship is a general contrast between a culture structured largely on kinship relationships and one that is less structured on kinship relations.

Notes

1. Fieldwork in Khalapur was done October 1954 to June 1956 and February to June 1984; fieldwork in the Jaipur villages was done September 1966–January 1967, May 1967, June–July 1969, and for a week or two in 1974

and 1978; fieldwork in the Kanyakumari hamlets was done in February-April 1967, July-August 1969, January-March 1974, May-August 1978, and May-August 1980. My fieldwork has been supported by the following institutions: Cornell University, Ford Foundation, American Institute of Indian Studies, National Science Foundation, Smithsonian Institution, and University of Houston. I owe thanks to them, as well as to many research assistants, most importantly Usha Bhagat Dave, Indira Sapru, Prema Nathaniel, Prabha Roy Joshua, Saroja Chelliah Srinivasan, Mary Fainsod Katzenstein, and Wilda Campbell.

2. In a study of marriage among 14 different caste-communities in the village of Khalapur, J. M. Mahar found that about two-thirds of women had the experience of marrying into a village in which she found no previously known kinswoman (Mahar 1966: 156).

3. The term *purdah* comes from the Hindi word *parda,* or curtain. It refers most noticeably to the requirement that women veil themselves, particularly their heads and faces, in the presence of strange men and in the presence of older men related through the husband; it is required also that they keep silent in such circumstances.

In Khalapur, purdah involves strict segregation of the sexes among all caste-communities, both high and low, and both Hindu and Muslim (about 10% of the population in the village of Khalapur is Muslim). A married couple is separated, with the wife living in a women's quarters and the husband in a men's clubhouse or cattleyard. A woman is required to leave her natal village upon marriage and live in her husband's village, in a compound of rooms built around a courtyard, with no windows looking outside and only a single doorway (locked at night), with her husband's mother, his brothers' wives, his sisters, and possibly more distant female relatives of the husband. The men, who share a men's clubhouse or cattleshed, always at some distance from the women's quarters, are father and sons, sometimes a father's brother or brothers and sons, and possibly more distant male relatives. Males over the age of six enter the women's quarters for only two purposes—to eat and to have sexual relations. A mother, sister, or daughter is more likely to bring a man his food than is his wife. Sexual relations are carried out surreptitiously, when a man slips into his wife's room in the middle of the night. Husband and wife never share a bed for the whole night; a woman often sleeps with her small children. A companionable relationship between husband and wife is not a cultural ideal in north India and the architectural arrangements do not encourage companionship between them.

In the Jaipur villages, the women of all castes also cover their heads and faces from strangers and older male relatives of the husband, but there are not separate women's quarters and men's quarters. Two brothers, their wives, and their children are likely to share a household, with the men sleeping at night in an alcove at the locked entrance to the courtyard, and married women and their small children sleeping in rooms around the inside of the courtyard. Thus, the house is built like a small fortress, with the men as guards. Separation between the sexes is maintained in the fields where both men and women work, women working together or with children, the men at a distance but keeping an eye on the women. Whenever my research assistant and I would go up to a cluster of women working in the fields of the Jaipur villages and start to talk to them, their menfolk would immediately come over and take over the conversation, expecting the women to remain silent.

In the south Indian hamlets of Kanyakumari, there is no requirement that women veil themselves. Households are usually nuclear in composition, husband, wife, and children inhabiting a small, clearly separate house. While the women and children are expected to remain quiet while the husband talks to strangers, there is much more conversation between the sexes and across the generations within the Kanyakumari household than in north or central India.

An excellent treatment of purdah in South Asia is Papanek and Minault (1982).

4. Only large villages in India have high schools, so children from villages without high schools may reside with relatives who live in villages that do have them. This was the case with these two students.

5. Adult men were excluded during the day from the inner courtyard, where each of the three wives had her own cooking area and spent most of her time. Around three sides of the inner courtyard were the women's private rooms for sleeping and storage of food supplies, clothing, and other belongings. The fourth side was the entranceway from the outer courtyard, a much larger open area where the old mother of the three married sons often sat with elderly women friends sunning herself in winter, where clothes were dried, and where men sat on cots to take their food brought to them by one of the children. Individual husbands slipped into their wives' rooms through the inner courtyard at night, something that was never openly spoken about.

6. Carstairs (1957), Wiser (1978), Sharma (1980), and Bennett (1983) have written about rivalrous relations among brothers. Carstairs suggests that the rivalry is related to the perception on the part of one or all sons that their father prefers one son, usually the eldest, over the others, or else to the quarrels over partitioning the jointly owned land. Wiser portrays a rivalry between two brothers over decades.

7. The term *dowry*, as used in India, refers both to personal and household goods that a bride takes with her to her new home, what might be covered by the term *trousseau*, as well as valuables and money handed over to the groom's father or elder to be spent as he sees fit. The dowry in the second sense was given in premodern times by royal communities and some high castes, and it is given increasingly nowadays when the bridegroom is educated and is considered to have good future prospects. Equal exchange of gifts and/or the giving of bride-price was and is usual among middle and lower Hindu castes (see Sharma 1980: 137–43; Kolenda 1967, 1989).

Nuckolls states that in the Andhra communities (numbering over 50,000 people) where he worked, "there was only one wedding in four years." He continues.

> Most people seemed to think they were too expensive. Marriages were commemorated simply and unceremoniously by a payment of fifteen rupees to the

> headman. More important seemed to be the earlier rituals which commemorated the alliance when the marriage partners were still children. In the first ritual, a sister and brother confirm the future marriages of their children when the sister takes her brother's newly born daughter and bathes her with turmeric water on her lap. . . . In the second ritual, the brother takes the umbilical cord of his sister's newly born son and puts it in his house, under the pot where his family keeps its "cold rice gruel" (the staple food of this area). These rituals confirm that the cross-cousin marriage of the siblings' two children will take place. Villagers easily dismissed the importance of formal weddings, but agreed that early promissory rituals were absolutely indispensable. (Nuckolls, personal communication, June 15, 1989)

The two Andhra customs Nuckolls describes can be seen as parallel to the two marriage rites in north India and central India, one before puberty and one after; the infant rites by the aunt and uncle seem to be roughly equivalent to the first wedding rite in north and central India, the payment to the headman the rough equivalent to the second rite. One could argue just as well that the first Andhra rite is equivalent to the engagement ceremony in north India. The lack of ritualization of cross-cousin marriages in Sri Lanka was noted by Yalman (1967). In Kanyakumari, in south India, the puberty rite for the girl after her first menstruation seems to replace the first rite, the wedding itself is the second rite (see Kolenda 1984). In the village in Karimnagar District, Andhra Pradesh, studied by Philip and Carol Bousley, there were infant and child weddings, roughly equivalent to the north and central Indian *shadi*, with cohabitation not taking place until after the girl had reached puberty (Bousley 1969).

There are places and communities in South Asia in which weddings are not celebrated or only minimally celebrated. Yalman (1967) suggested for Sri Lanka that wealthy families tried to make advantageous marriages with non-relatives and to celebrate these lavishly, while marriages between cross-cousins, especially among the poor, were not ritualized at all. I have attended lavish weddings between cross-cousins in Kanyakumari, and even poor families extended themselves to celebrate weddings, whether between cross-cousins or between an unrelated bride and groom.

8. Sharma (1980) gives an excellent account of the arrangement of marriages in rural Punjab and Himachal Pradesh, where negotiations tend to be in the hands of the older women.

9. Sharma, talking about villages in the northern Punjab and eastern Himachal Pradesh, puts it this way:

> The most honorable form of marriage is that where there is no element of prior sexual attraction between the partners. There should also be the appearance of maximum trust between the two families, and hence the minimum need actually to subject the boy or girl to any kind of "looking over" (although this almost always does take place in practice, however discreetly disguised as a casual social visit). (Sharma 1980: 40)

10. Spinsterhood is common in a few communities such as the Parsis, some Christian groups, and the Nambudiri Brahmans (of Kerala) among

whom, until the twentieth century, only eldest sons could marry, so many Nambudiri women were left without husbands.

11. The term "mated again" is purposely used in this passage, because even middle- and lower-caste people generally accept the Hindu idea that a woman should only be married once to a single husband. Dumont (1970) has referred to the remarriages among middle- or lower-caste people as secondary marriages. The people themselves have special terms for these secondary marriages, distinctly different from the term used for the first and only true marriage (see Kolenda 1982).

12. Sharma (1980: 155–66, 176) presents nine cases of divorce in northwest India initiated by women. She makes the point that where bride-price is given for women, men are unlikely to desert or evict their wives, since it is costly for them to try to get another, but where there is dowry they may allow wives to leave (Sharma 1980: 163–64).

13. B. D. Miller (1981) has explored various explanations for the disproportionate sex ratio in India. In Kolenda and Haddon (1987) the correlation between the prevalence of joint families and a preference for sons is noted, based on statistical data in the Census of India for 1961. Ajit Kumar Sinha (1974) explains son-preference as due to a Hindu requirement for salvation. He writes, "It is believed by the Hindus that a man may attain salvation or *moksha* only when a son is born to him." He adds that a wife is seen as an instrument for the procreation of a son.

14. In her description of a Maharashtrian Brahman landed family over 60 years, Irawati Karve (1963) found it common for several brothers to do no work: "The idleness of certain males in the joint family might be owing to the deliberate policy of the head who, owing to this, gets a sort of moral right to divide the property in an unequal way" (Karve 1963: 260–61).

15. Various researchers have given attention to siblings as child caretakers. See, for example, Weisner (1982) and Watson-Gegeo and Gegeo (1989).

16. Hershman (1981: 218) reports that in the Punjab a sister does not allow her brother to circumambulate the wedding fire until he has paid her an amount of money.

17. Sale of a woman must be distinguished from bride-price. With bride-price, a sum of money is given by the groom's people to the bride's, but a ceremonial wedding and feasting, along with other gift-giving, takes place. The bride-price is just one of several prestations exchanged. With sale of a woman, there is no celebration, and the woman is suspected of having behaved immorally. In some cases, she has become pregnant outside of wedlock, but in other cases, a male relative has found it to his advantage to sell the woman.

References

Bennett, L. (1983). *Dangerous Wives and Sacred Sisters*. New York: Columbia University Press.

Bousley, P. (1969). *A Study in Caste Ranking*. Master's thesis in Sociology and Anthropology, University of Houston.

Carstairs, G. M. (1957). *The Twice-Born*. London: Hogarth Press.

Cicirelli, V. G. (1982). Sibling Influence throughout the Lifespan. In M. E. Lamb & B. Sutton-Smith (Eds.), *Sibling Relationships: Their Nature and Significance across the Lifespan* (pp. 267–84). Hillsdale, NJ: Erlbaum.

Dumont, L. (1966). "Marriage in India: The Present State of the Question. Part Three: North India in Relation to South India." *Contributions to Indian Sociology* 7: 99–102.

Fabian, J. (1983). *Time and the Other*. New York: Columbia University Press.

Gould, H. (1960). "The Micro-demography of Marriages in a North Indian Area." *Southwestern Journal of Anthropology* 16: 476–91.

Gould, H. (1961). "Further Note on Village Exogamy in North India." *Southwestern Journal of Anthropology* 17: 297–300.

Hershman, P. (1981). *Punjabi Kinship and Marriage*. Delhi: Hindustan Publishing.

Karve, I. (1965). *Kinship Organization in India*. Bombay: Asia.

Karve, I. (1963). A Family through Six Generations. In L. K. Bala Ratnam (Ed.), *Anthropology on the March* (pp. 241–62). Madras: The Book Center.

Kolenda, P. (1967). Regional Differences in Indian Family Structure. In R. Crane (Ed.), *Regions and Regionalism in South Asian Studies* (pp. 147–225). Monograph 5. Durham, NC: Duke University Program in Comparative Studies of Southern Asia.

Kolenda, P. (1978). Sibling-set Marriage, Collateral-set Marriage and Deflected Alliance among Annana Jats of Jaipur District, Rajasthan. In S. Vatuk (Ed.), *American Studies in Indian Anthropology* (pp. 242–77). New Delhi: American Institute of Indian Studies.

Kolenda, P. (1982). Widowhood among "Untouchable" Chuhras. In A. Ostor, L. Fruzzetti, & S. Barnett (Eds.), *Concepts of Person: Kinship, Caste, and Marriage in India* (pp. 172–220). Cambridge: Harvard University Press.

Kolenda, P. (1984). "Woman as Tribute, Woman as Flower: Images of 'Woman' in North and South India." *American Ethnologist* 11: 98–117.

Kolenda, P. (1987a). *Regional Differences in Family Structure in India*. Jaipur: Rawat.

Kolenda, P. (1987b). Living the Levirate: The Mating of an Untouchable Chuhra Widow. In P. Hockings (Ed.), *Dimensions of Social Life: Essays in Honor of David G. Mandelbaum* (pp. 45–67). Berlin: Mouton de Gruyter.

Kolenda, P. (1989). The Joint-Family Household in Rural Rajasthan: Ecological, Cultural and Demographic Conditions for Its Occurrence. In J. N. Gray & D. J. Mearns (Eds.), *Society from the Inside Out: Anthropological Perspectives on the South Asian Household* (pp. 55–106). New Delhi: Sage.

Kolenda, P. (1990). "Untouchable" Chuhras through Their Humor: "Equalizing" Marital Kin through Teasing, Pretence and Farce. In O. Lynch (Ed.), *Divine Passions* (pp. 116–53). Berkeley: University of California Press.

Kolenda, P., & Haddon, L. (1987). Marked Regional Differences in Family Structure in India. In P. Kolenda, *Regional Differences in Family Structure in India* (pp. 214–88). Jaipur: Rawat.

Lewis, O. (1958). *Village Life in Northern India.* Urbana: University of Illinois Press.

Mahar, J. M. (1966). *Marriage Networks in the Northern Gangetic Plain.* Ph.D. dissertation in Anthropology, Cornell University.

Marriott, M. (1959). Social Structure and Change in a U.P. Village. In M. N. Srinivas (Ed.), *India's Villages* (pp. 96–109). Calcutta: Development Department of West Bengal.

Miller, B. D. (1981). *The Endangered Sex.* Ithaca: Cornell University Press.

Minturn, L., & Hitchcock, J. T. (1966). *The Rajputs of Khalapur.* New York: John Wiley.

Papanek, H., & Minault, G. (Eds.). (1982). *Separate Worlds: Studies of Purdah in South Asia.* Columbia, MO: South Asia Books.

Rosin, T. (1978). Peasant Adaptation as Process in Land Reform: A Case Study. In S. Vatuk (Ed.), *American Studies in the Anthropology of India* (pp. 460–95). Delhi: American Institute of Indian Studies.

Rosin, T. (1987, December). *Set Marriage and the Continuity of the Joint Family in Rajasthan.* Paper presented at Rajastan Studies Conference, Jaipur.

Ross, H. G., & Milgram, J. I. (1982). Important Variables in Adult Sibling Relationships. In M. E. Lamb & B. Sutton-Smith (Eds.), *Sibling Relationships: Their Nature and Significance across the Lifespan* (pp. 225–49). Hillsdale, NJ: Erlbaum.

Rowe, W. L. (1960). "The Marriage Network and Structural Change in a North Indian Community." *Southwestern Journal of Anthropology* 16: 299–311.

Sharma, U. (1980). *Women, Work, and Property in North-West India.* London: Tavistock Publications.

Troll, L. E. (1971). "The Family of Later Life. A Decade Review." *Journal of Marriage and the Family* 33: 263–90.

van der Veer, K. W. (1971). *I Give Thee My Daughter: A Study of Marriage and Hierarchy Among the Anavil Brahmans of South Gujarat.* Assen: van Gorcum.

Vatuk, S. (1969). "A Structural Analysis of Hindi Kinship Terminology." *Contributions to Indian Sociology* (n.s.) 3: 94–115.

Watson-Gegeo, K., & Gegeo, D. W. (1989). The Role of Sibling Interaction in Child Socialization. In P. G. Zukow (Ed.), *Sibling Interactions across Cultures* (pp. 54–76). New York: Springer-Verlag.

Weisner, T. (1982). Sibling Interdependence and Child Caretaking: A Cross-Cultural View. In M. E. Lamb & B. Sutton-Smith (Eds.), *Sibling Rela-*

tionships: Their Nature and Significance across the Lifespan (pp. 305–27). Hillsdale, NJ: Erlbaum.

Weisner, T. (1989). Comparing Sibling Relationships Across Cultures. In P. G. Zuckow (Ed.), *Sibling Interaction across Cultures: Theoretical and Methodological Issues* (pp. 11–25). New York: Springer-Verlag.

Wiser, C. V. (1978). *Four Families of Karimpur*. Foreign and Comparative Studies/South Asian Series 3. Syracuse, N.Y.: Maxwell School of Citizenship and Public Affairs, Syracuse University.

Yalman, N. (1967). *Under the Bo Tree*. Berkeley: University of California Press.

Photo by Victor C. de Munck

CHAPTER 6

The Dialectics and Norms of Self Interest

Reciprocity among Cross-siblings in a Sri Lankan Muslim Community

Victor C. de Munck

This chapter provides an examination of adult cross-sibling relationships in the Muslim community of Kutali (a pseudonym used in previous writings) located in the southcentral region of Sri Lanka. My primary goal is to describe and explain intracultural variability in the practice of sibling relationships. Additionally, I intend to show that material ties shape sibling relationships in general. I view practice not in Bourdieu's (1977) sense of reflexive behavior but as the outcome of the interplay of social norms and the individual's version of his or her culture, what Schwartz (1978) referred to as the "idioverse."

Social norms are shared historical constructions that authenticate cultural "truths," systems of ethics, and "fields of power" with which individuals constitute themselves through experience (Foucault 1984: 351–54). Fields of power consist of situationally specific modes of compliance and support, punishment and discipline. Social norms are verbally expressed as "should" statements that provide general guidelines of conduct and are used to evaluate actions ethically (Bailey 1969: 5). The idioverse, as I understand it, is a loosely orchestrated system of biological, cultural, and experientially "coded" effective, cognitive, and behavioral complexes (de Munck 1992); it is "the individualized texture of a culture" (Schwartz 1978: 425). The relationship of the idioverse to social norms is analogous to the relationship between *parole and langue.* Idioverse refers to each individual's understanding (or version) of different social situations and implies cognitive and behavioral variability rather than conformity. Practice, as action, is the outcome or synthesis of these dual and interpenetrating systems of the normative system and the idioverse of individuals within a culture.

My aim is to analyze this relational system in reference to cross-sibling relationships. To do so, I begin with a brief review of the literature on siblingship and a description of the community. I then proceed with a discussion of the normative system of cross-sibling relations in South Asia in general and Kutali in particular. This is followed by the presentation of six case studies of adult cross-sibling behaviors and a concluding analysis of the relation between the normative system and individual sibling behaviors.

The cross-sibling bond in South Asia has been described as "durable" and "without calculation" (Mandelbaum 1970: 67). I will argue that this characterizes the normative system of cross-siblingship and that cross-sibling relationships vary along a continuum of generalized reciprocity to negative reciprocity. Generalized reciprocity refers to an enduring bond based on loyalty and "without calculation"; negative reciprocity refers to actions that symbolically express opposition to another such as theft, malicious gossip, and verbal or physical abuse. My hypothesis is that material interests mediate and underlie sibling relations.

This economic argument is hardly new, yet it is not usually associated with sibling relations, particularly in South Asia where social hierarchies and norms are thought to determine rather than be determined by personal interests (Bharati 1985; Dumont 1970; Inden & Nicholas 1977; Marriott 1976; Mines 1988; Shweder & Bourne 1984; Yalman 1976). Bharati (1985: 219), for example, notes that the Indian "self" is bound to follow its *svadharma*, its proper duty as determined by caste and birth. Marriott (1976: 111) refers to the Indian person as a "dividual" who absorbs and gives of culturally "coded substances" in social transaction and ritual offerings. Through the six cases presented in this chapter I will show, by counterexample, that such "context-dependent" explanations of Indian and, by extension, Sri Lankan social behavior are unidimensional and account only for the normative aspects of a culture. These explanatory schemes neglect the multifarious ways individuals interpret, manipulate, and act in and on these cultural contexts.

The economic basis of social relationships varies depending on the nature of the relationship. Sibling relations must also articulate with those norms that formulate appropriate and inappropriate forms of intrasibling behavior. Accountability is expressed within the framework of social norms, but it does not necessarily follow that behavior accords with these expressions of accountability.

Studies of sibling relations have tended to focus on their rivalrous nature during childhood. Sibling rivalry may be based on competition for parental affection (Adler 1959); be motivated by desires to "deidentify" with one's sibs and establish one's own identity (Schachter & Stone 1987); be a consequence of parental favoritism (Brody & Stoneman 1987; Felson & Russo 1988; Ross 1981); be formed by perceptions of relative strengths and weaknesses between siblings in terms of some valued skill or behavior (Ross & Milgram 1982); be a consequence of birth order (Sutton-Smith 1982). Studies of sibling relations also note that aggressive and/or rivalrous behaviors tend to be exhibited among siblings of the same sex (Cicirelli 1975; Bryant 1982; Schachter, Gilutz, Shore & Adler 1978). Cicirelli writes, "Rivalry is least between cross-sex siblings, with sisters in an intermediate position" (1982: 276). Allan (1977) notes that sibling rivalry tends to dissipate during adulthood as siblings moved away from one another.

Recent studies have focused on the prosocial aspects of the sibling bond (Abramovitch, Pepler, & Corter 1982; Bank & Kahn 1982; Cicirelli 1982; Dunn & Kendrick 1982). Siblings, as Bank and Kahn note, manifest their "loyalty" in contexts in which one is threatened by an outside agent (1982: 259).

This brief excursion into the sibling literature points out, by its absence, the neglect of cross-cultural and, more specifically, non-Western studies of sibling relations. This neglect is partly a result of the anthropological concern with socialization processes and social reproduction (e.g. descent), both of which focus on parent–child or adult–child relationships. Weisner notes that in anthropological studies, data on siblings are to be found but "in the context of or service of other institutions [such as] corporate kin groups; time-limited ceremonial groups . . . ; age grades; and so forth" (1982: 306). To my knowledge, there are only two, mostly descriptive, published anthologies on siblings in non-Western cultural contexts: Marshall (1981) examines siblings in a variety of Oceania island cultures, and Kensinger (1985) provides brief ethnographic expositions of sibling relationships in lowland South America. The studies in these two anthologies are primarily ethnographic in theme and content.

It is not altogether surprising that no such anthology or exhaustive study of siblings exists for South Asia. In particular, in the Dravidian kinship system of the south Indian subcontinent, the cross-cousin component has been the focus of analysis and debate. In south India and Sri Lanka, cross-cousin marriage practices not only occur but are expected and desired. Yalman (1967, 1969), Dumont (1957), Tambiah (1965), Trautman (1981), and de Munck (1988, 1992) have emphasized the intrinsic and logical centrality of cross-sibling relationships to the

Dravidian kinship system. However, the focus has tended to be on kinship terminology as a structural dimension that predicates the Dravidian preference for and practice of cross-cousin marriages.

Yalman, quite rightly, argues that the brother–sister tie is "crucial" because of the respective claims each has on the other in terms of "the whole complex of dowry, (1969: 624). It is, as Yalman notes, the dowry that "sets up powerful claims between brothers and sisters and thereby provides a most vital lateral spread to kinship relations" (1969: 624). However, Yalman's interest like Dumont's, is limited to describing, rather than exploring, the relationship between the dowry and cross-siblings since the two scholar's theoretical interest is in demonstrating structural consistencies at the categorical/terminological level of kinship. Briefly, their argument goes as follows: Brothers and sisters retain close ties because they will eventually invest their family wealth, in the form of a dowry, in each other's offspring.

The central importance of the sibling bond in Dravidian culture has also been the cause for considerable strain between siblings. Srinivas referred to this as the "myth of fraternal solidarity" (1980: 276). Brothers are bound together by principles of kinship and economic interdependence but are often at odds with one another because of these obligatory ties. Cross-siblings, on the other hand, are not assumed to be in competition with one another. Relationships between parallel-siblings in the South Asian literature, as described by researchers and their informants, oscillate between mutual support and hostility, with support being the norm and hostility being situational and incidental.

These examinations of sibling relationships remain on the categorical and normative level. I expect, however, that the importance of the dowry and the pooling of family labor described above and by Weisner (1982) and Mandelbaum (1970) will be pertinent to our examination of cross-sibling behavior. The maintenance of cross-sibling cooperative and affiliative bonds is, in part, contingent on the socioeconomic interests of the respective siblings. These interests are articulated within a moral code as part of the community's normative system. Before I discuss the normative system, I shall present a brief description of the village of Kutali.

Ethnographic Context

The village of Kutali is located in the Moneragala District of Sri Lanka. It is a rural peasant community with a population in 1982 of 1,100, 1,000 of whom are Muslims. The remaining 100 are Sinhalese

Buddhist who live on the outskirts of the village and are not discussed in this paper.

The Muslims of Kutali make their living by farming rice paddies and *chena* (i.e. swidden) fields. Villagers obtain farming lands primarily through the dowry. Lands may also be obtained by clearing unclaimed forest lands or by leasing lands from other villagers. Land is seldom, if ever, sold and is the primary index of a person's wealth. The dowry, thus, serves as a form of "pre-mortem" inheritance (de Munck 1988; Goody & Tambiah 1973) in which family wealth devolves to the daughter and, by extension, her husband, at the time of her marriage.

Kutali is an encapsulated village, isolated from the Sri Lankan Muslim populations living along the west and east coasts, and surrounded by Sinhalese Buddhist populations. Villagers noted that cultivation lands surround the village as a protective buffer against possible attacks by outsiders.

The Normative System of Cross-sibling Relations

Throughout South Asia brothers are ritually obligated to provide services and gifts to their sisters with no thought of a return in kind (Mandelbaum 1970: 69). Conversely, sisters may make claims for the services, resources, or help of a brother on the basis of need without returning these favors in the future. While brothers provide material and political support, sisters provide nurturance and affection.

In north India the nature of the cross-sibling bond is symbolically expressed during the annual *raki* ceremony in which the sister gives a decorative thread to her brother, who wears it around his wrist. In turn, he gives her gifts of cash and food and vows to help and defend her in any crisis situation.

In north India, there is a gradual generational dispersal and attenuation of kinship ties descendent from the sibling bond. In the Dravidian cultural region, there is a cross-generational pattern of bifurcation and merging as cross-siblings separate at marriage and their offspring unite in marriage (Yalman 1967: 374–75). In the north postmarital cross-sibling bonds are manifested through symbolic and affective displays. In the south postmarital sibling bonds are compounded by the vested interest both have in the future welfare of each other's children because the offspring of adult cross-siblings are potential mates.

In Kutali, for example, first cross-cousins, nieces and nephews, are socialized to think of each other as potential mates, while adolescent cross-siblings are socialized to avoid one another. A sibling will never

bathe at a well where a cross-sibling is bathing but will at one where a cross-cousin is present. Cross-cousins flirt with one another when they are not being watched by adult family members. For example, one adolescent boy told me that when he was bathing with his female cross-cousin his sarong accidentally fell down. Thereafter she nicknamed him "snakecharmer." After circumcision, usually when a boy is in his teens, his female cross-cousins are expected to visit while he is healing and inquire after the health of his "little friend."

Adolescent cross-siblings are expected to develop a symbiotic relationship. Elder sisters serving as caretakers for their younger siblings, running errands, cooking, and making tea for brothers and parents. Brothers, on the other hand, are ever vigilant of their sister's behavior in public and protect them both from abuse and the wiles of their male age-mates.

Unless there is a large discrepancy in age, sisters are expected to marry before brothers. Brothers are expected to help provide a suitable dowry for their sisters. It is also in the brother's interest that a sister is provided with a large dowry, for he and his family may then reasonably demand a comparable dowry when his marriage is arranged. A brother also recognizes that the dowry wealth provided his sister may, in the future, be given to his son.

After puberty, cross-sibling interactions are routinized in terms of formal role behavior based on cultural conceptions of gender distinctions. These conceptions may be succinctly expressed by the following set of normative rules: males are dominant over females; male and female intimacy necessarily leads to sex; males inhabit the public domain and females the private domain (Nelson 1974). These norms regulate gender relations and are necessarily conflated in the cultural expectations of how cross-siblings should interact (Schneider 1981: 398–99).

The complementary services of nurturance and cooking by the sister and protection and aid by the brother, initiated during childhood, are compounded in their adult years by their vested interest in each other's offspring as potential mates for their own children. Villagers view the brother–sister bond as enduring, affectionate, and complementary. One villager, comparing relations between brothers and brother and sister observed.

> "A brother marries another woman who is far off and not of our blood. But you can go to the sister's house whether her husband is home or not and open the pots to see what's cooking. Brothers are never home and are married to someone else. But your sister's house is like your own. For any emergency she will beg or borrow

to get you money, the brother easily says, 'No, I don't have any money.'"

Adult cross-siblings need not avoid each other. Brothers freely visit their sister's domicile and eat there. This house was typically bequeathed to her as part of the dowry and may be the house in which she and her siblings were raised. Her brother, therefore, thinks of it as "his" house. He also has paternal rights over her children, who may become his son- or daughter-in-law. The terms for nieces and nephews is *marumagan* and *marumagal*. *Maru* means "again" or "other," and *magan* and *magal* mean "son" and "daughter," respectively. Thus, *marumagan* literally means "other/again son", and *marumagal* literally means "other/again daughter." A woman's brother may assume the role of the authoritative father over her children, in part, to establish his dominance. Further, one informant remarked that parents in their later years may separate with the father moving into the house of his daughter and the mother into the house of her son, thus physically separating husband and wife and reuniting brother (i.e., the wife's father) and sister (i.e., the husband's mother).

Kutali cross-siblings are ideally conceived of as "alter egos"—complementary parts of a sibling unit, with the actions of the one reflecting on the public reputation, personal esteem, and future welfare of the other (Lambert 1981). The sense of cross-siblings as alter egos of a collective identity is alluded to by an informant who said plaintively, "I don't care what happens to me, my sister must prosper; my sole interest is in getting her married justly and without disgrace."

Of 62 marriages for much I have data, 33 (53%) were between first cross-cousins. Generally, the incidence of cross-cousin marriages in Darvidian communities falls between 10% and 30% (McGilvray 1988; Trautman 1981). In an earlier paper I argued that this high frequency of cross-cousin marriages is tied to the geographical isolation if Kutali and to the economic importance of the dowry as a form of "premortem inheritance" (de Munck 1988). For Sri Lankan Muslims, dowry composition includes a house, cultivation land, and cash, the first two being permanent sources of wealth and serving as the economic foundation for the new couple. Dowries are legally transferred to the daughter, though her husband obtains proprietary rights over the cultivation lands.

The provisioning of a house as part of the dowry composition entails a residence pattern where sisters "stay put" within the natal compound, brothers disperse, and parents move about as they build houses for their daughters (McGilvray 1988). The natal home is given to the first daughter who marries, usually the eldest. Her parents and unmarried siblings may live in the house, though usually in a separate room, until the next house, typically smaller, is built. As a cost- and labor-saving strategy, villagers will often build duplexes, with each half mirroring the other.

Goody and Tambiah (1973) and Schlegel and Eloul (1988) have posited a direct correlation between dowry and arranged marriages: the greater in value the dowry, the greater the parental control over selecting a bridegroom. The logic of this correlation is based on the parental strategy of marrying their daughter to a "client son-in-law" over whom they can exercise some control.

In summary, the cultural norms discussed above include gender relations, cross-cousin marriage, matrilocality, the economic importance of the dowry, and the socialization process of cross-siblings. It is within this complex cultural milieu that individuals act.

Six Case Studies

Case 1

> This case involves two brothers and their younger sister. Bas was the elder brother, Hamsa was the younger brother, and Mukuluth was the sister. All three siblings maintained separate households. Bas and Mukuluth were poor by village standards. Hamsa, however, was successful shopkeeper, owned five acres of paddy land, and had been elected treasurer of the village mosque.
>
> Their father was deceased, and Hamsa had assumed the role of family patriarch. Hamsa had arranged the marriage of Mukuluth to a Muslim trader from the east coast. Hamsa had provided the bulk of the dowry, which consisted of a house with a garden compound, one acre of paddy land, 1,501 rupees, and sundry moveable furniture. The marriage had not been a happy one; Mukuluth had complained to her brothers of her husband's verbal and physical abuse, his habitual drinking and gambling, the lack of home funds, and his long absences from the village. After Mukuluth had been married for five years and had given birth to three sons, Hamsa had accosted her husband and demanded that he leave the village. The husband had left and did not return.
>
> There was no official registration of divorce, and Mukuluth did not remarry. Hamsa provided her with food, worked her acre of paddy land, and her eldest son (in his early teens at the time of my departure in 1982) managed the day-to-day business at his small store.
>
> In 1981, I witnessed an argument involving Mukuluth, Bas's wife, and Bas's eldest daughter. Mukuluth accused these two

women of stealing some ears of corn from her garden. Bas was present but did not participate in the dispute. When Hamsa appeared, he first scolded his sister for cursing in public and ordered her to leave. He then turned to Bas's wife and daughter and scolded them.

Some evenings hence, Bas appeared at Hamsa's store and offered him some ears of corn. Hamsa was seated as his elder brother stood. I assume the ears of corn were subsequently given to their sister by Hamsa.

Case 2

In 1981 Sithi lived in a dilapidated one-room shed with four of her children ranging in age from 2 to 12. Their home was constructed of branches tied together by bark with roofing made of palm fronds. She had been deserted by her husband 10 years earlier. I asked the village headman (*grama sevaka*) about her, and he said that Sithi was known to villagers as a "keep" (he used the English term), meaning she provided sexual favors to males in turn for cash, food, and other goods.

Her eldest son, Hakkim, in his mid-twenties, lived in the town of Moneragala, 25 miles from Kutali. Hakkim was married and was employed as a handyman in a large merchandising store in Moneragala. He was also a vocal supporter of the SLFP (Sri Lankan Freedom Party), at that time the major opposition party. The party in power was the UNP (United National Party). The SLFP is roughly analogous to the liberal party, and the UNP the conservative party.

Sithi had three brothers who lived in Kutali. The eldest, Mohideen, was a rich and politically powerful man; he had served as the mosque trustee (the administrative head) and was the village representative of the UNP. Mohideen owned a shop, 12 acres of paddy lands, was a successful contractor for development projects, and was involved in various petty enterprises. The two younger brothers were also well off by village standards; the youngest had inherited Mohideen's position as mosque trustee.

In conversations with Sithi, she said that her brothers never visited or helped her out. Hakkim provided her financial and material support and was expected to eventually arrange the marriages and provide the bulk of the dowry for her two daughters.

The trustee acknowledged Sithi's statements but explained that she was promiscuous and added that he was not in a position to help her. In interviews with Mohideen and Hakkim, it became apparent that their political differences exacerbated tensions between Sithi and her brothers. Hakkim and Mohideen had frequently argued in public and on occasions had come to blows.

Case 3

This case involves Bibi and her three younger brothers. Bibi, in her mid-thirties at the time of the study, had been married twice. Her last husband had been a Sinhalese man who had allegedly converted to Islam. He subsequently deserted her. Bibi lived with her four children, her parents, and a younger sister, who had been stricken by polio and was mentally impaired. Her three brothers were all married and lived in neighboring houses. The entire family was poor. Bibi earned a meager living by weaving mats that were sold at local fairs and by hiring herself out for day labor in paddy and *chena* fields.

When Bibi's youngest son became ill, she had wanted to take the child to the hospital. My field assistant, Mr. Muthulingam, and I discussed the matter with her and her father, and it was decided that we would give her eldest brother 50 rupees to take the child to the hospital which was about 16 miles away by bus. On the appointed day, I was informed that Bibi, her mother, and the sick child were seen walking to the hospital and that her elder brother had pocketed the 20 rupees. When I asked her brother about the matter, he did not respond.

Case 4

This case involves an elder sister, Mynah, and her younger brother. Mynah, in her mid-twenties, lived with her husband and two children in a three-room house. In the adjoining house, connected like a duplex, lived her parents, her elder sister's husband and their children.

Mynah's younger brother was unmarried and slept and ate at either house. Mynah's husband was an unassuming and industrious man who worked at a gem store in a neighboring town. By village standards, she and her husband were well off. One night Mynah had caught her younger brother in the act of pocketing her husband's watch. He pleaded with her not to tell her husband, and she agreed. When her husband noticed his watch missing, she pretended not to know anything and he made no accusations. Her younger brother continued to live and eat at her house, and the subject of the watch was apparently never again discussed.

Case 5

On July 14, 1980, during the month of *Ramadan*, the Islamic holy month of fasting, two male friends had made arrangements to meet two girls in the jungle. The two boys, Omar and Jailan, and the two girls, Aziah and Nachi, were between 16 and 20 years of age. Adam, Nachi's elder brother, had spotted Omar in the jungle and asked him what he was doing. Adam became suspicious and forced Omar to lead him to the other three. The double affair became public knowledge and was all the more scandalous because it had occurred during *Ramadan.*

For Aziah and Jailan, one of the couples, there were no problems as both families agreed to a marriage. Jailan's elder brother had married Aziah's elder sister and had mediated between the two families. A dowry was agreed upon and the two were married shortly after *Ramadan.*

Omar's family balked at the marriage fearing he would receive a meager dowry. Adam urged the mosque leaders to force an immediate marriage between the couple. The mosque officials agreed, stating that both couples should, in any event, be punished according to the religious custom. During the debate, a member of Omar's family argued that no one had actually witnessed the couple together and that Omar had sworn that they had never had sexual intercourse. According to the *Sharia,* the Islamic code of law, the couple must be witnessed in *flagrante delicto* before any legal action may be taken.

It was decided that Omar would secretly be brought to Nachi so that they could be witnessed together, and this would suffice. Nachi was taken to her mother's brother's residence. In the middle of the night, Omar was led to this house by Adam. Omar's younger brother heard about this plan and helped Omar escape. The mosque officials reconvened and decided to take Nachi to the house where Omar was hiding. The two were then forced to spend the night together, though care was taken that they sleep in separate rooms.

Thereafter the two were married. Wedding ceremonies generally take place at the groom's house, but Omar's parents wanted to express their opposition to the wedding. The dowry consisted of 500 rupees and no lands. As marriages are not permitted during the month of *Ramadan,* the official registrar of marriages was not invited. Adam promised to build a house and provide paddy lands in the future.

Case 6

This case involves an elder brother, Latif, his younger sister, Sakhina, and her husband Ishmael. Latif had arranged the marriage of his sister with his best friend Ishmael. He had also provided them with a dowry consisting of one large house with a tiled roof, an acre of fenced garden land, an acre of irrigated paddy land adjacent to the house, and 1,000 rupees. Latif was in his late-twenties and Sakhina in her early-twenties.

In 1980, Latif had opened a bakery and, as he had other business ventures, gave Ishmael 1,050 rupees to start up the business. A Sinhalese baker was hired, and Ishmael managed the buying of provisions and selling of loaves of bread.

After the first month, Ishmael earned a gross income of 700 rupees; he kept 300 and reinvested the remainder. During the second month of operations he noticed that supplies were disappearing. One morning he caught Latif's wife, Aisha, leaving the bakery with goods. Ishmael claimed that she was siphoning off goods to her parents' household and said he could no longer manage the bakery under such conditions. Latif insisted that Ishmael continue to manage the bakery, but Ishmael refused and quit. (Aisha later told me that she was, unbeknownst to Latif, providing her family with food and cash as her father was consumptive and could not support the household.)

Shortly therafter, Ishmael and Sakhina were walking to their *chena* field when they met Ishmael's mother and elder sister. His mother, addressing Ishmael, said, "You should give us some money instead of spending everything on them." Sakhina responded with sharp words and there was a brief public argument among the three women.

Following the argument, Latif hurried to his sister's house and said to Ishmael, "I heard about what happened to my sister. I didn't even have a cup of tea but thought of getting a knife (to avenge my sister). Why didn't you prevent the attack? You can't live here anymore . . . get out!"

Ishmael yelled back but vacated the house. Sakhina placated Latif by noting her indebtedness to him and acknowledging that her husband was a "lazy but good man." She then concluded that if Latif drove her husband out she would have no means to support herself and her children. Over time Latif and Ishmael resolved their differences.

These case studies illustrate the rich and varied textures of community life within which cross-sibling relationships are managed and shaped. What follows is an analysis of these normative and behavioral depictions of cross-sibling relationships with reference to modes of reciprocity.

Discussion of the Case Studies

These case studies provide numerous instances of reciprocal modalities of behavior between cross-silbings. Table 6.1 summarizes these instances in terms of quantitative measures of reciprocal modalities. I

TABLE 6.1. Cross-sibling Interaction Scores of Reciprocity

	Generalized	Limited	Zero	Negative	Total
B→S	3	2	5	2	12
S→B	2	1	0	0	3

have adopted a version of Sahlin's (1958) concept of reciprocity to score and tabulate these data. Initiation of an interaction, even the decision not to act, is significant by an arrow directed from one cross-sibling to another (i.e., B→S, or S→B). Four behavioral categories are presented: (1) generalized reciprocity—signifies the unidirectional flow of goods and services; (2) limited reciprocity—signifies the unidirectional flow of one particular good or service; (3) zero reciprocity—signifies the absence of any observable flow of goods or services; (4) negative reciprocity—signifies the taking of goods against the best interest of the other. Each cross-sibling interaction that could be unambiguously subsumed under one of these categorical headings was tabulated.

The "limited" category includes: (1) Bas's offer of some ears of corn to Hamsa, intended to be given to their sister (Case 1); (2) Adam's arrangement of Nachi's marriage without concomitantly providing an adequate dowry (Case 5); (3) Sakhina's attempt to placate Latif (Case 6). Each cross-sibling interaction was assessed according to the criterial definitions of the respective categories.

Two observations that require explanation stand out. First, the relative lack of interactions initiated by the sisters (3) as compared to those initiated by the brothers (12). Second, the less-than-expected quantity of generalized reciprocity normatively assumed to characterize cross-sibling relationships.

The low incidence of sister-initiated interactions conforms to the cultural pattern of male dominance and segregation of the sexes. Postmarital residence patterns in conjunction with the dowry norm of building or deeding a house to a daughter further inhibits the sister from contacting her married brother(s). Brothers feels no such compunction in visiting a sister's house over which they retain proprietary interest. Within these residential and normative parameters, the brother has the advantage of regulating the frequency and managing the quality of his relationships with his sister(s). Should be neglect his sister, she or a spokesperson, as in the case of Ishmael's mother (Case 6), may remind him, but cannot demand his attention or support. The brother's obligations are based on moral rather than jural codes of behavior.

The two instances of generalized reciprocity initiated by a sister were both accomplished through clandestine means. In one instance, the sister allowed her brother to steal her husband's watch (Case 4). Her loyalty to her brother was expressed through inaction. In another instance, a wife brought food and money to her family without the knowledge of her husband (Case 6).

In both these instances, it was an elder sister who provided support. As the eldest sister nearly always marries first, she also tends to receive the largest dowry relative to her younger sisters. While families want to provide dowries of equal value, their wealth diminishes with each dowry and they are less able to afford dowries of equivalent value. The eldest daughter is, therefore, more likely than other daughters to be in a position to provide patron-like services to her family. As a consequence, the patriarchal nature of Sri Lankan culture described by Obeyesekere (1970, 1983) can be counterbalanced by the economic patronage of the eldest married daughter (see McGilvray 1988 for a more complete analysis).

Moreover, by receiving the most valued dowry, the eldest daughter is likely to marry hypergamously, that is, to marry a man from a family with a higher socioeconomic-political rank than her own family. In this case, it benefits both the sister and her brother(s) to maintain a close relationship "without calculation." The sister, in this instance, benefits, because her brothers will provide support and protection should her husband or in-laws mistreat her. Reciprocally, her brothers will receive food, aid, and various benefits from her and her husband.

In three cases where the brother was of superior socioeconomic status to his sister's husband, the former sought to assert his dominance over her household by extending patronage to his brother-in-law. Hamsa (Case 1), for example, expressed his authority over his sister.

In two other cases (Case 5, Adam; Case 6, Latif) the brothers were primary donors of their sister's dowry and sought to reorient their brother-in-law's loyalties toward his new wife and the matrilineal estate by extending their patronage. In both instances, generalized reciprocity between brother and sister entailed the subordination of the brother-in-law, who is perceived by the brother as potentially expendable. The sister literally functions as an alter ego, with her brother investing a portion of his wealth, self esteem, and public reputation in her at the time of marriage. The greater this investment, the greater the brother's desire to control its management.

Conversely, in cases of zero and negative reciprocity, either the sister or brother was impoverished. One sister, Sithi (Case 2), occupied a nonstatus in the village. The absence of any economic aid by her three brothers foreshadowed the dissolution of the cross-sibling bond. By socially excising her from the family, the brothers had redefined their sibling set to exclude her.

If, as I have argued, the reciprocal nature of cross-sibling relationships is influenced by material interests, then the value of the dowry, as an index of the wealth of a married sister, should correlate with the patterns of reciprocity presented in Table 6.1. The presence of absence of a full dowry, consisting of a house and agricultural land, is compared with the scores of reciprocity in Table 6.2. If my argument is correct, then cooperative cross-sibling relations are more likely to be maintained when the sister receives a new dowry. Generalized and limited reciprocity are combined as one category and zero and negative as the other. The presence or absence of a dowry is scored in terms of the transfer of permanent sources of wealth that remain in possession of the sister. The cash portion of the dowry was excluded as these sums were not always available and because villagers consider money to be an impermanent, easily disposable, source of wealth. The Fisher's exact test for small samples indicates that there is a significant relationship between dowry and cross-sibling postmarital relationships. That is, generalized or limited reciprocal relationships were maintained among cross-siblings when the sister received a dowry. When a sister did not receive a dowry, there was only one instance of positive reciprocity and seven instances of zero or negative reciprocity. The data suggest that personal material interests predictively affect cross-sibling interactions in ways that contradict the social norms of solidarity and cooperation among cross-siblings.

Conclusion

The six cases presented in this chapter indicate that cross-sibling relationships are more complex and diverse than would be presumed

TABLE 6.2. Comparison of Dowry and Cross-sibling Interaction Scores

	Generalized and limited reciprocity	Zero and negative reciprocity
Dowry	7	0
No dowry	1	7

$p < .01$.

by an acceptance of normative statements as factually descriptive of behaviors.

A reliance on categorical data neglects the significance of personal autonomy and motivations. Most recently, Mines (1988) has argued against South Asian social scientists who have sought to explain personal motivations in terms of the "compelling influence" of the Indian hierarchy of caste and family. Similarly, in this chapter hierarchically salient criteria such as gender, seniority, kinship, and wealth were shown to crosscut each other and, thus, confound placement within a hierarchy.

Two sets of normative parameters that constrain cross-sibling interaction were identified; one set delimits gender relations, the other delimits cross-sibling relations. These norms were viewed as conflated and negotiable. Males, for example, were presumed dominant, but the oldest sister may be in a position to extend patronage toward her brothers. Her seniority, in essence, counterbalances her subordinate status as a female.

Central to my analysis was the economic importance of the dowry. The greater the dowry, the greater the brother's stake in his sister's family and the more likely their pattern of interaction would conform to the cultural norms of generalized reciprocity. This may occur because the brother(s) provided the major portion of the dowry, which signifies an immediate and enduring interest in the welfare of his sister. If her dowry was provided by her parents, then the brother still retains an interest in maintaining close ties with his sister. Whether or not his or her motivations accord with social norms of generalized reciprocity, the results are the same.

Conversely, the lower the value of the dowry, the less likely the cross-sibling relationship will accord with social norms. The data suggests that this is due to the brother's recognition that his sister simply has nothing to give him. Despite the absense of cooperative social interactions, brothers cannot ignore the social norm of generalized reciprocity and rationalize their neglect with other explanations. As in Case 2, Mohideen and his brothers may justify their neglect of Sithi either in terms of her son's political views or her promiscuity. Whichever they choose, the result remains the same: Their ties with her were severed. Moral turpitude was used to justify the breech of another normative rule—that brothers should provide for and protect their sister(s). In the case of the brother who pocketed the 50 rupees earmarked to take his sister's son to the hospital (Case 3), normative claims were subverted by material interest.

In Kutali, as everywhere, social norms provide means for interpreting behaviors. Through socialization and the accumulation of experience, we interpret, reinterpret and adapt these norms as we construct our own idioverse. Idioverses, by definition, are not shared. In social encounters each person finds a common framework, a shared locus, or shared loci, of distributive experiential and social representations (Schwartz 1978). The level at which these representations are shared, represents the conjunction or intersection of idioverses. Of necessity this is a generalized abstracted level, removed from experience. The intersection of idioverses is made manifest in discourse as representations of commonality (Schwartz 1978) from which cultural constructs are inferred.

If brothers represent one group of idioverses and sisters another group, then it is reasonable, as each idioverse is idiosyncratic, that the pattern of intersections between sets of brother–sister dyads will be distributive and heterogeneous rather than uniform and homogeneous.

Kutali cross-sibling relationships are distributive, they vary along a generalized–negative reciprocity continuum. By representing the idioverse in terms of interactions, rather than by statements about interactions. I have tried to describe the distributive pattern of adult cross-sibling relationships in Kutali. I showed that the pattern of distribution can be explained in terms of the interplay among social norms, material conditions, and interests. In this interplay, the social norms provide a set of ethical propositions that are manipulated and adapted to justify material interests. Social norms do not explain behavior but are used by individuals to provide an explanation for behavior. Brothers and sisters in Kutali, as elsewhere, may act like brothers and sisters should out of love and loyalty but wealth seems a more durable adhesive.

References

Abramovitch, R., Pepler, D., & Corter, C. (1982). Patterns of Sibling Interaction among Preschool-Age Children. In M. E. Lamb & B. Sutton-Smith (Eds.), *Sibling Relationships: Their Nature and Significance across the Lifespan* (pp. 61–86). Hillsdale, NJ: Erlbaum.

Adler, A. (1959). *Understanding Human Nature.* New York: Premier Books.

Allan, G. (1977). "Sibling Solidarity." *Journal of Marriage and Family* 39: 177–84.

Bailey, F. G. (1969). *Strategems and Spoils.* Oxford: Basil Blackwell.

Bank, S., & Kahn, M. D. (1982). *The Sibling Bond.* New York: Basic Books.

Bharati, A. (1985). The Self in Hindu Thought and Action. In A. Marsella, G. De Vos, F. L. K. Hsu (Eds), *Culture and Self: Asian and Western Perspectives* (pp. 185–230). New York: Tavistock.

Bourdieu, P. (1977) *Outline of a Theory of Practice.* Cambridge: Cambridge University Press.

Brody G., & Stoneman, Z. (1987). "Sibling Conflict: Contributions of the Siblings Themselves, the Parent–Sibling Relationship, and the Broader Family System." *Journal of Children in Contemporary Society* 19: 39–53.

Bryant, B. (1982). Sibling Relationships in Middle Childhood. In M. E. Lamb & B. Sutton-Smith (Eds.), *Sibling Relationships: Their Nature and Significance across the Lifespan* (pp 68–122). Hillsdale, NJ: Erlbaum.

Cicirelli, V. (1975). "Effects of Sibling Structure and Interaction on Children's Categorizing Style." *Developmental Psychology* 45: 1–5.

Cicirelli, V. (1982). Sibling Influence throughout the lifespan. In M. E. Lamb & B. Sutton-Smith (Eds.), *Sibling Relationships: Their Nature and Significance across the Lifespan* (pp. 267–84). Hillsdale, NJ: Erlbaum.

de Munck, V. (1988). The Economics of Love: an Examination of Sri Lankan Muslim Marriage Practices. *Journal of South Asian Studies* 11: 25–38.

de Munck, V. (1992). "The Fallacy of the Misplaced Self: A Study of Gender Relations and the Construction of Multiple Selves among Sri Lankan Muslims." *Ethos* 20(2): 167–89.

Dumont, L. (1957). *Hierarchy and Marriage Alliance in South Indian Kinship.* Occasional Papers of the Royal Anthropological Institute, no. 12. London: RAI of Great Britain and Ireland.

Dumont, L. (1970). *Homo Hierarchicus.* Chicago: Chicago University Press.

Dunn, J., & Kendrick, C. (1982). Siblings and Their Mothers: Developing Relationships within the Family. In M. E. Lamb & B. Sutton-Smith (Eds.) *Sibling Relationships: Their Nature and Significance across the Lifespan* (pp. 36–60). Hillsdale, NJ: Erlbaum.

Felson, R. B., & Russo, N. J. (1988). "Parental Punishment and Sibling Aggression." *Social Psychology Quarterly* 51: 11–8.

Foucault, M. (1984). *The History of Sexuality* (Vol. 1). Harmondsworth, England: Penguin.

Goody, J., & Tambiah, S. J. (1973). Bridewealth and Dowry in Africa and Eurasia. *Cambridge Papers in Social Anthropology* (Vol. 7). Cambridge: Cambridge University Press.

Inden, R. B., & Nicholas, R. W. (1977). *Kinship in Bengali Culture.* New York: Bantam.

Kensinger, K. M. (1985). *The Sibling Relation in Lowland South America.* Working Papers on South American Indians, Vol. 7. Bennington, VT: Bennington College.

Lambert, B. (1981). Equivalence, Authority, and Complementarity in Bukaritari-Makin Sibling Relationships. In M. Marshall (Ed.), *Siblingship in Oceania* (pp. 149–200). Ann Arbor: University of Michigan Press.

Mandelbaum, D. G. (1970). *Society in India: Vol. 1. Continuity and Change.* Berkeley: University of California Press.

Marriott, M. (1976). Hindu Transactions: Diversity without Dualism. In B. Kapferer (Ed.), *Transaction and Meaning: Directions in the Anthro-*

pology of Exchange and Symbolic Behavior (pp. 109–42). Philadelphia: Institute for the Study of Human Issues.

Marshall, M. (1981). Introduction. In. M. Marshall (Ed.), *Siblingship in Oceania* (pp. 1–33). Ann Arbor: University of Michigan Press.

McGilvray, D. (1988). "Sex, Repression, and Sanskritization in Sri Lanka?" *Ethos* 16: 99–125.

Mines, M. (1988). "Conceptualizing the Person." *American Anthropologist* 3: 568–79.

Nelson, C. (1974). "Public and Private Politics: Women in the Middle Eastern World." *American Ethnologist* 1: 551–63.

Obeyesekere, G. (1970). "The Idiom of Demonic Possession: A Case Study." *Social Science and Medicine* 4: 97–111.

Obeyesekere, G. (1983). *The Cult of the Goddess Pattini.* Chicago: University of Chicago Press.

Ross, H. G. (1981). *Critical Incidents and Their Perceived Consequences in Adult Sibling Relationships.* Paper presented at the meeting of the American Psychological Association, Los Angeles.

Ross, H. G., & Milgram, J. I. (1982). Important Variables in Adult Sibling Relationships: A Qualitive Study. In M. E. Lamb & B. Sutton-Smith (Eds.), *Sibling Relationships: Their Nature and Significance across the Lifespan* (pp. 225–50). Hillsdale, NJ: Erlbaum.

Sahlins, M. D. (1958). *Social Stratification in Polynesia.* Seattle: University of Washington Press.

Schachter, F. F., Gilutz, G., Shore, E., & Adler, M. (1978). "Sibling Deidentification Judged by Mothers: Cross-validation and Developmental Studies." *Child Development* 49: 543–46.

Schachter, F. F., & Stone, R. (1987). "Comparing and Contrasting Siblings Defining the Self." *Journal of Contemporary Society* 19: 55–75.

Schlegel, A., & Eloul, A. (1988). "Marriage Transactions: Labor, Property, and Status." *American Anthropologist* 90: 291–309.

Schneider, D. M. (1981). Conclusion. In M. Marshall (Ed.), *Siblingship in Oceania* (pp. 389–404). Ann Arbor: University of Michigan Press.

Schwartz, T. (1978). Where Is the Culture? Personality as the Locus of Culture. In G. Spindler (Ed.), *The Psychological Anthropology* (pp. 419–41). Berkeley: University of California Press.

Shweder, R. A., & Bourne, E. J. (1984). Does the Concept of the Person Vary Cross-culturally? In R. A. Shweder & R. A. Le Vine (Eds.), *Cultural Theory: Essays on Mind, Self, and Emotion* (pp. 137–57). Cambridge: Cambridge University Press.

Srinivas, M. N. (1980). *The Remembered Village.* Delhi: Oxford University Press.

Sutton-Smith, B. (1982). Birth Order and Sibling Status Effects. In M. E. Lamb & B. Sutton-Smith (Eds.), *Sibling Relationships: Their Nature and Significance across the Lifespan* (pp. 153–65). Hillsdale, NJ: Erlbaum.

Tambiah, S. J. (1965). "Kinship Fact and Fiction in Relationship to the Kandyan Sinhalese." *Journal of Royal Anthropological Institute* 95: 131–73.

Trautman, T. (1981). *Dravidian Kinship*. New York: Cambridge University Press.

Weisner, T. (1982). Sibling Interdependence and Child Caretaking: A Cross-cultural View. In M. E. Lamb & B. Sutton-Smith (Eds.), *Sibling Relationships: Their Nature and Significance across the Lifespan* (pp. 305–28). Hillsdale, NJ: Erlbaum.

Yalman, N. (1967). *Under the Bo Tree*. Berkeley: University of California Press.

Yalman, N. (1969). The Semantics of Kinship in South India and Ceylon. In T. Sebeok (Ed.), *Current Trends in Linguistics* (pp. 607–626). The Hague: Mouton.

PART TWO

SIBLINGS IN MYTH, RELIGION, AND ETHNOPSYCHOLOGY

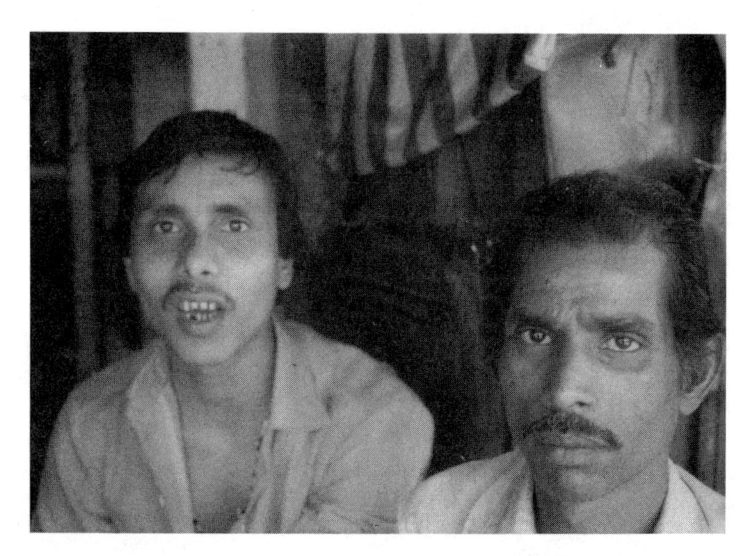

Photo by Steve Derné

C H A P T E R 7

Equality and Hierarchy between Adult Brothers

Culture and Sibling Relations in North Indian Urban Joint Families

Steve Derné

Cross-cultural studies recognize that culture shapes human behavior, including relations between siblings (Zukow 1989: 3). In the United States, while many siblings become close to one another in adulthood and old age, psychologists usually focus on sibling conflict. Indeed, even in adulthood, few American siblings consult with each other on important decisions, and rivalry—especially between brothers—often continues unabated (Dunn 1985: 156–57). By contrast, cross-cultural examinations of siblings often focus on sibs as supporters as well as competitors (Ervin-Tripp 1989: 185). Weisner (1989) suggests that differing cultural beliefs regarding the roles and responsibilities of siblings, and differing cultural emphases on hierarchy, are important in shaping sibling relations. This chapter focuses on how the emphasis north Indian Hindu men place on hierarchy, and their expectation that adult brothers will continue to live harmoniously in a joint family, shape relations between adult brothers.

Unlike North Americans (Bellah, Madsen, Sullivan, Swidler & Tipton 1985; Bryant 1989; Hewitt 1989; Varenne 1977), but like, for instance the Kwara'ae (Weisner 1989: 17), north Indian Hindu brothers are encouraged to pursue lifelong shared obligations and relationships, usually by continuing to live in the same household along with their parents, wives and children, and brothers and sister-in-law. Unlike North Americans, who focus on individual autonomy and privacy

(Bellah et al. 1985; Varenne 1977), but like, for instance, the Mandinka (Weisner 1989: 17–8), Hindu men learn the importance of hierarchy and the appropriate deference within it. How do these cultural elaborations shape relations between adult Hindu brothers?

This chapter argues that the emphasis on hierarchy shapes the relationship between brothers not only by demanding that younger brothers be deferent to their elder brothers but also by leading Hindu brothers to find relief from hierarchy by constructing equal relationships with one another. While Hindu men usually distrust nonhierarchical relationships, they often construct equal relationships with their brothers. These relations seem nonthreatening because they are safely embedded in the hierarchy of a joint family headed by their father. Brothers' attachment to the "sweet" relationships they develop with each other, and the cultural emphasis on brothers continuing to stay together, prompt many men to strive to maintain harmonious relations with their brothers throughout their adult lives.

However, Hindu culture also emphasizes hierarchy between brothers. In understanding how culture shapes human relations, we must try to understand how individuals deal with culture's inconsistencies and contradictions (Hewitt 1989). How do Hindu men reconcile the conflict between the cultural emphasis on hierarchy and the equal relations brothers often build together? This chapter focuses on how the resulting disputes between brothers sometimes lead to enmity between brothers and the breakup of the joint family but also sometimes lead to a focus on compromise and cooperation between brothers who find a way to continue to live together. In this sense, culture does not constrain with an iron hand, but rather suggests the contradictions people must resolve in constructing their lives (Hewitt 1989). Culture provides a "tool kit" (Daniel 1983; Swidler 1986), of conflicting choices that people use in diverse ways.

I proceed in five broad steps. First, I briefly describe the qualitative interviews I conducted with north Indian Hindu men. Second, I describe the importance Hindu men place on being guided by their elders rather than by their own individual volition. In a third, lengthy, section, I illustrate the Hindu focus on hierarchy and emphasize the importance Hindu men place on brothers continuing to live together by describing Hindu men's attachment to joint-family living. Fourth, I emphasize the satisfactions of equality between brothers who live as junior members of joint families. In this section, I focus on how a cultural emphasis on equality, while less elaborated, complements the dominant focus on hierarchy. Finally, I conclude by discussing how the disputes that sometimes arise between adult brothers often lead brothers to de-emphasize hierarchical relations between them and focus instead on compromise and cooperation.

Interviews with North Indian Hindu Men

In 1986 and 1987 I conducted intensive interviews with 49 caste Hindus who live and work in the city of Benares. The men are of Brahman (20 men), Kshatriya (8 men), Vaishya (17 men), and Shudra (4 men) castes. Roughly 80% (40 out of 49) of them live in joint-family households with more than one married couple. They range in age from their twenties to their seventies and include both junior and senior members of joint households: 12 men head joint households with more than one married couple; 21 men live with their wives as junior members of a household; 10 men are unmarried, most of these living in joint households; and 6 men head nuclear families. Slightly more than half of those younger than 45 have some college education and most of the rest had been to high school. While none of those over 45 had attended college, more than a third are high school educated. Most of these men are merchants, although 6 work in white-collar jobs in government or industry. The men are fairly well off: The families of most of the men own scooters and/or televisions. None of them, however, is spectacularly well off: None owns an automobile or has been abroad.

In open-ended interviews, I asked men to tell me about the advantages and disadvantages they found in joint-family living and about relations they had with their parents, wives, and brothers. Interviews lasted from 40 minutes to more than 2 hours and were sometimes supplemented with follow-up interviews. I taped the interviews, all of which were conducted in Hindi, and translated them into English with the help of a research assistant.

While my selection of respondents was not systematic—I approached respondents at their places of business in several neighborhoods—the rate of refusals was very low (less than 15%), and there is no obvious reason why this group of men would be unrepresentative of upper-caste Hindu merchants of Benares. These men's general preference for joint-family living, arranged marriages, restrictions on women's movement outside the home, and limitation on interactions between husband and wife are typical of upper-caste Hindu men throughout north India (Mandelbaum 1988). Joint-family living is more typical in the Benares region than in other places in India (Kolenda 1987: 243), but most Indians probably spend at least the first years of married life in joint households (Kakar 1981: 14; Kolenda

1967: 386). These men's understandings of self and of what shapes actions are similar to the commonsense understandings reported by other investigators (Derné 1992; Roland 1988). In short, there is no reason to believe that these men are atypical of upper middle-class, urban, caste Hindus in the Hindi-speaking region of north India.

The Hindu Emphasis on Hierarchy

Dumont's (1966/1980) argument that Hindus focus on hierarchy rather than equality still provides a useful account of the values of upper-caste north Indian Hindu males. While it is clear that lower-caste people do not embrace the value on hierarchy (Appadurai 1986; Berreman 1971; Derné 1990; Mencher 1974), hierarchy is still the dominant value for many upper-caste males. Each individual feels that he must act out predetermined roles that are seen as contributing to the functioning of the social order as a whole (see also Shweder & Miller 1985). By contrast, Dumont argues, in Western societies, the individual rather than the social whole is given primary importance. In these societies—which Dumont sees as emphasizing equality—the individual is presumed able to choose the roles he or she will play according to what the individual thinks will bring him or her the most individual happiness (see Varenne 1977; Bellah et al. 1985). Where hierarchy is the dominant value, primary importance is attached to following the duties associated with institutionally anchored roles (see Turner 1976; Shweder & Miller 1985). In Hindu society, as Kakar (1981: 121) puts it, "to conform is to be admired; to strike out on one's own . . . is to invite scorn or pity."

Hindu men live with the cultural ideal of hierarchy. They examine it, talk about it, find it useful to them, and struggle against it if it impedes them. While the men I interviewed did not invent the cultural ideal of hierarchy, most come to possess the cultural ideal as their own. In their own talk with each other they reconstitute the ideal in their own interactions. (This approach to culture follows Hewitt [1989: 69–71]).

For instance, the men I interviewed embrace the ideal of hierarchy by focusing on how they are guided by tradition and a concern with their honor—rather than on individual choices. Hindu men repeatedly refer to the maintenance of honor as a rationale for diverse actions (see also Roland 1988: 242–43). More than 20% (10 out of 49) of the men I interviewed mention the dishonor of living separately from one's parents as one reason they live in joint families. Nearly half (24 out of 49) of the men I interviewed spontaneously mention that maintenance of honor is a principal reason that marriages must be arranged by the parents. Nandu Gupta,[1] a 35-year-old heading a nuclear family, says, for instance, that:

> "The man who marries for love loses his honor. Society kicks him away, and he becomes utterly worthless."

Men also commonly justify restrictions on women's movements outside the home as necessitated by a concern with their family's honor (Derné 1988: 108–11, 207–11). Phoolchand Mishra, a 28-year-old married Brahman living in a joint family, says, for instance, that if a woman takes "any type of unlimited step in any field [it] could destroy the honor of her family."

Men's references to tradition are just as common in their accounts of why they live in joint families, why marriages are arranged, and why women should be restricted to the home. Sunil Gupta, a 35-year-old living in a large joint family headed by his older brother, says, for instance, that he likes living in the joint family because "this tradition of joint-family living has been running from the beginning." Two thirds (33 out of 49) of the men I interviewed spontaneously mention that they value arranged marriages because they are in accord with the Hindu religious tradition. Men also cite the dictates of tradition as an important reason for restricting women's movements outside the home. Shobnath Gupta, an unmarried 20-year-old, refers to these restrictions as an "old tradition," that "therefore should be accepted." In focusing on following tradition and protecting their honor, the Hindu men I interviewed emphasize being guided by their social group.

Hindu men often explicitly state their preference for being guided by their social group. Typically, for instance, men explain their actions by referring to what is appropriate for their caste. Ramchandra Mishra, a married 32-year-old living with his wife and children, parents, and brother and his family, explains arranged marriages by saying:

> "We have to move under whatever is the family's society. We cannot go outside the society. Whatever customs are there in the society of Brahmans, we move according to those customs."

Men often do not evaluate whether their caste's customs are right in an abstract way, but feel simply that established customs must be followed *whatever they may be.* A married 35-year-old Vaishya, who commented that women go outside the home more now than they did in his youth, refuses to consider whether the times of his youth or modern times are right, saying only that "whatever situation is moving right now is right." A married Brahman in his thirties solves the "problem of understanding what is right" by answering the question "what is the time saying?" As Roland (1988: 271) argues, "Indians are constantly sensitive to how others regard them and seem quite open to be guided and directed by an elder or other superior in their hierarchical relationships."

The Hindu men I interviewed distrust those who are not controlled by such hierarchical relationships. Dileep Singh is a 54-year-old heading a nuclear family. He is very religious and enjoys talking not just about Tulsi's *Ramcaritmanas* but also about religion in America. Dileep, who has lively eyes, a warm face, and salt-and-pepper hair, decorates his cloth shop with numerous religious pictures, all of which show signs of his active devotion. He states his distrust of the individual outside of hierarchical control in general terms:

> "It is for the respect of society that people keep their character. If people don't see the society, then many people here will be bad. If one understands that the society is nothing, then one can do anything. Only by fear of society are we educated from doing wrong."

Prem Singh, an unmarried 24-year-old whose marriage has been set, believes the thoughts of unmarried college women are suspect simply because these women are not directly supervised by their families:

> "Today's environment is such that 60% of the girls in colleges are victims of their own bad thoughts during their study time. The bad thoughts are that 'I am free. I have no restrictions. I am not under anybody.'"

One reason that Hindu men avoid directly criticizing unrelated people who act inappropriately is that they see these people as dangerously uncontrolled by their family. Deepak Mishra, a 30-year-old junior member of a joint family headed by his father, says, for instance, that if criticized directly, the individual "may fight or quarrel with you. He can beat you up. But if you tell someone else, he'll not fight with you."

These common ideas about the dangers of individuals free of hierarchical control are enforced by and reflected in cultural nightmares of individuals outside this control. This is strongly evident in the common idea that love marriages—marriages decided by a man and a woman without parental input—inevitably fail. Two-thirds (32 out of 49) of the men I interviewed spontaneously mention that most love marriages fail. The reason they fail, as one married 27-year-old puts it, is that neither the husband nor the wife will "understand themselves as lower than anybody else." Free of social hierarchy, without the "fear of public shame," as one 60-year-old puts it, the husband and wife "fight uncontrollably."

The Preference for Joint-Family Living

Joint-Family Living as Providing Hierarchical Control

The Hindu preference for being guided by their elders is one reason that Hindu men prefer joint-family living. The Hindu men I interviewed—like urban and village Hindus throughout north India (Kakar 1981; Rao & Rao 1982: 131–45; Sharma 1989; Vatuk 1989)—say that the ideal state of affairs is living under one roof with one's parents, brothers, wife, and children. Kumar Yadav, a married 25-year-old eldest son, relies on his father's guidance for even the smallest tasks:

> "I wouldn't even do the smallest bit of work without asking father. If the work will be spoiled [because he can't be asked], let it get spoiled. We don't act according to our own mind without asking. We only do the types of work he tells us to do."

Most men prefer that elders provide guidance about whom to marry and what occupational and educational opportunities to pursue (Derné 1988: 42–6; Roland 1988: 98–100).

Some men see the presence of elders as necessary to check their own antisocial impulses. Prem Singh not only fears that women uncontrolled by their families will be attacked by bad thoughts of freedom, but he also relies on his parents to check his own sexual urges. He believes that no young man can "control himself when it comes to matters of sex," and says that unless young men such as himself are controlled by their families, they cannot help but "run behind the back of girls" and lose themselves in the "intoxication of sex." Prem laments his own sexual urges as destructive to his "power of thinking and understanding" and is thankful his family checks these urges. He says that because he lives with his parents he has "the emotional calculation that my parents are above me. There is somebody to guide me, and I am under somebody."

Some men also emphasize that they can be certain their wives will be under control if they live within the joint family. One reason that Prem Singh will continue to live with his parents after he marries is that by living in the joint family, "it remains safe that [my wife] will not be able to go anywhere." Ravi Mishra, an unmarried 24-year-old living with his older brother and *bhabhi* (older brother's wife), says that if a young husband and wife live outside the joint family, their fighting "will never be tamed, but rather increases." By contrast, if husband and wife live with the husband's parents,

> "if any fight happens, the parents come between them and hold it down. Or for several days they may send their son outside or send the girl back to her house. Because of this, fighting [between husband and wife] happens rarely."

During my stay in Benares, I knew of several families who curbed fighting between husband and wife by sending the wife back to her parents' household, indicating the importance of such hierarchical control. As Surjit Singh, an unmarried 33-year-old, puts it, because of joint-family living, "the influence of [the wife's] father, [the husband's] father, and the whole joint family is on the woman. The woman is kept down a little from all sides."

Among many men, the image is of a group of brothers directing each individual's actions. Arjun Gupta, a 44-year-old heading a large joint family that includes three of his younger brothers as well as his adult and near-adult sons, describes such a process in typical, if idealized, terms:

> "When any tension arises in the family, we sit together, think, and solve the problem. Suppose I made a mistake, then I will accept my fault. Or if my younger brother made a mistake, then all three brothers will say to him, 'you are doing wrong.' This has a mental effect on him. When he realizes what he has done, he comes again to his place."

One reason that men prefer joint-family living, then, is because they rely on the family—often represented by a committee of brothers—to guide their actions.

By living in a joint family, men say that they feel confident of their strength, honor, and place in the society. College educated Ashok Mishra is a 26-year-old living in a small joint family with his parents, wife and small child, and brother's family. Ashok, who already has grey in the unshaved stubble that covers his face, aspired to be a high school teacher like his father, but eventually decided he could make more money by running a blanket store, which his father set up for him at an important downtown crossing. Religion is important to Ashok, who talks enthusiastically about the depictions of Shiva and Vishnu that he keeps in his shop. Ashok emphasizes that

> "By living in the joint family, man's honor [*izzat*] will always remain. Man's esteem [*man*] will never be damaged. [When the

> joint family is strong], people know to which *khandan* [family lineage] a man belongs."

Deepak Mishra, who feels "very bad" that two of his brothers live separately, frets that

> "People think we have become weak. If all five brothers live together, then all people are afraid of them and no one dares to stand up to them."

Deepak emphasizes the point by clenching his five fingers into a fist to highlight the strength of five brothers living together. Vinod Gupta, a married 38-year-old father living in a joint family headed by his brother, says that by contrast "the feeling of insecurity is very much among those who live separately."

The preference for being directed by respected elders in the joint family, and the feeling that joint-family living secures one's honor, sometimes leads Hindus to feel uneasy when forced to live separately. Ashok Mishra fears, for instance, that if he lived separately, he would "start to do bad things." A few men mention particular instances of discomfort when suddenly forced to act outside of their joint family. Anil Gupta, 76, has operated a tobacco and *pan* shop for many years. He continues to live with one of his sons in a quiet house in close proximity to the residences of his other sons. He has a white beard and healthy, lively, bright eyes. He loves to talk about his activities in the independence movement. Anil is an only child whose mother died when he was just an infant, leaving him with just his father and grandmother. When his father and grandmother died, Anil experienced intense anxiety:

> "I became completely helpless. Even for an ordinary thing, I had to act according to my own mind! Because I didn't have any relatives, there was no one to advise me. I did whatever came into my mind with whatever results! The situation was very terrible because when I looked around my neighborhood, I saw that someone had two brothers, someone else had three brothers, and some others had four brothers. Then, this came into my heart: 'How unfortunate I am because I don't have anyone!'"

Despite being married to a woman with whom he was particularly close, Anil was distressed that no elders were available to guide his actions. His distress was acute since he was accustomed to receiving guidance from his father and since others around him had many older relatives on whom they could rely for advice. Psychoanalysts Kakar

(1981: 20–1) and Roland (1988: 103) found such distress following separations from the joint family common among Indian men.

Emotional Satisfactions of Joint-Family Living

Men prefer joint-family living not only because it places them in a larger hierarchy but also because they find comfort and satisfaction in living jointly. Sureshwar Mishra, the 60-year-old father of Deepak Mishra, emphasizes that the "badness in living separately is that then one does one's actions for oneself separately!" Sureshwar suggests that because "everyone lives together and loves each other," joint-family living is emotionally satisfying. Raj Kumar Singh, a recently married 23-year-old who lives with his parents, wife, and older brothers and their families, comments, for instance, on the satisfaction he receives by living in a joint family. "Everyone," Raj says, "lives laughing and talking. Every brother shares each other's pains and sorrows." Tej Gupta, Arjun Gupta's 21-year-old eldest son, is a college graduate who expects to be married soon. He operates a small flour mill on the outskirts of Benares near the Benares Hindu University. When I interviewed Tej, he was covered with flour but had a bright smile. He wore fashionable glasses and had a dark red *tika* on his forehead. Tej expressed a similar satisfaction: "If anyone [in the family] has any trouble, everyone bears it together."

For some, good relations between brothers are so central that they are as important as joint-family living. Thirty-year-old Deepak Mishra, two of whose brothers live separately while two others remain living with him and their parents within the joint family, emphasizes that it is "sweet" relationships with his brothers that are most important. "You can all live and eat together," he says, "but if everyone is of his own mind, this is very bad."

The feeling that one is pleasing one's elders is also an important emotional satisfaction of joint-family living. After commenting on how everyone in the joint family bears each other's troubles, Tej Gupta adds that he is satisfied with joint-family living because his parents are "happy to see us living together." Just as younger men routinely comment on the satisfaction they get from fulfilling their obligations to their parents, their fathers often comment on the pleasure they get from watching their sons continue to live happily within one joint family. Shom Mishra is a 45-year-old whose sons have recently married, bringing two daughters-in-laws into the household Shom heads. Shom is a religious man who has returned to daily meditation after a hiatus of many years. He occasionally publishers articles in the local Hindi paper and sees himself as a literary person.

Shom enjoys seeing his sons prosper. Parents, he says, "always have happy imaginations about our sons and their children," adding that he is satisfied to see his sons living happily together with wives he himself chose for them.

Besides this emotional attachment to joint-family living, men also typically mention a variety of practical advantages of living jointly. They see the division of labor between women of a large joint family as preferable to wives performing all tasks in separate households. To cite one preferred arrangement, a mother might organize household tasks, while a wife sews clothes, a younger brother's wife cooks meals, and an elder brother's wife takes children to school. Men find such arrangements convenient in comparison to the burden of having their wives do all such tasks. Men who live in joint families also claim that they benefit from the ability to pool money for large wedding expenses, the availability of family members to help out if a husband or wife falls ill, and the economy of operating the single stove that is required for joint-family living (Derné 1988: 35–6).

Some men also mention that brothers can help each other in times of financial difficulty. Krishna Das Singh, 25, and living with his wife, parents, and older brother's family, describes the help that brothers can offer each other:

> "Today, my brother may have food and money when I have none. We can both live from what he earns. If my brother does not have these things, then I can feed him, just as he feeds me. If I am ill and cannot walk around, then my brother can look after me and take me to the doctor. When I become well again, I can take him to the doctor [should he become sick]."

The practical advantages of joint-family living, then, can extend to the financial security provided by pooling the multiple incomes of several brothers in the family.

The Idea That Hierarchy Protects the Joint Family

One reason that men value joint-family living is because of their belief that individuals must be embedded in larger hierarchies. But some men embrace hierarchy within a family *because* of the importance they place on joint-family living. For these men, joint-family living is a more primary value than hierarchy. The comments of Ramesh Mishra, a 35-year-old eldest son living in a large joint family with his wife and children, parents, and brothers and their children, typify the position that the successful operation of the joint family requires a clear hierarchy:

> "In the household in which there is only one *malik* [head of household], the family will not break, while in the house where there are two or three *maliks*, everyone wants to impose his own point. It is very natural that in those places separations will occur."

Valuing joint-family living, Hindu men believe the harmony of the family can best be protected by maintaining the authority of men over women and elder over younger within the family (Derné 1988: 31–61; Dumont 1966/1980; Kakar 1981: 116–20; Roland 1988).

Longing for Joint-Family Living

The strength of the cultural ideal of harmonious relations between brothers in a joint family is apparent in the continued longing for such relations even by men who find satisfaction in living separately from their parents and brothers. Nandu Gupta, a 35-year-old high school graduate who heads a nuclear family, operates a small, dusty luggage shop that he decorates with depictions of various gods and goddesses. Nandu decided to remarry after his first wife died partly because his relations with his brothers provided him little satisfaction:

> "I used to feel uneasy when I went home at night. Whom did I have to talk to? None of my brothers were mixing with each other. None of us had a good relation with each other. There should be someone to talk to, with whom I can share my joys and sorrows. Because there was no one, I decided to remarry."

After remarrying, Nandu continued to be dissatisfied living with his parents, and he decided to establish a separate household:

> "Living in the joint family where four women live together, there are always quarrels, such as 'She has no work; she is sitting and doing nothing.' Because all these quarrels were happening daily, I was very unsettled. Furthermore, although I came home on time, I didn't get any special food. When the cooking is done for all, there is nothing special for me. I have separated my family and myself so that I will be separated from all these problems. I have peace from what was happening before among the women. I have much peace and satisfaction."

Although Nandu describes his relationships with his brothers as poor, he nevertheless continues to be drawn to the cultural ideal of harmony between brothers:

> "I wish that my brothers and I would go home at night after doing our business and put our problems in front of our father and take advice from him. But these things are not in my brothers."

The cultural emphasis on harmonious solidarity of brothers in a joint family is so strong that Nandu finds that he, too, desires these relations with his brothers, even though he himself decided he is happier living separately from them.

Nandu's continuing consultation with his parents, and his efforts to fulfill his obligations to them, are further indications that he continues to be attached to the ideal of joint-family living. Like others who have separated from their parents (Roland 1988: 211), Nandu continues to consult his father about important actions. Nandu insists that his father "is the one who directs the family. We are all under him." Nandu is similarly careful to meet the obligations implied by joint-family living, especially the obligation to care for his parents:

> "I have to look after my father and mother. My wife also has to serve my parents. We understand that he who is serving his parents is very fortunate. The result of this will be given by the master of the upper side [God]."

The strength of the cultural ideal of joint-family living is such that even some men who find relief in separation from the joint family continue to consult their parents, serve their parents, and recognize that close relationships with their brothers under their father are to be desired.

Tactics for Minimizing Joint-Family Splits

Despite the value placed on hierarchy, joint-family living, and the solidarity of brothers, joint families often break. Although the separation of brothers into separate households is not a desired act, it is—especially after their parents' death—an expected one (Derné 1988: 47–55; Shah 1973: 31; Sharma 1980: 4–5). Indeed, among the men I interviewed, it is rare for brothers to continue to live together sharing one hearth after their parents' have died and their own children have become adults. Thus, only three of the ten men who head households that include their married sons have any of their brothers still living with them. Few of the men I interviewed who were living with their parents were also living with their uncles. Yet, the salience of the ideal of brothers living harmoniously under one roof is so strong and the potential dishonor of the appearance of contentious relations between brothers are so fearful that men take elaborate steps to explain in favorable terms apparent deviations from the ideal.

Most commonly, men refer to the difficulty of living under one roof as families grow in size. For instance, a young married Vaishya now living with his wife and child, his parents, and his brothers in a joint family comments that his father had separated from his uncle many years before because the house became too small for all of them to live in, insisting that it was "not for the reason of any fight."

Other men emphasize that separations do not reflect enmity between brothers by focusing on tensions between wives as the fundamental reason behind any separation (see also Berreman 1972: 175; Luschinsky 1962: 423–76; Mandelbaum 1988; Sharma 1978: 226, 1980: 4–5). Phoolchand Mishra, a 28-year-old living with his wife and children along with his parents and younger siblings, now works as a printing press operator, but once used his B.Com. degree to work as a journalist. Phoolchand presents himself as close to his brother who has left the family. He describes his relationship with his brother as "sweet," explaining the separation by pointing to the brother's wife's unwillingness to do the joint family's work:

> "Because there is only one stove, a lot of food needs to be cooked in the joint family. Some of today's women don't like to do much work. They like to roam [*ghumna*] around too much. They want to cook food for fewer people so that they have to work less. Therefore, my brother has become separate."

Ashok Mishra similarly blames women for most breakups of joint families. He says,

> "Women create fights between brothers and talk in such a way that mutual tension is born. Without [this talk], there is no tension between brothers."

That men often blame separations from the joint family on intruding wives, rather than the often real enmity between brothers, is an indication of the importance men place on the harmony of brothers.

Another tactic some men use to explain breakups of the joint family is to deny that any separation has occurred at all by pointing, for instance, to the lack of animosity between brothers or, alternatively, to the sharing of important occasions and social projects such as weddings. It is almost as if these men conceptualize themselves as living in joint families despite the separation of living and eating. Five men who had brothers working in separate cities all insist that the families must still be seen as joint, despite what they call "temporary" separations based on the demands of their brothers' work—"temporary" separations that in some cases had endured for more than 15 years! Deepak Mishra's 60-year-old father, Sureshwar, minimizes the fact that two of his sons live in separate cities by emphasizing that they live jointly when visiting Benares. Sureshwar insists that the family must continue to be seen as joint. In two households in which brothers continue to live together with their grown children, the men insist that the food be seen as cooked in common even though meals are, in fact, cooked separately. As a 50-year-old Vaishya insists, although two stoves burn in the house, "they must be considered one."

Men who have moved to Benares from the surrounding villages are similarly reluctant to admit that they have separated from their joint families. Dileep Singh admits that he has taken his family to live in the city because he can provide for his young children better than if they lived in the joint family. Yet, he still insists, "I don't live separately from anyone." To back this up, he emphasizes his participation in agricultural work in the village, points out that his relatives sometimes stay with him on festival days, and underlines that "works of the family such as marriages" are completed jointly.

Even Nandu Gupta, who separated from his family for his own peace and satisfaction, minimizes his serious tensions with his brothers as transitory:

> "Tensions happen, but it always becomes right again. If there is ever any fighting between brothers, it ends the next day. Anger comes, but it cools down after one or two days and brothers meet again. Even if tensions rise up, they do not last forever."

Men are so strongly attached to the ideal of harmonious joint-family living in which adult brothers continue to live under one roof that they continue to imagine harmonious relations even where they do not exist. This ideal of continuing, lifelong relations between brothers, like the attachment to hierarchical relations, is an important element of Hindu culture. How do these ideals shape the relationship between Hindu brothers?

Experiences of Equality between Brothers

The cultural emphasis on harmony between brothers leads men to emphasize their relations with their brothers as important, and the emphasis on the hierarchy of old over young suggests that relations between brothers will be one of respectful obedience of the younger. But, Hindu values are more complex than this, As Hewitt (1989) argues in his recent discussion of culture, cultures are often divided.

"Culture shapes throught, action, and feeling," Hewitt (1989: 72) argues, "not only by emphasizing certain tendencies but also by permitting people to imagine their opposites." If people emphasize, "duty," for instance:

> "People will not only talk about it and devote their energies to it, but they will worry about its opposite, however they conceive it—as 'selfishness,' as 'sloth,' or as 'desire.' They are likely to be anxious about whether they are doing their duty, daydream about being released from duty, and be on the lookout to punish those who stray too far from its demands."

Thus, the Hindu focus on duty, obedience, and hierarchy allows people to imagine opposites—freedom, desire, selfishness, and equality. They are not only concerned with how to control those who are dangerously free from social hierarchy but also sense, even if vaguely, their own desire to be free from hierarchy, even as they feel safe by being embedded within it.

The Complexity of Hindu Ideals

The importance of obligations to others and the importance of acting based on one's own desires reflect *universals* of human experience (Heelas 1981). All individuals have the experience, even if vaguely understood, both of being nourished and controlled by their society and of being able to choose actions on their own. Because of the Hindu focus on hierarchy, Hindu men more easily recognize how they are nourished by their society than how they also have individual volition. But because total passivity or powerlessness runs counter to the human experience of being able to act in the world (Heelas 1981: 47), the constraint of hierarchy presses people to desire freedom. While the American focus on the individual's freedom and separateness leads many Americans to desire limits and the security of social groups (Hewitt 1989; Varenne 1977), the Hindu focus on the individual being controlled by his or her social group leads many Hindus to desire freedom.

Indeed, various "second languages" recognizing the importance of the individual complement the dominant Indian "first language" that sees the individual as rightly situated within a family hierarchy (Derné 1992). (The discussion of "languages" uses the terminology of Bellah et al. [1985]). The Hindu "second language" recognizing individual volition is apparent in the Indian constitution's provisions making individuals an important bearer of rights and obligations (Béteille 1983). Roland (1988: 228–29) argues that Indians are similarly often very aware of individual libidinal and sensual desires. But the "second language" that is most powerful is in the spiritual realm. While it has long been recognized that the tradition of religious renouncers in Indian society represents the possibility of the individual free of social hierarchies (Dumont 1966/1980: 184–85), Roland (1988: 228, 240) has argued recently that common Indians, too, recognize "particular proclivities of a person" with respect to "spiritual strivings." While individualism is not recognized in a person's hierarchical role in the family, most Indians have an "inner spiritual self" (Roland 1988: 289) that valorizes the individual. This Hindu "second language" of individualism in the spiritual realm is apparent in *bhakti* (devotional) sects that allow the individual to achieve salvation through devotion irrespective of caste, gender, or other social groupings; in pilgrimages in which familial responsibilities become subordinate to an inner spiritual quest; and in Hindu religious philosophies that urge detachment from family ties that are deemed mere illusion (Ramanujan 1989: 54, Roland 1988: 307–10).

Equality between Brothers

Relations with one's brother is another arena in which Hindu men often find refreshing equality in a hierarchical world. Despite the emphasis placed on hierarchy in the family—including the hierarchy of elder over younger brother—many experiences of Hindu brothers are characterized by equality. Similar in age, brothers often live as near-equals under their father in the joint family. While men feel comfortable living within a family hierarchy so that there is someone elder than them to give them guidance, the relationship of brothers often provides relief from hierarchy. Indeed, the constraints of following social roles may be one reason that relationships between brothers are so savored.

Ramesh Mishra, 35, is an eldest son who lives with his parents, wife and children, and his brothers and their families. Ramesh's hair is turning silver, and his round face is engaging. Although Ramesh married for love, he says that his father still respects him the most of all of his brothers. College educated, Ramesh has abandoned teaching to operate a successful general store. Ramesh describes his relationship with his brothers as "a relationship of friendship more than a relationship of brothers." By emphasizing friendship, Ramesh recognizes the equality he feels with his brothers. By contrasting such a relationship with the expected relationship between brothers, he emphasizes that the relationship between brothers is ideally a hierarchical one—with elder brother superior to younger, with younger brother obliged to obey his elder.

For Ramesh, like a few other men, sports is an arena for acting out the equal relationship between brothers. Ramesh talks with relish of the pleasure he gets from playing soccer with his brothers. "We are sportsmen," he says, "and we enjoy playing football together." Newly married Kumar Yadav, who is also an eldest son living with his parents in a joint family, similarly enjoys sports with his brothers. Kumar decorates his milk shop with pictures of wrestlers, as well as religious images. Kumar is a strong, handsome man, with a moustache and a tough smile. Kumar loves wrestling with his brother:

> "We do exercises together in the morning. When we do it for two hours, we get such bliss as if we are in heaven. My main rival in wrestling is my [younger] brother. My brother has become a very good wrestler, and we pull and push with each other."

These shared leisure activities are an indication of the pleasure and closeness that sometimes exists between brothers, pleasure that may provide relief from a ruthlessly hierarchical world.

Are the easy, equal relations Ramesh Mishra and Kumar Yadav have with their brothers dependent on being situated within a clear hierarchy? Ramesh and his brothers, and Kumar and his brothers, live under their fathers within the joint family. Thus, Ramesh, Kumar, and their brothers can rely on their fathers to provide the stable hierarchy that they think insures the proper functioning of the family, allowing them to emphasize equality with each other. Indeed, both Ramesh and Kumar clearly recognize the importance of obeying their parents in the joint family. Recall Remesh's statement that a family requires one *malik* if it is to run smoothly, and Kumar's statement that he would not do even "the smallest bit of work" without asking his father. Ramesh's and Kumar's relationships with their brothers are less likely to be spoiled by a conflict between the expectations of hierarchy between brothers and the perception of equality between them, since both see themselves as working together with their brothers under a father who alone heads the joint family.

Resolutions of the Conflict between Equality and Hierarchy between Brothers

While brothers may find equal relationships refreshing, they also may find these relationships threatening if they are not firmly situated within a family hierarchy. Just as men distrust the relationship of husband and wife if it is not controlled by their joint-family group, so men similarly distrust equal relationships between brothers if they are not embedded in a larger family hierarchy. The similarity of age and position that helps men construct equal relations with their brothers also makes it difficult for a younger brother to offer his older brother the respectful obedience that is demanded by their difference in age.

Newly married Raj Kumar Singh is a college graduate who lives in a large joint family, whose electronics shop he helps operate. An image of the goddess Lakshmi is displayed in the shop along with the radios Raj sells—radios that allow him to listen to cricket matches while he works. A younger son who has long enjoyed interactions with his elder brother's wives, Raj is delighted with his marriage and enjoys talking with his wife about their childhoods. Raj enjoys joint-family living because he can share his pains and sorrows with his brothers. "Each brother," he says, "has someone to talk with about any concerns." He also enjoys close, joking relationships with his older brother's wives. Despite these close ties, Raj recognizes that from time to time there are tensions with his brothers "because they are in my age." He emphasizes that he never has any tensions with his father because his father is so much older than him. While Raj feels a degree of equality with his brothers and enjoys living with them under his father in the joint family, these feelings of equality may prove an impediment to harmonious relations should his eldest brother come to head the family and expect Raj's unwavering obedience. Raj recognizes that his harmonious relations with his brothers may deteriorate as soon as he has children:

> "Now everyone is one. But if my wife has a child, then the relationship will spoil a little. It is natural that the blood will pull the blood."

Even Raj Kumar Singh, a man who values joint-family living enough to be careful to teach his wife to "look after each brother equally," nonetheless believes disputes are inevitable between those of similar age.

The harmony Raj feels with his brothers is strengthened by his relationship with his parents. Raj emphasizes that it is his father who "runs the whole family" and admits it is difficult to obey his brother's orders in the same fashion that he respects those of his father. Raj counts on his mother to lighten the load of disputes with his brothers by talking them over with him. "Any time there is any trouble with any of my brothers," he says, "I tell it to my mother. I have the most love for my mother—more even than for my father." This suggests that a joint family may not run long after the parents' death. When parents die, it is difficult for a man like Raj Kumar Singh to accept an eldest brother, who was often seen as a near-equal, as the undisputed head of the family.

Enmity and Dissolution of the Joint Family

Most of the men I interviewed believe disputes between brothers are common as brothers grow older and take on more responsibilities (Derné 1988: 53–9; see also Das 1976: 5; Shah 1973). An unmarried 33-year-old's comments are typical: "When the family grows," he says, "there are naturally disputes. The feeling of dislike comes, and the joint family automatically breaks."

One outcome of the tension between eldest brother's authority and the feeling of equality between brothers is enmity that leads to separation. This enmity is apparent in a number of the cases discussed above, most notably the case of Nandu Gupta, who moved himself out of the joint family because of the lack of cooperation he received from his brothers. Phoolchand Mishra, similarly, has a contentious relationship with his brother, although he, too, is reluctant to admit this tension. While Phoolchand emphasizes that it was his brother's wife who caused the joint family to break, he nevertheless admits to lingering bitterness with his brother over the split. Phoolchand says that his brother separated from the family because the brother had become "selfish," adding that this was a "corruption" that he dislikes very much. A few other men spoke more openly about their disputes with their brothers. Narayan Singh, a 34-year-old who continues to live with his wife and parents, also admits to disappointment that his elder brother has established a separate household. Narayan focuses on how his brother's wife poisoned his brother's mind, saying, "as the woman comes out, man's mind works in this way." "Now," Narayan laments, "we do not have much relationship with them."

Maintaining "Sweet" Relations: A Focus on Compromise in Joint-Family Living

Because of the ideal placed on harmonious relations between brothers and the real attachment to the relations of equality that have developed, many men try to counter tensions between brothers by emphasizing compromise rather than obedience to authority within the joint family (Derné 1988: 44–46; Kakar 1981: 119). Such a shift to a focus on compromise may be essential to the maintenance of joint families that include several adult males. Deepak Mishra emphasizes, for instance, the importance of freedom within the joint family. While emphasizing the fact that his father is the *malik,* Deepak says that "since the family is full of adults, the *malik* does not obstruct us in any way. We are free to do whatever we want—roam around [*ghumna*], see films, whatever." A 76-year-old *malik* who heads a very large joint family with many adult sons, also reasons that compromise is important to the successful operation of the joint family:

> "If I don't do things according to my son's wish or if his wife's wants aren't fulfilled, then they will go separately because they will feel my pressure on them. They should feel [this pressure] as shade. [They should understand] that from living under me they are getting shelter and comfort."

While many men, then, think that hierarchy is the foundation of the joint family, a substantial number see the joint family's existence as dependent on give-and-take between superior and subordinate within the family hierarchy.

This focus on compromise is especially important when brothers continue to live together after their father's death. Anand Singh, 47, who is living in a joint family headed by the eldest of his six older brothers, emphasizes that hierarchy must be tempered with compromise. "Our elder brother is our boss," Anand says. But because "tensions arise,"

> "We [also] try to create tolerance of one another. [We tell each other to] listen to our elders. But sometimes the elders accept the points of those who are junior. Only then can the family move on."

Sunil Gupta, a 35-year-old who also lives in a joint family headed by an elder brother, similarly focuses on the importance of compromise, while accepting that the eldest brother should always be consulted first:

> "We tell our thoughts to the *malik*, and we listen to his talk. Somewhere he is flexible, and somewhere we are flexible."

Vinod Gupta, a 34-year-old living in a joint family headed by his brother, also focuses on the importance of compromise in keeping a family together:

> "We can live for a long time in the joint family if we compromise with each other. Everyone meets together and solves a problem by making compromises. While there are difficulties in the joint family, if we compromise with each other in the right way and cooperate with each other, then the joint family is a very good thing."

Many men, then, accept the importance of compromising to maintain the joint family. These men emphasize that obedience and hierarchy must be tempered by compromise and discussion.

Conclusions

How does the focus on hierarchy and on brothers living harmoniously together for their whole lives affect the relationship between brothers? The cultural ideal of harmonious ties between brothers leads many brothers to construct fulfilling relations with each other. The focus on hierarchy leads them to construct equal relations with their brothers, providing valued relief from the hierarchy that dominates their lives. Such fraternal equality is often constructed easily because of the life brothers share as junior members of the joint family. But the emphasis on hierarchy also leads some men to expect that older brother will have authority over younger.

Tensions arise because the valued equality between brothers contradicts the respectful obedience younger brothers owe elder brothers. As elder brothers take on more responsibility in running the joint family, the dictates of hierarchy may sour relations between brothers, but the outcome of these tensions is not self-evident. In many instances, these tensions speed the breakup of the joint family. But in some instances, brothers try to maintain joint-family living by balancing a younger brother's obligations to his elder brother with a degree of democracy within the joint family. While the dominant understanding of what constitutes proper relationships between adult brothers still emphasizes hierarchical ordering, a focus on the importance of compromise and cooperation among brothers becomes an important secondary understanding in some families. Men emphasize the necessity of compromise not merely to save the joint family, but also to rescue the relation between brothers many men have come to value.

Neither hierarchy nor equality, then, is the sole principle that shapes the relationships between brothers. For some brothers one principle or the other is primary. For Kumar Yadav and Ramesh Mishra, for instance, the focus on "sweet," equal relationships between brothers is primary. For Kumar and Ramesh, this focus on equality is not poisoned by the contradictory demands of hierarchy largely because of the continuted presence of their father in the household. For most men, however, relations between brothers reflect the tension between these principles. For some, like Phoolchand Mishra, Nandu Gupta, and Narayan Singh, the tension between hierarchy and equality between brothers is so great that brothers separate and relations between them remain acrimonious. For others, like Raj Kumar Singh, the tension is felt, although it has not yet split the family. For many men, like Vinod Gupta, Deepak Mishra, and Sunil Gupta, the tension between hierarchy and equality does not split the family, but leads them to temper the focus on hierarchy with recognition that compromise must also govern relations between brothers.

Following Hewitt (1989: 72), culture provides not just core values but contrasting values, as well. In Hindu culture, hierarchy is a core value, but there is a fascination not just with the dangers of freedom but also with the seductiveness of equality. Individuals live with their culture's central contradictions and struggle to resolve them. An individual may make "hierarchy" central and "equality" peripheral; or the individual may make "equality" central and "hierarchy" peripheral; or the individual may try to strike a balance between the two. (See Hewitt's [1989: 72] discussion of the conflict between "duty" and "desire.") Men, then, can construct diverse relationships with their brothers by manipulating "core" and "contrasting" values in Hindu culture in different ways. Thus, the tension between hierarchy and equality leads not only to the disputes so common between brothers but also to the diversity of relationships between brothers that characterize north India.

Acknowledgments

The U.S. Department of Education supported this research with Foreign Language and Area Studies fellowships, which financed my study of Hindi, and with a Fulbright-Hays Doctoral Dissertation Research Abroad grant, which funded the research itself. Awadesh Kumar Mishra, Nagendra Ghandi, Parvez Kahn, and Ramchandra Pandit assisted me in conducting and translating interviews. Gerald Berreman, Kenneth Bock, Arlie Hochschild, Pauline Kolenda, Charles Nuckolls, and Ann Swidler provided useful comments on earlier drafts of this chapter.

Note

1. I have changed the names of those I interviewed to protect their privacy. The Brahmans, Vaishyas, and Kshatriyas I interviewed were of various *jatis,* or subcastes. In order to identify each respondent's *varna* caste, I have given each member of each *varna* caste grouping a shared surname. Some, but not a majority of the respondents, actually had this surname. I have given all Brahman respondents the surname Mishra, all Vaishya respondents the surname Gupta, all Kshatriya respondents the surname Singh, and all Shudra respondents the surname Yadav. All of the Shudras were, in fact, Yadavs or *ahir*s.

References

Appadurai, A. (1986). "Is Homo Hierarchicus?" *American Ethnologist,* 13: 745–61.

Bellah, R. N., Madsen, R., Sullivan, W. M., Swidler, A., & Tipton, S. M. (1985). *Habits of the Heart: Individualism and Commitment in American Life.* New York: Harper & Row.

Berreman, G. D. (1971). "The Brahmanical View of Caste." *Contributions to Indian Sociology* (n.s.) 5: 18–25.

Berreman, G. D. (1972). *Hindus of the Himalayas: Ethnography and Change.* Berkeley: University of California Press.

Béteille, A. (1983). Homo Hierarchicus, Homo Equalis. In A. Béteille (Ed.), *The Idea of Natural Inequality* (pp. 33–53). Delhi: Oxford University Press.

Bryant, B. K. (1989). The Child's Perspective of Sibling Caretaking and Its Relevance to Understanding Social-Emotional Functioning and Development. In P. R. Zukow (Ed.), *Sibling Interaction across Cultures: Theoretical and Methodological Issues* (pp. 143–64). New York: Springer-Verlag.

Daniel, S. (1983). The Tool Box Approach of the Tamil to the Issues of Moral Responsibility and Human Destiny. In C. F. Keyes & E. V. Daniel (Eds.), *Karma: An Anthropological Inquiry* (pp. 27–62). Berkeley: University of California Press.

Das, V. (1976). "Masks and Faces: An Essay on Punjabi Kinship." *Contributions to Indian Sociology* (n.s.) 10: 1–30.

Derné, S. (1988). *Culture in Action: Hindu Men's Talk About Women, Marriage, and Family.* Ph.D. Dissertation, Department of Sociology, University of California, Berkeley.

Derné, S. (1990). "The Kshatriya View of Caste." *Contributions to Indian Sociology* (n.s.) 24: 259–63.

Derné, S. (1992). "Hindu Men's 'Languages' of Social Pressure and Individualism: The Diversity of South Asian Ethnopsychologies." *International Journal of Indian Studies* 2:40–71.

Dumont, L. (1980). *Homo Hierarchicus: The Caste System and Its Implications.* (M. Sainsbury, L. Dumont, & B. Gulati, Trans.). Chicago: University of Chicago Press. (Original work published 1966)

Dunn, J. (1985). *Sisters and Brothers.* Cambridge, MA: Harvard University Press.

Ervin-Tripp, S. (1989). Sisters and Brothers. In P. G. Zukow, (Ed.), *Sibling Interaction across Cultures: Theoretical and Methodological Issues* (pp. 184–96). New York: Springer-Verlag.

Heelas, P. (1981). Introduction: Indigenous Psychologies. In P. Heelas & A. Lock (Eds.), *Indigenous Psychologies: The Anthropology of the Self* (pp. 3–18). New York: Academic Press.

Hewitt, J. P. (1989). *Dilemmas of the American Self.* Philadelphia: Temple University Press.

Kakar, S. (1981). *The Inner World: A Psycho-analytic Study of Childhood and Society in India* (2nd ed.). Delhi: Oxford University Press.

Kolenda, P. M. (1967). Region, Caste, and Family Structure: A Comparative Study of The Indian 'Joint' Family. In M. Singer & B. S. Cohn (Eds.), *Structure and Change in Indian Society* (pp. 339–96). Chicago: Aldine.

Kolenda, P. M. (1987). *Regional Differences in Family Structure in India.* Jaipur, India: Rawat.

Luschinsky, M. S. (1962). *The Life of Women in a Village of North India: A Study of Role and Status.* Ph.D. Dissertation, Cornell University. Ann Arbor: University Microfilms.

Mandelbaum, D. G. (1988). *Women's Seclusion and Men's Honor: Sex Roles in North India, Bangladesh, and Pakistan.* Tucson: University of Arizona Press.

Mencher, J. (1974). "The Caste System Upside Down or the Not-So-Mysterious East." *Current Anthropology* 15: 469–92.

Ramanujan, A. K. (1989). "Is There an Indian Way of Thinking? An Informal Essay." *Contributions to Indian Sociology* (n.s.) 23: 41–58.

Rao, V. V. P. & Rao, V. N. (1982). *Marriage, the Family and Women in India.* New Delhi: Heritage.

Roland, A. (1988). *In Search of Self in India and Japan: Toward a Cross-cultural Psychology.* Princeton: Princeton University Press.

Shah, A. M. (1973). *The Household Dimension of the Family in India.* New Delhi: Orient Longman.

Sharma, U. (1978). "Women and Their Affines: The Veil as Symbol of Separation." *Man* (n.s.) 13: 218–33.

Sharma, U. (1980). *Women, Work and Property in North-west India.* London: Tavistock.

Sharma, U. (1989). Studying the Household: Individuation and Values. In J. N. Gray & D. J. Mearns (Eds.), *Society from the Inside Out: Anthropological Perspectives on the South Asian Household* (pp. 35–54). New Delhi: Sage.

Shweder, R. A., & Miller J. G. (1985). The Social Construction of the Person: How Is It Possible? In K. J. Gergen & K. E. Davis (Eds.), *The Social Construction of the Person* (pp. 41–69). New York: Springer-Verlag.

Swidler, A. (1986). "Culture in Action: Symbols and Strategies." *American Sociological Review* 51: 273–86.

Turner, R. (1976). "The Real Self: From Institution to Impulse." *American Journal of Sociology* 81: 989–1016.

Varenne, H. (1977). *Americans Together: Structured Diversity in a Midwestern Town.* New York: Teachers College Press.

Vatuk, S. (1989). Making New Homes in the City: Urbanization and the Contemporary Indian Family. In C. M. Borden (Ed.), *Contemporary Indian Tradition* (pp. 187–202). Washington: Smithsonian Institution Press.

Weisner, T. S. (1989). Comparing Sibling Relationships across Cultures. In P. G. Zukow (Ed.), *Sibling Interaction across Cultures: Theoretical and Methodological Issues,* (pp. 11–25). New York: Springer-Verlag.

Zukow, P. G. (Ed.). (1989). *Sibling Interaction across Cultures: Theoretical and Methodological Issues.* New York: Springer-Verlag.

Photo by Charles W. Nuckolls

Temple image of the goddess Ramanamma.

CHAPTER 8

Sibling Myths in a South Indian Fishing Village
A Case Study in Sociological Ambivalence

Charles W. Nuckolls

The idea that social structures generate what Merton (1976) called "sociological ambivalence" is not new (see Coser 1976; Durkheim 1964; Freud 1964; Grathoff 1970; Langer 1942, 1953; Whiting 1953). Ambivalence of this kind exists among people in conflicting institutions and complex interrelationships such that no single commitment dominates one's life. Unlike psychological ambivalence. Merton wrote,

> [sociological ambivalence] focuses on the ways in which ambivalence comes to be built into the structure of social statuses and roles. It directs us to examine the processes in social structure that affect the probability of ambivalence turning up in particular kinds of role-relations. And finally, it directs us to the social consequences of ambivalence for the workings of social structures. (Merton 1976: 5)

Some scholars have chosen to view this ambivalence as socially functional. Merton, for example, considers it a device "for helping people in designated statuses to cope with the contingencies they face in trying to fulfill their functions" (Merton 1976: 18.) Others focus on the psychological consequences of ambivalence, finding that it generates anxiety, dysphoria, or other pathological states (see Coser 1976; Wexler 1983). They observe that cultures typically provide patterns of representation and interpretation that predefine resolutions to felt contradictions. Some of these patterns include joking and humor (Coser

1976), narcissism (Slater & Slater 1965), religion (Weigert 1988), and membership in countercultural groups (Yinger 1982).

This chapter addresses the ambivalence of conflicting role expectations in a south Indian fishing village. It describes those expectations as emergent properties of the kinship system and traces their differing representations and resolutions in "myth." It has long been recognized, of course, that myths may provide a *reconciliato oppositorum*, representing and reconciling contradictions that social systems create. Contradictions and their attendant ambivalences may even be at the heart of the religious experience (Otto 1923; van der Leeuw 1933). But it is not my purpose here to make or support such a claim. In this chapter, I focus exclusively on one system of relations (sibling relations), along with its systemically induced ambivalence, and on the myths that seem to represent this phenomenon.

Sociological Ambivalence and Mythic Representation

Sociological ambivalence creates problems for which mythic representations seem to fall into at least two groups. Some myths deny reality by asserting the existence of social roles that completely fulfill normative ideals. The popular and long-running American television show "Leave It to Beaver" is an example: The mythical Cleavers fully realize the family norms of harmony, responsibility, and mutual affection. Other myths substitute reality by asserting the existence of alternative worlds in which problems emergent in everyday social roles never arise. The myth of Peter Pan is a case in point: Hard to achieve normative ideals are ignored in favor of the fantasy motif that, as perpetual children, we never have to assume adult responsibilities. Myths of the first sort represent conscious desires, which correspond to stated objectives that are socially sanctioned. They speak to an overt reality that is normative: What we *say* the world should be and what the world is become the same. Myths of the second sort represent unconscious desires, which correspond to unstated objectives that are nonnormative and perhaps forbidden. They speak to a covert reality that is driven by desire: What we *want* the world to be and what the world is become the same.

Myths of Denial

Denial defends normative social roles simply by asserting that real problems do not exist. Idealized fictions are deployed to mask unwanted elements. This is the realm of "family myth" that, according to

Stierlin (1973: 119), "paints a rosy picture of past and present family togetherness, family harmony, and happiness—in contast to what a perceptive observer often notes within his first minutes of contact with such families." As an example, Stierlin cites the following case:

> In one family, the parents had on one occasion battered a child so severely that he needed surgical treatment. This was some fifteen years before the family entered treatment. By this later time, the members had created a myth of harmony that made appear unreal and incomprehensible such intra-family brutality. The incident was unearthed only during the course of lengthy family therapy. Typically, the battered victim, no less than his victimizing parents, had shared in the construction and maintenance of this myth—i.e., had made it into a true myth of harmony. (Stierlin 1973: 119)

The family myth helps members deny unwanted emotions by representing reality *as if* it corresponded perfectly to a consciously stated, normative ideal: the ideal of family harmony. Unpleasant memories, based on past experience of these emotions, are ignored.

Myths of Substitution

Substitution exchanges current reality for an alternative one in which emotions denied in real life are "acted out" through characters in a life of fantasy. Problems created when contradictory role expectations conflict are not denied, as they are in family myth, but projected outside into the world of fantastic beings and supernatural experiences. The best example is still the Oedipus myth. The wish to be merged with the mother is projected onto the alternative reality the Oedipus myth provides: There, Oedipus acts out the primal fantasy, achieving unity with the desired but forbidden mother. Of course the myth offers no permanent solution to the problem. As soon as Oedipus finds out what he has done, he is doomed. South Indian goddess myths also involve incest themes, but unlike the Theban trilogy, they provide resolutions that do not end in tragic annihilation.

Goals and Interpretive Method

In the first part of this paper, I describe a patrilineal ideology and the structurally induced ambivalences it creates. In the second part, I show how myths fulfill the patrilineal ideology 1) by deploying consciously espoused idealizations to deny social problems, and 2) by constructing alternative worlds in which social problems emergent in the "real world" simply never come up. I do *not* claim that myths function exclusively to achieve these ends, or that myths, by themselves, are the only places we find such themes played out. To claim that would be to engage in a form of functionalist reductionism that opponents to psychoanalytic interpretation rightly disparage. Shamanic diagnosis, for example, in which sibling relations are "mapped onto" relations between household spirits, is arguably more important in everyday life (Nuckolls 1987, 1991a, 1991c, 1992a). But while diagnosis tells us what people *do* about sibling relations, myths tell what people *feel* about sibling relations, both consciously, as overtly realized idealizations, and unconsciously, as covertly realized fantasies.

The method I use—an interpretive approach synthesized from the work of Heuscher (1974), Roheim (1974), and Reik (1956)—takes seriously the proposition that myths resemble dreams. A dream often develops from or depends on events that make no manifest sense. Such events, as Merkur (1988: 65) notes, "obtrude from the otherwise naturalistic character of the narrative and provide the impression that the narrative has an interior logic of its own." But that logic may be concealed because the wishes it represents are somehow problematic. In dreaming, the "dream-work" (as Freud called it) accomplishes the concealment through devices known as "displacement," "condensation," and "representation by symbols" (Freud 1965). In myth, mechanisms that could be called the "myth-work" accomplish similar ends, systematically altering ideas and meanings that are too problematic to appear undisguised. Knowing something about these mechanisms helps us use "obtrusive events" to reveal these ideas and meanings.

For example, in a myth concerning her origin (discussed at length below), the goddess Ramanamma suddenly changes herself into a demon and then back again, resuming her form as a beautiful maiden as her brothers come to rescue her. The myth itself offers no explanation for these obtrusive events, which seem logically inconsistent with the myth's manifest content. After all, Ramanamma wants to be rescued as much as her brothers want to rescue her, so why does she undergo these changes? But the myth's interior logic reveals a hidden meaning. Appearing alternately as a demon and as a maiden, the goddess represents in her two personas a "split" in her emotional orientation to her brothers. The "demon" image represents her anger, and the "maiden" image represents her love. Ramanamma's transformation into a village goddess, however, resolves the conflict between the two by licensing her to alternately manifest both in a single role.

As a goddess (but not as a sister) she is *supposed* to be an angry demon and benign protector, each at different times, depending on how she and her brothers (now defined as "devotees") are getting along.

Description of Region Studied

This discussion, though generalizable in its results to other parts of south India, is specific in its details to a Jalari-caste fishing village on the northeastern coast of Andhra Pradesh. There are at least one million Telugu-speaking Jalaris who live in villages that dot the eastern coast from north of Puri (in Orissa) to south of Madras (in Tamil Nadu) I worked in Jalaripet, a coastal hamlet near the port city of Visakhapatnam, were the men fish for their livelihood in the Bay of Bengal. The women collect the fish on the beach and sell it at several sites in the city. Since the port was opened to seagoing container vessles a few years ago, more and more Jalari men have turned to smuggling, trading fish for consumer goods not legitimately available in India. Few, however, have moved away from the village, and almost none have entered urban occupations. The situation may have begun to change since the end of 1984, when the village was destroyed by fire and the Visakhapatnam city government (which controls the village as part of its administrative district) took over the site for redevelopment.

Key Concepts and Organizing Principles

In the Jalari kinship system, sibling relations are very important. Brothers, as codescendents of the same patriline and as coresidents of the same extended family, must fulfil obligations to each other and to the patriline they constitute. The most important of these obligations is the provision of material support and the preservation of agnatic unity. If they fail, they face dissolution of the patrilineal group and division of its constituent families. Brothers and married sisters, as sources of their children's future marriage partners, must honor the obligations to trade with each other and to arrange marriages between their children. If they fail, they face disruption of their alliance relationships that bind the brothers' lineage and the lineages into which their sisters married. However, Jalaris cannot simultaneously and satisfactorily fulfill all normative obligations in their roles as brothers and sisters. This is the source of the deep ambivalence that suffuses

Jalari sibling relations and that Jalari sibling myths represent and partially resolve.

The Structures of Agnation and Affinality

Clan and lineage are important agnatic groups, but they figure less prominently in everyday life than do the individual patrilines that they incorporate. The smallest patriline consists of only one conjugal family (*kutumbamu*), while the largest comprises seven families. Rarely, however, do patrilines extend more than three generations in depth. Most patrilines in the village are in the process either of increasing to the usual three generation limit or breaking down into their constituent families, forming new patrilines, and thus starting the whole process over again.

As long as the patriline endures, its members associate with each other as coresidents of a single *peddillu* ("big house.") Usually the senior male member (father or elder brother) occupies the "big house" with his own conjugal family, while his married brothers and their children occupy adjacent *gaddillu*s or "room houses.'" Room houses are either physically part of the big house, separated from it only by partitions, or satellite structures built nearby. The big house, however, contains everything that is essential to the definition of the patriline as a unit. There is, or should be, only one "hearth" (*poyi*), where the wives cook the joint meal, one "pot" (*kundi*), from which all members take their food, and one "goddess money" (*ammavari dabbu*), a fund to which all male members contribute part of their earnings to support offerings to the patrilineal spirits.

Family Myths

Jalari men refer to themselves as "birds of a single nest" (*oka guduki paccilu*). The "nest" is the patriline into which men are born and to which they owe their first allegiance. There they receive protection, nurturance, and succor in times of distress. As "birds," they occupy one "nest" until they fly away, "like birds to separate trees (*okoka cettluki erigi poyai*)," to start their own families and, later, found their own patrilines. Jalari men employ avian metaphors to call up the feelings of codependency, mutual support, and close affection that should characterize patrilineal relations.

The vocabulary for affinal (marriage) relations, by contrast, indicates that relationships *between* patrilines differ markedly from relations *within* patrilines. The house is no longer called a "nest," but a "court" (*divanamu*), and all associations to a protecting and nurturing environment are gone. They are replaced by something that is, if anything, almost militaristic. "*Divanamu*" comes from the Hindi word, *divan*, and refers to the person, place, or system of relations among rulers. By implication, then, *divanamu* refers to potential adversarial relations among affinally linked households. Consider the household goddesses, usually seen as nurturing mothers with respect to their own household members. Between affinally related households, however, they are not "mothers" at all, but watchful protectors, ready at a moment's notice to leave their own "corners" and "rush" (*daudi vellu*) to the households of affinal kin, to "beat" (*kottu*), "bind" (*kattu*), and "correct" (*savarincu*) them. Here is a shaman's description of the goddess Nukalamma, the household goddess of one Jalari clan, as she prepares to attack an affinally related family: "To the sound of knives and spears, her eyes bulging, she screamed like a cock from the battlements as she rushed to their *divanamu* and shot them full of burning hot arrows." There can be no doubt that potentially adversarial relationships are understood to exist between affinally linked families, that is, families related by ties of cross-cousin marriage.

What we are talking about here are family myths—emotionally tinged idealizations family members use to represent to themselves the symbolic structures of agnatic and affinal relationship. It does not matter that the patriline is something else in everyday life—a strife-torn combination of competing interests always on the verge of collapse. The idealization expressed in the equation "the patriline is to a nest what patriline members are to birds" represents the family not as it is, but as it should be, and provides for family members an emotional reference point that remains constant despite everyday life's vicissitudes. The myth of the "courts" is similar, in that it identifies outsiders, especially affines, as potentially inimical: It is *they*, says the myth, and not family members, who threaten the integity of the patriline. Together the two mythic structures support the patrilineal idology that holds that the patriline is good and worth preserving.

Such splitting of social groups into "good" and "bad" can be understood as an outcome of the ambivalence the kinship system generates. Brothers and sisters have obligations to themselves and to each other that naturally and inevitably conflict. Ambivalence results as pressures mount to fulfil these expectations. Such pressures become particularly intense at certain points in family development. To understand the resolution myths offer, then, it is necessary to appreciate how the Jalari system generates these pressures and why, at certain moments, they are likely to overwhelm the family system and lead to the breakdown and division of the patrilineal unit.

Kinship and Contradiction

Perhaps the best way to understand the perspective just described is to imagine the Jalari patriline as a matrix whose development over time causes it to pass through several crisis moments. For reasons I explain below, these "moments" constitute periods in the development of the family when both kinds of relationship—agnatic and affinal—come into conflict. Eventually, they cause patrilineal fission and the creation of new patrilineal units.

The patriline can be viewed as a matrix crosscut by axes representing agnatic and affinal relationships. Changes on one axis necessarily affect and are affected by changes on the other axis. Of course, the symbolic constitution of the system makes important conceptual distinctions between agnatic and affinal relationships, so that, for example, it is possible to talk individually about the "nest," with its implicit symbolic network of associations to the patriline, or to talk about the "court," with its associations to affinal relations. But by conjoining agnation and affinality, the axial model calls attention to the processes of interaction, to change over time, and to specific "moments" in the development of the patriline when the axes conflict.

As soon as brothers marry and bring their wives, vast structural changes begin to occur within the patriline they constitute as members. New wives are notoriously jealous and (in a scenario familiar throughout South Asia) quarrel among themselves over the distribution of family resources. At the same time that wives come, sisters leave by marrying out. Married sisters are their brothers' primary trading partners, buying their fish and selling it in the market downtown. They expect favorable trading terms that their brothers, either individually or collectively, find difficult to meet or agree on. Both groups—wives and sisters—compete for the brothers' assistance and support, making the effort to balance their competing needs increasingly difficult. The agnatic axis—consisting symbolically of brothers as the heads of their own constituent families—necessarily changes to accommodate the pressures that arise from within and from without.

Because of the "sudden" juxtaposition of competing agnatic and affinal expectations, I refer to the copresence of intense affinal obligations at this point as the first "crisis moment." Of course, the moment may take months or years to develop, as all the brothers and sisters marry, and begin their own families. It comes to an end when brothers can no longer agree on the distribution of resources—including money, food, and fishing equipment—among their dependent affines. Factions usually develop. Several brothers (usually the younger ones) advocate greater individual control and other brothers (usually the older ones) advocated continued collectivization and control of resources by an elder. The result is always the same: dissolution of the patriline as a residential and coparcenary unit.

Following division of the patriline's property, the brothers leave their joint residence and live apart in physically separate *gadillus* ("room houses.") But the patriline remains joint under the authority of the senior male. To be sure, that authority no longer means control over or access to collective property or earnings. It pertains to the group's ritual identity—that is, to its members' identification with one "big house" (*peddillu*), where the senior male lives; one "goddess shrine" (*sadaru*), where patriline members worship patriline spirits; and one "goddess money" (*ammavari dabbu*), to which members contribute a portion of their income for the support of rituals. Patriline members remain, both in their own and in the community's eyes, "birds of a single nest."

Time passes and the deaths of senior males weaken the solidarity of the patriline, leading to changes that now begin primarily on the agnatic axis. Family problems have shifted from the women who marry into and out of the patriline—the cause of the first crisis moment—to the men whom they marry. The shift reflects a change in structural focus, from concern with the incorporation and exodus of members through marriage to a concern with the continuation of the patriline through the bearing and raising of children. The more serious disputes now begin and end among men and they concern the allocation of ritual identity, not living expenses. The reason is that Jalari men become increasingly familocentric as their children grow up, devoting more and more of their resources to their children's (especially their sons') care and training. Men feel increasingly disinclined to contribute any of their heavily committed funds to the "goddess money," the last collective resource patriline members possess. Serious quarrels between patriline members eventually focus on this money—on how much each member is or is not contributing and on how the collected money should be spent. Since the goddess money represents the ritual identity of the patriline, disputes of this kind are really disputes about patrilineal solidarity.

As pressures mount within the patriline for its dissolution, they necessarily affect relations between the patriline and its affinally linked households, especially the households of married sisters. Cross-siblings may find trading with each other less profitable than trading with others. Brothers may not respond to their sisters' demands for help or, if they do, may respond in ways their sisters do not like. Finally, either a brother or a sister may abrogate an alliance relationship, deciding to marry their children to other related households or (in a growing trend) to unrelated households. But even if such problems do not develop, normal obligations for support and assistance add considerably to brothers' extrapatrilineal obligations and so further diminish the amount of time, money, and emotional energy they can devote to the maintenance of the patrilineal group. To support affinal relations to the extent of normative obligations means reducing the amount of support allocatable to the patriline—and that, because obligations to the patriline are most intense at this "moment," becomes extremely difficult. The opposite is true also: Fulfilling patrilineal obligations means abrogating some or all of the obligations owed to affines. The patriline, as a unit caught in the middle, is less and less able to hold its own ground against the fissiparous pressures exerted by cross-sibling bonds.

Kinship tensions between patrilines, like tensions within them, cause arguments among patriline members that again, center on contributions to the goddess money. Because of competing affinal obligations, brothers stop contributing altogether or demand the return of certain sums to meet personal expenses. Jalaris recognize these acts as symptoms of underlying tension and the result of competing role expectations. Such acts signal members' growing disaffection from the group.

The centrality of the goddess money attests to the importance of spirit-human relations as one of the influences codetermining the family's passage through crisis moments in its development. Household spirits require periodic offerings that family members pay for from the goddess money. When family relations are unsettled, family members cannot join together to make offerings. As a result, the spirits become angry and attack, usually by inflicting illness or by causing a sudden drop in the fish catch. Family members then reexamine their social relations, for the purpose of identifying and addressing the social problem that caused them to neglect the offering in the first place. Early in the patriline's development, disaffected members may reunite and resume regular contributions to the goddess money. But later, when the brothers are older and their contributions to the patriline are more difficult to maintain, patriline members claim that dividing the patriline, rather than keeping it together, is the best way to avoid future attacks. The result is a complete breakdown of the patriline. Brothers then enter the "big house" for the last time and split off chunks of the goddess shrine (*sadaru*). Each brother takes a chunk to his own house where, if he has the money, he consecrates it as a new *sadaru*, thus making his house into a "big house," the symbolic nucleus of a new patriline. The second crisis moment is now over and fission of the old patriline is complete.

Family Myths as Myths of Denial

People feel very strongly about the bonds that bind them together and pull them apart. They express these feelings in distinctive language. When brothers say, "We are birds of a single nest," they represent to themselves the intense bonds that constitute the "patrilineal ideology" and that bind them together as members of the same patriline. Considerable emotive force is bound up in this expression. A Jalari man expresses his love for, and complete dependence on, the patriline by referring to himself as a "bird" and to it, the patriline, as his "nest" or "branch." Most men cannot discuss this subject without being visibly moved.

Similarly, when Jalaris talk about "courts" (*divanamus*) they refer to people who, in their view, most contribute to the strife and tension patriline members feel. "Courts," of course, are where the affines are, and the most prototypic of affines are the families of married cross-siblings, since these families are sources for all the patriline's marriage partners. Brothers and sisters, obviously, are "courts" with respect to each other, but so are husbands and wives since they are related to each other as the children of adult cross-siblings. Consequently, when Jalaris blame "courts," that is, affinal groups, for their patrilineal strife, brothers blame their sisters and sisters blame their brothers—and everybody, of course, blames their spouses.

The symbolic idealizations of patrilineal and affinal relations I have described correspond to family myths, the functions of which are to defend and protect family members. Defensive functions come into play when family members employ the myth of mutual and harmonious support (the "nest bird" myth). Its purpose is to ward off pain, to obscure conflict, and to deny that features endemic to patrilineal clan structure must eventually destroy the clan by causing it to subdivide. Protective functions come into play when family members use the myth of military assault (the "courts" myth) to assert that the only permanent threats to patrilineal integrity come from outside, from married sisters and wives, who compete for support and attention with patriline members. The two myths and their respective functions complement each other and together support the ideology of patrilineal cohesiveness, harmony, and continuity through time.

Goddess Myths as Myths of Substitution

Family myths, like those described above, provide a framework for values and attitudes strongly congruent with the dominant patrilineal ideology. They enhance patrilineal solidarity by denying internal divisiveness and identifying outsiders as inimical, and so insure that the clan will always be seen as good and worth preserving. Not all myths, however, are structurally congruent, at least not in the same way. There is a hierarchy on which myths can be ranked according to the "status" they assign reality. The "normative" myths I described earlier alter social reality very little; they simply assert the ideal forms toward which social reality should tend. Other myths—goddess myths and the like—alter social reality itself to conform to unexpressed, but powerful desires. Incongruent fantasies are acknowledged, not denied, and then acted out in alternative realities, among beings and in places far removed from the conventional and the everyday.

The Ramanamma myth is a good example. It provides an answer to the question, how would the patrilineal ideology be fulfilled in a world in which contradictory obligations and competing allegiances had been eliminated?

Ramanamma, like most Jalari goddesses, arrived in Jalaripet as an epidemic disease (in this case, smallpox) in 1964. Her temple is situated to the north of Jalaripet near the beach and not far from the only other monolithic Jalari temple, which is dedicated to the goddess Gatilamma, who arrived with the last cholera epidemic in 1955. The Ramanamma temple, a large stone-built structure situated near the beach, consists of two rooms. The first is a long hall occupied by a crude model of an ocean tanker. Like most Jalari goddesses, Ramanamma is said to have arrived by boat "from the east," from a place usually identified as *konda desam*, the "hill country" (recently, however, some Jalaris have asserted that she really comes from New York—this being a far more exotic place to come from than "the east.") In this temple formerly—and currently in many Jalari temples in remoter areas—the boat was not a modern tanker but a three-masted sailing vessel typical of the European ships that first visited coastal south India in the mid-17th century. The model is carried by a succession of individuals possessed by the goddess, in the festival performed once every three years. The second room is occupied by the image of the goddess Ramanamma. She is flanked on both sides by figures representing her male companions. One, "Koya Raju," figures prominently in the Ramanamma myth. He is the father of her illegitimate child. The other, "Konda Raju," could not be further identified. Offerings at the temple are made on Sundays, the goddess's favorite day. Such offerings consist of fruit, distilled liquor, and (sometimes) a raw egg broken over the goddess's nose.

The story of Ramanamma was related by a Jalari possession-medium (*pati*). In most respects it resembles the tales told about other Jalari goddesses. During the smallpox epidemic the medium revealed that the afflicting goddess's name was Ramanamma and that she had come to settle among the Jalaris. Here is the full text of the medium's version.

The Story of Ramanamma

"That *amma* ('woman,' 'mother') had 7 brothers. She was from the east, the daughter of Cencu Naidu. There were 7 brothers and one sister. What happened was was this: After the 7 brothers were born, Cencu Naidu performed *tapas* (ascetic acts) because he had no daughter. When he performed *tapas*—when he performed *tapas* to Visnu, Brahma, and Isvaradu—that girl was born as a boon.

"The child was born already 12 years old. They built a house of 12 windows and put her in that house. After they put her there, the 7 brothers went out on a bird hunt. After that, she took 12 ministers and 7 companions to a flower garden. When she went to the flower garden, the Koyavadu (literally, 'the Koya man') saw her. He was desirous of her. She saw him and thought, 'He is a magician, he is coming for me!' She climbed a green tree. After she climbed it, he remained until evening, waiting to catch her. She was not to be found. After a while, she again went on the path. He met her and said, 'Little girl, what is your city, which is your village?' She answered, 'This is not my city, this is not my village. Mine is the Cencu people's town. I have 7 brothers. I was the only one born after 7 brothers. My elder brothers went to hunt birds. I came to pick flowers. I have 7 brothers, 7 companions, and 12 ministers. I have a 7-storied house with 12 windows.' She told him the place where she lived.

"He felt excited. He did not go, but thought, 'I can have sex with her anytime.' After she told him where she lived, she left. Taking 12 Koyas, he went to her house. When he went to her house, he said 'This is the foundation, and this is the foundation of the wall.' So to the place where she stays, he dug a tunnel and went through it, to where she stays. She was sleeping pleasantly on her bed. He went in and without touching or contacting her, she became a woman 9 months pregnant. In 9 minutes, the Koya formed a 9 months' pregnancy.

"At midnight, she woke up. She saw that her sari blouse was open, that the edge of her sari had slipped, and that her makeup had been rubbed off. There was no more eyeliner around her eyes. All these had been spoiled. Then what did she do? 'While my brothers were not here, that man came and spoiled me. When I get up in the morning, all the neighbors will hear of it. When my parents hear, they will not approve,' she said and crossed the *yugas* (a great distance) into the forest.

"She went to the 7 wells and to one well, the 'ilabuddi' well. At the 7 wells she took a bath. In that well, at the time of childbirth, she was suffering. She went to the big 'ilabuddi' well. As she suffered, who heard her suffering? Parvati Devi, Sarasvati Devi, and Laksmi Devi heard it. The 3 of them came. Saravati assisted as midwife in the delivery. Parvati Devi prepared the milk mixed with castor oil. Laksmi Devi prepared the bed. Then, in this well, they made her into a golden flower ball (*bangara puvula banti*). They made the child into a marantha (*parijati*) flower. They kept these two—the mother (*talli*) and the child—in the well.

"Meanwhile, the brothers were searching for her. They had come back from hunting birds. They searched from village to village. She was nowhere—not here, not anywhere. That *amma,* that sister, was not there. They searched and searched, and finally they came to sleep under a shade tree.

"When they slept under the tree, that *amma* saw them. 'My elder brothers came. They came searching and searching,' she said and went into the dream of the youngest elder brother. 'Brother, I am here! You are searching in the villages. That Koya man spoiled me. I became the mother of a child. My child and I, together, are in the 'ilabuddi' well. Why are you searching?' she said.

"The younger one woke and alerted the eldest brother, 'Elder brother, our sister is in the 'ilabuddi' well. Come, we'll go!' When he said this, the 7 brothers came. When they were coming, she assumed the form of a *raksasa* ('demon') and stood near a lake. She thought, 'They might be afraid of me and run away,' and she changed her form. 'Brother, it is I,' she shouted. 'Ramanamma, let's go! Let's go to our village. Let's go to our house!' they said. 'I won't go just like that to our village.' she said. 'I will come from here only for a festival. I will come to my parents, to the king's city. I will come to the city of my birth.'

"'What do you want? What shall we offer?' they asked. 'You must go to the weaver's house, to the potter's house, to the cane worker's house, to the eye-shadow maker's house, to the makeup seller's house. Then you must apply cow-dung water and draw *muggulu* (designs, made of lime dust, drawn on the ground as enticements to the goddess Laksmi to enter the house). That is the time when I shall come.' She wanted many things: bangles, beads, eye shadow, boxes, mirrors, and combs. She said, 'And for those who want meat, meat; to those who want bread, bread; to those who want toddy, toddy; to those who want marijuana, marijuana; to those who want brandy, brandy. Give these to those who want them. If you perform a 9-day festival, with costumes, flags, and toddy, then—if you do all this—I will come to your village.'

"Then the brothers went to their father and told him what their sister had said when they asked her to come back. 'What do you say?' they said. 'If we give all these sorts of things, she will come. If not, she won't come.' Then the sons asked, 'Father, please take our money and do it,' the father said, 'You should bring the sister to our house.'

"She came to Jalaripet. From East Mayagiripatnam (*maya*, "illusion," *giri*, "hill," *patnam*, "town"), so she came to Jalaripet. She came to Bhimlipatnam (another fishing village). After a few years, she ate some number of people. She stayed here. We give flowers to her there, don't we? That night she came here and for 3 months cholera came. She ate 570 people. Then, at the beach, the people came to know. After our elders knew, they went to possession-mediums (*pati*s) and to diviners (*kaniki*s) and found out. Then they built a temple for that *amma*. They built it, and now they perform a festival for her once every 3 years."

Analysis of the Story of Ramanamma

The integrity of the patriline is threatened from within by fraternal interests that, for senior brothers, center increasingly on their constituent nuclear families and not the patriline. The patriline is threatened from without by affinally related families and especially by married sisters, who demand their brothers' support and attention, and who frequently play off brothers against each other in order to get what they want. Family myths defend and protect the patrilineal ideology by splitting these camps into "all good" and "all bad" groups: The patrilineal clan (the "nest") is all good and the affinal group (the "court") is "all bad."

Both kinds of myth—family and goddess—start from the position of women as the dominant patrilineal ideology defines it. Brothers, of course, reluctantly admit their divisiveness, but quickly point out that it is not they, but their wives, who are to blame. Wives, they say, bicker constantly over alleged inequalities in the distribution of patriline resources. Eventually, brothers must separate in order to preserve peace in their own homes. The meaning, at least implicitly, is clear: If there were no wives (an impossibility, given the need to produce sons and preserve patrilineal continuity), then brothers could remain together forever as "birds of a single nest." The myth is, in part, a speculation on just this theme: it answers the question, what would the world be like if there were no wives?

Now consider the affines. Here, too, according to the patrilineal ideology, women are to blame for patrilineal divisiveness. In Jalari culture, daughters are valued and esteemed. The natal family does not readily assent to the loss of its daughter/sister to another household and the daughter herself is torn emotionally about her new role as a mature woman and wife. She wants marital union, but fears it, and cannot conceive of pleasure outside the boundaries of her natal household, the only environment she knows, and beyond the realm of her own brothers, the only male figures she is sure she can trust. But worst of all, married sisters become arch-competitors for patrilineal resources. As their brothers' primary trading partners, they demand special buying terms. And as the source of their brothers' children's marriage partners, they each demand special and possibly conflicting consideration. Not only do sisters as a group create problems for the patriline, but individually as competitors for their brothers' resources they frequently conflict, and by enlisting brothers individually as allies, they produce fissions in the patriline. Here, too, the myth offers a fantasy speculation: What would life be like if sisters were never alienated from their brothers?

Consider how the myth begins. Jalaris want daughters, and so, in the myth, Cencu Naidu gets a daughter by performing *tapas* (ascetic acts) and compelling the gods to give him one. In the next scene, Ramanamma, now 12 years old and fully mature, is placed by her 7 brothers in large house with 12 windows. This is, to use Merkur's apt phrase, an "obtrusive event." There is no manifest reason why the story should provide this information. The size of the house and the number of its windows attest to the family's wealth and, more importantly, reemphasize the number "12." Twelve years is considered the age of sexual maturity, and sexual maturity initiates the crisis the myth attempts to resolve. Notice that it is the brothers who place her in the 12-windowed house. This is another obtrusive event. If the house is the father's (Cencu Naidu's) house, then surely there would have been no need to place Ramanamma there so deliberately. She would have been there already. But, if the house had been constructed for Ramanamma, it would suggest that the brothers saw some special need to confine her at this time. It really makes no difference which is true, as long as we note the fact that Ramanamma's brothers placed her in a special place (a house) at a certain time (the onset of womanhood.) What are the implications of this? Apparently, the brothers wished to keep Ramanamma in the house, under their control, and sequester her from outside influences, especially from those who might corrupt her at her present age of awakening sexual maturity. Notice that it is not the father, Cencu Naidu, who announces or enforces these strictures, but the brothers themselves. This is strange, since preserving a daughter's chastity is chiefly the parents' obligation. But the father plays no role and the mother, if she exists, does or says nothing.

For the brothers to assume the role of principal protectors suggests that for them Ramanamma's budding sexuality has special significance. We recall with Shulman the folk motif of the brothers who keep their sister or sisters unmarried in order to retain the power vested in the virgin. Discussing this power in relation to south Indian myths from the Tamil region, Shulman writes:

> This power is rooted in the erotic potential of the woman, in her threatening and enticing sexuality. The incest motif, especially in its appearance in folk myths in connection with the love of brothers and sisters, expresses clearly the idea of a dangerous eroticism, of sexuality gone awry, of the power that lurks in the virgin and that seeks an outlet in violent, potentially destructive and even forbidden behavior. (Shulman 1980: 153–54)

Possibly Ramanamma's brothers keep her, then, to guard against the loss of a great source of energy. On the other hand, Trawick's interpretation of Oedipal themes in south Indian family life is equally tenable: "The intense erotic love for the mother might, under some circumstances, be converted into intense attachment between older brother and younger sister" (1990: 172). Both could explain Ramanamma's brothers' desires to protect and isolate her. But even if this were true, what are they protecting her from?

In this version of the story, the 7 brothers leave their sister to go hunting for birds. Ramanamma, accompanied by 12 ministers and 7 companions, visits a flower garden. This is interesting for two reasons. First, Ramanamma's departure from the house takes place as soon as the brothers leave, suggesting that, if they had still been present, Ramanamma might not have been able or willing to leave. Second, her destination is a flower garden, a site with associations to romantic love and erotic behavior. In Telugu, Tamil, and probably other South Asian languages, the "garden" represents a woman's sexuality, which is said to "bloom" at the time she matures. Ramanamma's journey into the garden is a metaphor for entry into her own sexuality.

Her companions are not mentioned again, and appear not to be present beyond the first scene. Ramanamma is alone when the Koya man first sees her. "Koya," like "Cencu," is the name of a non-Hindu, non-Dravidian tribal group resident in the hills of far northern Andhra and southern Orissa. It is also the name that Telugu plains folk apply to all tribals generally. As far as the Jalaris are concerned, "Koya" means "tribal," or "from the hills." The Koya man resides in the garden or, according to another version, came there from the "Koya village" to hunt birds. Notice that he and the brothers are described as being on identical quests (this is true in a deeper sense, as I will later show). The Koya sees Ramanamma and feels a strong desire for her ("his eye fell," as they say in Telugu.) Ramanamma sees him and fears he may be a "magician" (*mantramuvadu*), one capable of casting spells (*mantras*). In Jalari belief, mantras originated among tribals. Jalari skill in the use of mantras, for good or for evil, is still thought to be acquired among tribal peoples. Ramanamma is afraid and climbs a tree, where she remains until evening. After climbing down, she is observed again by the Koya man. He approaches and asks her to name her native place. She complies.

The Koya man's intention is clear: "I can have sex with her any time." The text repeats that Ramanamma told him where she lives. The Koya man follows her directions and goes there, accompanied by 12 companions who, like Ramanamma's companions earlier, disappear as soon as they are mentioned. The Koya digs a tunnel beneath the wall and the foundation, to the room where Ramanamma stays. He finds her sleeping. The story takes pains to emphasize that he never touches her and that she never wakes up. But "in 9 minutes, the Koya formed a 9 months' pregnancy." He then leaves and no more is said about him.

In the story, Ramanamma symbolically enters her own sexuality when she enters the garden. There she finds a male figure, a tribal, waiting for her and wanting her newly developed sexuality for himself. The Koya, as a being from the "hill country," represents a being from beyond the domain Jalaris recognize as culture. Through magic or some other extrarodinary means, he can acquire something that is forbidden to his more culture-bound counterparts. The Koya man thus stands in for individuals still "in" culture, satisfying on their behalf desires that they are forbidden to experience. Ramanamma feigns reluctance, but not before letting slip the crucial information about where she lives. The Koya man then digs a hole—a powerful metaphor for the sexual penetration which follows but which, because it is forbidden, must be represented as or displaced to the act of digging. Ramanamma is impregnated without knowing what happened to her.

The impregnation occurs in Ramanamma's own house, where she has been placed by her brothers. The act represents not just the failure of the brothers' protection but possibly the fulfillment of the brothers' own unconscious and forbidden desire: to keep their sister to themselves. The Koya man is thus a transformation of the brothers. He acts for them, achieving merger with and control over the sister, and thus doing what they cannot acknowledge wanting to do themselves. Ramanamma, asleep during this process, notices that she has been "spoiled" when she wakes and sees her clothing and makeup in disarray. She knows that something bad has happened and that her reputation will be destroyed if she does not leave. So she "crosses the *yugas* (a great distance)" and enters the forest.

The forest is a land beyond the village and beyond the world of normal humans and their affairs. For the Jalaris, it is the abode of tribals, the locus of esoteric knowledge, and the birthplace of goddesses. It is only fitting that the *human* Ramanamma should enter this region to be transformed into the *goddess* Ramanamma. Once there, she travels to a series of wells and to one well in particular, the "ilabuddi" (of uncertain etymology.) In some versions, she jumps into the first 6 wells, but finds them too shallow, and so proceeds to the deeper "ilabuddi" well. In this version, she goes to the "ilabuddi" well and takes a bath. She prepares to give birth, and is assisted in the delivery by 3 great pan-Hindu goddesses—Parvati, Sarasvati, and Laksmi—who perform different tasks related to the birth. Afterward, the goddesses make Ramanamma into a "golden flower ball" and the child (whose name and sex are never mentioned) into a marantha flower, and the goddesses throw both into the well.

In another version, Ramanamma approaches the well and reflects on her past:

> "O, sinner Koya man! My parents are now uncared for. Why did you spoil my chastity (*pati vrata*)? What life will I lead? I am in such misery. I couldn't protect my chastity for even a short while

> following my maturity. Elder brother, what can I do? I came here. My parents will cry hard for me. How much they will suffer! I am the last child.
>
> "My parents climbed the hills, and made a vow. But a female child was not born. Then they received a boon. Having gone to Shiva, they received a boon. My father went to Vishnu. Vishnu gave a boon, saying, 'You will have one female child. But your daughter will acquire ill-fame (*apakirti*). Through your womb a daughter will be born. She will have trouble because of a Koya man. She will "eat" the kingdom. There's no need for you to fear. That *amma* will be there for you. Although she goes upon the kingdom (i.e., causes epidemic diseases), she will be there for you.' Like that I was born. After I was born, the sinner Koya man spoiled my chastity."

She prays to Visnu and he, not the 3 goddesses, assists her in the birth of the child (here unnamed but identified as female). Afterwards, Ramanamma throws the child into the well, to purify it, and then contemplates going home to her parents. But she realizes they will detect the odor of childbirth on her clothes. So she jumps into the well with her child.

Let us consider what has taken place so far. Ramanamma's first reaction to her deflowering is to leave the house that her brothers built for her and to flee into the forest, the domain of wildness, from which her illicit lover and father of her child first appeared. In the forest, she can act without constraint and outside everyday social strictures. She can call upon the deities to help her, and they respond. Perhaps more than a domain of wildness or "nature," the forest represents a realm of possibilities (a liminal zone) where people are reconstituted in new forms before returning to society. Such a realm is not empty, though. It contains all that is unacknowledged but secretly wished for. Other South Asian societies employ the image of the forest in a similar way. As Desjarlais, writing on Nepali shamanism, comments:

> The image of the forest represents a certain domain of human experience. It is a place "where life is dangerous" (Macdonald, 1976: 337), where rationality and culture are lacking, and where the beasts and goblins of the dark, wild side of human action run rampant. Westerns have another term for this experiential domain, an image equally metaphorical, located less among the shadows or our physical terrain and more within the symbolic matrix of our corporeal selves: we call it "the unconscious." (Desjarlais 1989: 295)

This is what the forest represents in the first place in the Koya who impregnates her: a part of socially unrestrained wildness that breaks through into culture in the form of a disguised breach of the sibling incest taboo. Ramanamma is part of that realm (through impregnation by the Koya), and so it is to that realm that she goes in order to be transformed.

She gives birth to a child in a well. The well is a frequently chosen site for committing suicide in India. But perhaps because of its intimate associations with death, the well also represents the possibility of life and life-giving: What "dies" in one form in the well can be reborn in another form. This is what happens in the Ramanamma story. She and her child become a "golden flower ball"—the image of goodness and purity—and become, according to the myth, the joint being "Ramanamma."

The 7 brothers search for their sister. Obviously they want her back. Notice that no mention is made at any point of the brothers' wives, if they have any, or of their own families. For them the sister constitutes the vital core of the family. They sleep for a while in the shade of a tree, and while they sleep the youngest brother has a dream in which Ramanamma appears to him. She tells him what happened and where to find her. As much as they want her, she wants them. The stage is set for their reunion.

Reunification, however, is impossible on the basis of their previously existing sibling relation. The *sister* Ramanamma has been impregnated by a tribal, given birth, and then undergone a miraculous tranformation. As if to underscore the magnitude of these changes, Ramanamma changes herself into a *raksasa,* or demon. Not only is she no longer a sister, she is the most horrific of female forms, the total reversal of the unmarried sister's role. The demonic form represents Ramanamma's old "self," made up of unfulfilled dependency wishes centered on her brothers. But she knows that if she appears to them in this form her brothers will fear her and refuse to return her to the village. So she assumes another form more appealing to her brothers. In another version of the story told by the same possession-medium, this form is described: "She has a lotus on the sole of her foot; she has a bell in her navel; she has a cestus as bright as the world at her waist. At her back there is a white whisk. On her forehead, there is a crown, as bright as the whole world." This is the description of a Jalari goddess, an *ammavaru.* The form she first assumed and then abandoned—her demonic form—remains hidden for now, to be revealed on future occasions, to chastise her "brothers" (now defined as "devotees") for failing to appease with offerings or fruit and light.

Ramanamma, the goddess, reveals to her brothers the conditions under which she will return to the village. These conditions include a festival, the collection and preparation of various festival items, and the distribution of festival gifts (meat, marijuana, brandy, etc.) to those who want them. The brothers relay these demands to their father, who agrees to accept the brothers' contributions. The father tells them "you should bring the sister to our house" and so Ramanamma returns to the village. She is installed as a goddess.

Finally, the myth reveals how Ramanamma came to Jalaripet and, presumably, to all the other villages where she is resident as a goddess. She arrived in what may be described as her alter ego, her demonic *raksasa* form, and inflicted a cholera epidemic, killing several hundred people. At first her identity was unknown. The villagers consulted possession-mediums (*pati*s) and diviners (*kanikis*). The medium who related the story also identified Ramanamma and spoke for her, demanding on the goddess's behalf that the festival be performed and a temple built. The villagers obeyed and Ramanamma has since been one of the two main village goddesses.

Mythic Representations and Mythic Resolutions

Myths, according to Malinowski, are "what they appear to be on the surface, and not symbols of hidden realities" (1955: 126). The foregoing analysis disputes Malinowski's characterization and concludes that at least some myths speak to a deeper order of experience. To be sure, myths do not simply reproduce kinship structures and the recurring social dilemmas such structures create. We find, instead, a particular conceptualization of kinship problems and the kind of resolution only mythic realities can provide.

The brothers wanted to keep their youngest sister, Ramanamma, to themselves. This is not surprising, given what we know about the psychodynamics of sibling relations in South Asia (Kakar 1978; Trawick 1990). The male child's intense erotic love for the mother may be converted into an intense attachment to the younger sister. A resolution of the Oedipal crisis is then possible when the mother is given up, but the sister retained, as the locus of earliest emotional attachment. An analogous dynamic might be at work for sisters. The female child's longing for her father may be displaced to her brothers. She avoids separation by retaining close affective ties with her brothers. But the problem still remains. How can these dependencies be resolved in a way that avoids permanent mutual frustration?

In real life it cannot. In the myth, the sister escapes social constraints on her sexuality by entering the garden, that is, by becoming a sexual being. She realizes her sexuality by unconsciously, but deliberately, inviting access by the tribal man and allowing herself (while asleep) to be impregnated by him in her own house. The agent of her downfall and transformation—a tribal—represents both the absence of constraint and the wish fulfillment no constraint permits. To be impregnated by him in her own house is the fulfillment of her wish to be merged erotically with her own brothers. Realization of the act, not the act itself, forces her to leave and to seek a new status that accommodates her roles *both* as sexual being *and* as sister, achieving, as it were, "the best of both worlds." In Jalari culture, that new status—and therefore the resolution to the dilemma—is the status of the *ammavaru*, the "goddess."

The brothers, on their part, cannot realize their desire for their sister except through confining her and keeping her to themselves. Although they keep her, they cannot remain close to her lest the forbidden object exert too powerful an attraction. So they leave the house and go hunting, shooting their arrows and killing birds—behavior subject to a psychoanalytic interpretation of erotic displacement.

When the sister departs, the brothers must bring her back. But she cannot return with them as their sister, having abrogated that status through an illegitimate impregnation and childbirth. Ramanamma's midwives, who are goddesses themselves, transform her into a new being. In her new form she is neither a sister nor an ordinary human female. She can return to her brothers on the new terms this new form establishes, if the brothers accept these terms. Although this makes her return possible, it does not free her and her brothers from the ambivalence that pervaded their earlier relationship. Rather, ambivalence is projected outward into a realm—the realm of goddess worship—where it can be transformed through rules that govern divine-human and not cross-sibling relations.

Ramanamma's new form represents her more positive sisterly feelings and conveys her willingness to protect and guard her brothers. But she is unwilling to bestow these on her brothers unless they satisfy her by making offerings and performing festivals. To signify her intention, she assumes her demonic shape. Henceforth she, and not her brothers, will be in control. Her relationship to her brothers will be "transactive," based on their giving of offerings and on her bestowal of good fortune. She is freed from them as they are freed from her—but only in terms of a new dependency that replaces with "religious" transaction the old dependency relationship's reliance on the sublimation of unrealizable desires (on the nontransaction of sexuality, so to say) for its maintenance.

The myth reveals how ambivalences generated by the kinship system and its patrilineal ideology work themselves out in a mythic form. Male patriline members inhibit attrition among themselves by excluding (from the patrilineal perspective) a potent source of discord—their wives. Whether Ramanamma's brothers are "really" married or not is of no consequence. They are represented as single in the myth, and this is what counts. They attempt to control and manipulate another source of trouble—their sister. The brothers keep her at home, out of contact with other men, attempting to preserve her sexuality for themselves. Of course, the solution is partial and ultimately fails. Brothers and sisters cannot remain a unit unto themselves without violating norms and creating contradiction (i.e., if keeping in the sisters and keeping out the wives solves one problem, it creates another—namely, the problem of producing the next patrilineal generation.) The myth solves this in an acceptable manner. It allows siblings to commit an act of unconscious and displaced incest. But no one survives the normative breach as he was before. The mother (with her child) is transformed into a goddess and readmitted to the family as a household deity. The brothers are transformed into her "devotees." And their relationship goes from an ambivalence-laden bond between sister and brother to a bond between deity and devotee that is much easier to transact because the roles it defines do not generate ultimately unfulfillable expectations.

Conclusion

Contradictory kinship norms induce ambivalence by putting at risk the consciously upheld values of patrilineal solidarity. Brothers are "birds of a single nest," but fight among themselves and with their married sisters over the distribution of resources. To defend patrilineal values, clan members deny internal divisiveness and consciously espouse the myth of cohesiveness and mutual support. To protect patrilineal values, members define affines (especially married sisters) as potential enemies whose interests run counter to their own. The inside remains all good while the outside remains all bad.

Ambivalence exists at a lower level, too. Here, brothers and sisters struggle against normative demands to fulfill strongly felt dependency needs for each other. Goddess myths provide resolutions by acknowledging such needs and satisfying them through culturally legitimate means. It is as if the myths say, "If Jalari brothers and sisters need each other, but Jalari norms forbid their union, then let brothers be transformed into devotees and sisters into goddesses." In that way, strong emotions can be resolved through the transactive language of worship. The Ramanamma myth provides such resolutions. First, as a goddess, the sister can be retained and her special power employed to benefit her brothers. Second, the sister never becomes a threat to patrilineal solidarity by marrying out. Third, wives are not present and, for all practical purposes, do not exist within the structure of the myth, thus eliminating another potent source of friction. As a result, the brothers remain together, as "nest birds," and as coworshippers of their sister-turned-goddess, without division through competing interests.

To what extent the patterns described here for Jalari myth can be found elsewhere (in other expressive media) remains to be seen. My study of divination, however, suggests that kinship structures that are productive of ambivalence frame almost all divinatory accounts (Nuckolls 1991a, 1991b, 1991c, 1992a, 1992b). Such accounts begin in the diagnosis of spirit–human relations but always end in the diagnosis of social relations that, it is believed, precipitate the crises that interfere in the relationship between people and deities. Not coincidentally, the social relations of greatest divinatory concern are those between siblings. My expectation is that sibling issues will be seen to crop up in other areas as well. If they do, it might lend support to the hypothesis that in Jalari culture sociological ambivalence and the ways people represent/resolve it frame and constrain most things, from kinship to religion to divination.

References

Coser, L. (1976). Authority and Structural Ambivalence in the Middle-Class Family. In L. Coser & B. Rosenberg (Eds.), *Sociological Theory*. New York: Macmillan.

Desjarlais, R. (1989). "Healing through Images: The Magical Flight and Healing Geography of Nepali Shamans." *Ethos* 17: 289–308.

Durkheim, E. (1964). *Essays on Sociology and Philosophy*. New York: Harper & Row.

Freud, S. (1964). *Civilization and Its Discontents*. London: Hogarth.

Freud, S. (1965). *The Interpretation of Dreams*. New York: Avon.

Grathoff, R. (1970). *The Structure of Social Inconsistencies*. The Hague: Nijhoff.

Heuscher, J. (1974). *A Psychiatric Study of Myths and Fairy Tales.* Springfield, IL: Charles C. Thomas.

Kakar, S. (1978). *The Inner World: A Psychoanalytic Study of Childhood and Society in India.* Delhi: Oxford University Press.

Langer, S. (1942). *Philosophy in a New Key.* New York: Mentor.

Langer, S. (1953). *Feeling and Form.* New York: Scribners.

Malinowski, B. (1955). Myth in Primitive Psychology. In *Magic, Science and Religion: and Other Essays.* New York: Doubleday.

Merkur, D. (1988). "Adaptive Symbolism and the Theory of Myth: The Symbolic Understanding of Myths in Inuit Religion," In B. Boyer & J. Grolnick (Eds.), *The Psychoanalytic Study of Society* (Vol. 13, pp. 63–94). New York: Psychoanalytic Press.

Merton, R. (1976). *Sociological Ambivalence.* New York: Free Press.

Nuckolls, C. (1987). *Culture and Causal Thinking: Prediction and Diagnosis in Jalari Culture.* Unpublished doctoral dissertation. University of Chicago.

Nuckolls, C. (1991a). "Culture and Causal Thinking: Prediction and Diagnosis in a South Indian Fishing Village." *Ethos* 17: 3–51.

Nuckolls, C. (1991b). "Becoming a Possession-Medium in South India: A Psychocultural Account." *Medical Anthropology Quarterly* 5: 63–77.

Nuckolls, C. (1991c). "Deciding How to Decide: Possession-Mediumship in South India." *Medical Anthropology* 13: 57–82.

Nuckolls, C. (1992a). "Divergent Ontologies of Suffering in South Asia." *Ethnology* 3: 1–18.

Nuckolls, C. (1992b). Notes on a Defrocked Priest: Comparing South Indian Shamanic and American Psychiatric Diagnosis. In A. Gaines (Ed.), *Ethnopsychiatry: The Cultural Construction of Professional and Folk Psychiatry* (pp. 69–84). Albany: State University of New York Press.

Otto, R. (1923). *The Idea of the Holy.* New York: Oxford University Press.

Reik, T. (1956). *The Search Within: The Inner Experiences of a Psychoanalyst.* New York: Farrar, Straus & Colby.

Roheim, G. (1974). *Children of the Desert: Western Tribes of Central Australia.* New York: Basic Books.

Shulman, D. (1980). *Tamil Temple Myths: Sacrifice and Divine Marriage in the South Indian Śaiva Tradition.* Princeton, NJ: Princeton University Press.

Slater, P., & Slater, D. (1965). "Maternal Ambivalence and Narcissism: A Cross-cultural Study." *Merrill-Palmer Quarterly* 11: 241–59.

Stierlin, H. (1973). "Group Fantasies and Family Myths—Some Theoretical and Practical Aspects." *Family Process,* 12: 111–25.

Trawick, M. (1990). *Notes on Love in a Tamil Family.* Berkeley: University of California Press.

van der Leeuw, G. (1933). *Religion in Essence and Manifestation.* New York: Harper & Row.

Weigert, A. (1988). "Joyful Disaster: An Ambivalence-Religion Hypothesis." *Sociological Analysis* 50: 73–88.

Wexler, P. (1983). *Critical Social Psychology.* London: Routledge & Kegan Paul.
Whiting, J. (1953). *Child Training and Personality.* New Haven: Yale University Press.
Yinger, J. (1982). *Countercultures.* New York: Free Press.

Photo by Judy F. Pugh

An astrologer checks a client's horoscope and palm.

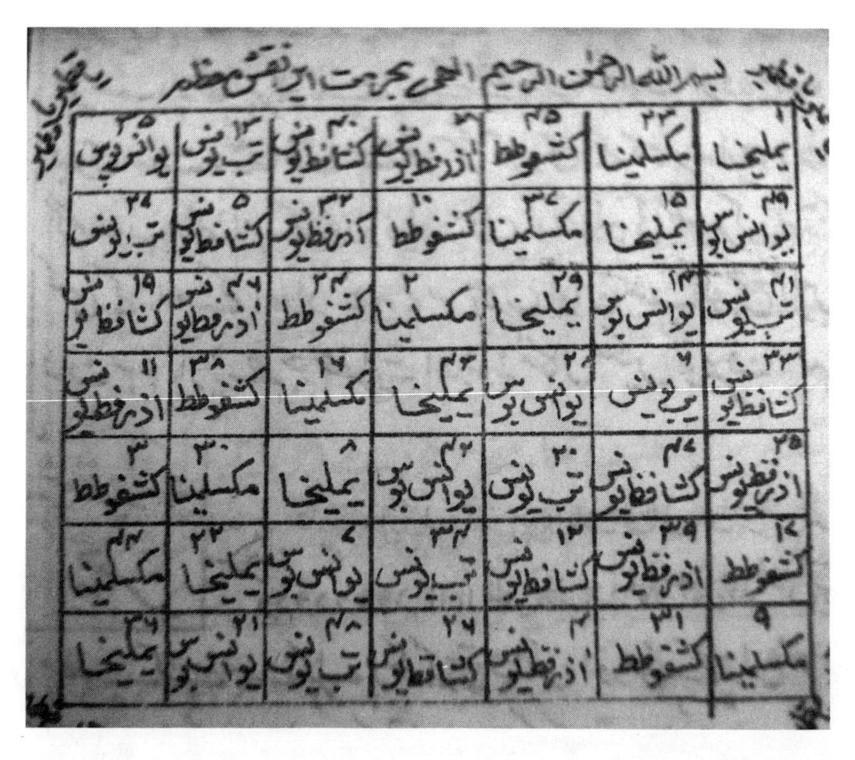

Photo by Judy F. Pugh

A talisman to promote family harmony.

CHAPTER 9

Brothers' Lives
Kinship and Ethnopsychology in North India[1]

Judy F. Pugh

Interpretive anthropology aims to explore local life-worlds. It presents the "native point of view" and analyzes the structures of experience that underpin a distinctive way of life (Geertz 1973). This perspective encourages the description of indigenous ideas of siblingship in the context of social life and personal experience. Anthropologists and psychologists have developed partial images of siblingship by focusing on social structure and psychological development, respectively. Examining indigenous concepts of siblings and their life experiences facilitates a more holistic perspective—one that construes siblings as persons.[2]

Indian society offers a wealth of materials for developing a holistic perspective. Myths, rituals, legal codes, ethical precepts, oral and written literatures, and counseling traditions all reflect and reproduce cultural views of siblingship (see Beck 1982, 1986; Inden & Nicholas 1977; O'Flaherty 1976; Wadley 1976). The indigenous counseling traditions of astrology, magic, and divination are exemplary in their concern with the vicissitudes of life experience. These practices—ancient, widely accepted, and used by people from all walks of life—constitute vital cultural resources for dealing with personal problems and crises. Their models of kinship, which articulate practitioners' knowledge, textual guidelines, and clients' interests, are oriented to the practical exigencies of social existence. What these models reveal is an experiential representation of siblings and other kinsmen set amidst the flux of life.

This chapter explores these experiential models and their images of brothers' lives and relationships in north India. An orientation to siblings' lives contrasts with mainstream approaches to the study of kinship and siblingship in South Asia. Anthropologists have often focused on kinship organization, which involves formal structural relationships, behavioral norms, interactional patterns, and kinship terminologies. These studies typically use an analytic distinction between norms and behavior, or between culture and conduct.[3] Cultural ideals describe the fraternal tie as a hierarchical relationship based on age and an egalitarian relationship based on shared descent and common property. Solidarity is its ideal state. Reports also note that the fraternal bond is highly vulnerable to disruption and that brothers often come into conflict over property claims and problems of authority and obedience.[4] Analysts tend to see such conflict as a behavioral deviation from the ideals of kin relatedness—an approach that reflects both indigenous valuations of social order and anthropological interest in the normative aspects of social life.

Anthropologists have also focused on the fraternal relationship in India as a cultural phenomenon. While they emphasize indigenous concepts and meanings, they share with analysts of kinship organization an interest in brothers' social structural relationships. The cultural model that they discern in myths, rituals, moral texts, and informants' statements stresses indigenous representations of the fraternal hierarchy and norms of solidarity, and treats ideas of fraternal conflict and enmity as subsidiary themes. Two prominent studies illustrate this point.

Inden and Nicholas's *Kinship in Bengali Culture* (1977) gives a description of kinship that emphasizes "the meanings connected with social solidarity . . . in the form of 'duties' and in the many differentiated forms of 'love'" (1977: xiii). Drawing on ethnographic accounts and medieval Sanskrit texts, they explore Bengali notions that all kin relations, including the fraternal bond, involve both "easy" and "difficult" enactments of "love." These enactments attend hierarchical relationships in which "an elder cares for a junior by commanding, instructing, and punishing him, and a junior shows his respect by obeying and serving his elders" (1977: 29)—tasks that involve older and younger brothers.

Beck's *The Three Twins* (1982), which deals with a folk epic from the southern state of Tamil Nadu, discusses themes of solidarity between an older and younger brother (the third twin is a sister). Beck comments on this orientation to fraternal solidarity in the Indian epic more generally, including the pan-Indian classics the *Ramayana* and the *Mahabharata*:

> Indian epics, a high-status genre, make unity a strong moral imperative for heroes, and the frame patterns in these accounts convey this norm of

> brotherly support most clearly. In the *Mahabharata* and the *Ramayana* this principle is embedded in the very structure of each story, since in each a pair of brothers are frequently seen together in cooperative roles. This basic principle is further reinforced by numerous dialogues that refer directly to a norm of unity and of mutual respect. The Brothers story is similar on both counts. (Beck 1982: 20–1)

These representations treat sibling conflict as a secondary phenomenon. Bengalis describe the "brittleness" of "difficult" love and say that "enmity" (*shatruta*) may result from a failure to fulfill duties, particularly for brothers. In this regard, Inden and Nicholas cite a Bengali proverb: "There is no friend like a brother; there is also no enemy like a brother" (1977: 31). In Beck's "Brothers" story, the younger brother sometimes exhibits physical aggression toward his older brother; in dream-like passages, he sees his older brother dressed in the clothes of enemies, and he throws his spear at him (1982: 21). The dream-like modality of this aggression subordinates it to the normative solidarity of fraternal relations.

The image of brothers in astrology, magic, and divination moves at a tangent to these more structural, normatively oriented accounts. It construes kin and fraternal relations as continuously articulated in a play of harmony and conflict, happiness and pain, support and betrayal. Discord carries equal, perhaps even greater, weight than the brighter experiences of family solidarity. The model's stance is best described as a melding of ethnosociological and ethnopsychological notions. It embeds such "structural" phenomena as hierarchy, birth order, and family norms, and it recognizes the sibling relationship as incorporating shared substance—a concept emphasized in South Asian ethnosociology.[5] Simultaneously and inseparably, it delineates the experiential dynamic of family and sibling relations in an ethnopsychological discourse of affect, temperament, and life experience.[6] Its representations stress each sibling's distinctive destiny as a powerful moral force that influences the unfolding of his own character and life fortunes. This perspective on sibling differentiation contrasts sharply with (Western) psychological theories of the determinative influences of birth order on siblings' traits, abilities, and achievements.[7]

The north Indian city of Benares is the ethnographic setting for this study. Astrologers, diviners, and talisman writers maintain active counseling practices in the Hindu and Muslim communities, and the astrological, divinatory, and magical texts that circulate in the city contain images of kin relations that are intended for use in the advisory process. By examining the discourse of these practitioners and their textual heritages, as well as the content of advisory sessions

involving brothers, we can outline an indigenous view of the sibling relationship in its experiential dimensions.

Ethnographic Background

Benares is a vibrant urban center with a population of over 600,000.[8] It is located on the Ganges River at the eastern end of the state of Uttar Pradesh in north India. Famous as a Hindu sacred city and pilgrimage center, it is dominated by religious, educational, and commercial institutions. Hindus form 74% of the population, Muslims 25%, and the combined numbers of Christians, Sikhs, Jains, and Buddhists 1%.[9] Alongside the Hindu community, the large Muslim community thrives in commerce and small industry, and Islamic educational and religious institutions are firmly established.

Like other Indian cities, Benares has hundreds of astrologers and diviners. Homes, offices, and even the roadsides serve as their "counseling chambers." Many practitioners are highly educated scholars, others are self-trained entrepreneurs, and some are hobbyists who advise friends and neighbors. These counselors help clients with their careers, livelihood, property, school exams, health, marriages, family problems, and court cases—all areas of high risk and high anxiety.

The logic of astrological, magical, and divinatory practices goes to the heart of local beliefs about misfortune and the problematic nature of life experience. Fate, stars and planets, malefic magic, ghosts, and other such forces can have a powerful impact on the unfolding of people's lives. Dealing with these influences frequently figures into strategies for misfortune management—strategies that also involve hard work, calculated planning, and religious devotion. Astrology's links with Indian concepts of fate imbue it with a special salience: Destiny is written in the heavens, and astrologers interpret celestial patterns in order to look into a client's past, present, and future. Hindus see fate (*karma*) as a manifestation of the consequences of a person's actions in a previous lifetime, while Muslims believe that God plays an overarching role in deciding each individual's destiny (*qismat*) (Pugh 1983a).[10]

Black magic (*sihr, jadu-tona*) may also contribute to people's misfortunes. Worked through talismans and incantations, it is believed to effect illness, conflict, financial setback, political defeat, loss of love, and other distresses. Its motivations are envy, hostility, and a sense of wrongful suffering. People who suspect its afflicting presence may seek advisory help in order to acquire magical means to protect themselves and sometimes to strike back at presumed perpetrators. The evil eye (*nazar*) also is directed by envy and may cause sickness, especially in infants and children.

Numerous divination techniques are available for identifying causes of affliction and gaining insight into problem situations. Practitioners may have their clients toss dice, pick a number on a chart, select a labeled token from a dish, or open the Quran to a random verse. These procedures identify malefic forces and suggest assessments of a situation's outcome. Some divinatory texts contain a variety of stock questions, including queries about specific family relationships. A dice toss or number selection pinpoints one answer from a list of possible answers to the client's question. Some specialists examine clients' dreams or read their palms. The palm's lines and mounds are associated with many different phenomena, including kinsmen, and these signs can be read for clues to the content of a person's various kin relationships.

Astrologers often use horoscopes as diagnostic devices. The horoscope's 12 houses, or compartments, represent key domains of life, including kin relationships (Figure 9.1). Casting a horoscope begins with an almanac, used to determine planets' and constellations' positions at a person's birth time and birthplace; these positions are then mapped into the horoscope to indicate specific qualities and events that will characterize each domain. Some overlap exists among various houses' indications. For instance, the second, eleventh, and twelfth houses can be read for signs of financial matters. The third

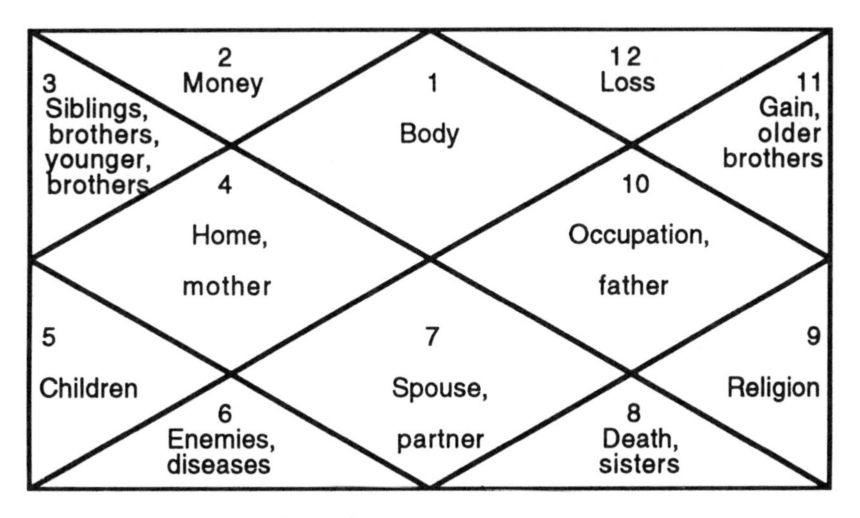

FIGURE 9.1. The horoscope.

house gives general indictions about siblings and more especially about brothers, such as how many brothers a person will have, and whether the relationships will be happy ones. The third house also gives more specific clues to a person's relationship to younger brothers, the eighth house to sisters, and the eleventh house to older brothers.

Informed by their divinatory inquiries, astrologers, diviners, and magicians may direct their clients to practices aimed at managing misfortune. Commonly suggested measures involve selecting auspicious times (*muhurtta, sa'at*) for important activities, wearing gemstone rings (*anguthi*) to protect against dangerous planets, and employing talismans (*ta'wiz*) and special verses (*mantra, du'a*) to enhance good fortune and counteract magical influences, afflicting spirits, or the evil eye. These "remedies" work on people's personal situations and their contextually relevant familial and social relationships.

Brothers and the Life Cycle

The life cycle constitutes a basic articulatory framework for fraternal relations and the development of brothers as persons. Birth marks the emergence of the fateful complexities of this relationship. Hindi terms for "brother"—*sahaja* ("those born together") and *sage bhai* ("those born from the same womb")—pinpoint brothers' shared origins. Their common womb gives brothers a special bond of destiny, while differences in their birth time and birthplace establish each one's distinctive karmic identity.

The whole thrust of astrology is to describe each person's particularity and distinctiveness, and hence the key dictum is this: Brothers are interconnected but never identical. The conundrum of twinship posses a special challenge for astrological interpretation.[11] Small differences in birth time, even up to twenty or thirty minutes, do not produce different horoscopes. This contravenes the idea of the uniqueness of a person's destiny and the important principle of the differentiation of siblings. An astrologer who examined roughly a dozen pairs of twins found that "although the birth chart [horoscope] is exactly the same in each case, actually the characteristic features and the lives of twin children in each case were perceptibly different" (Vaidya 1973: 58). He developed what he terms a microscopic horoscope in order to refract sibling differences that are set in motion by even slight differences in birth times.

Childhood is a phase in the ongoing manifestation of fraternal destinies. From an astrological perspective, brothers' childhoods may show a great variety of configurations, and each fraternal cohort will have its own distinctive pattern of experiences. Sickness may strike all the brothers of a family, or only one, leaving the others whole and healthy. One brother may succeed in school, while a second fails miserably. One brother may be outgoing and enjoy a happy childhood, while another may be shy and lonely, or perhaps all the brothers will be confident and happy. Astrology links these fundamental similarities and differences in health, temperament, and accomplishment to brothers' karmic inheritances, and not to their birth order, in contrast with Western psychological theories about the relationship between siblings' birth order and their personality traits, professional successes, and other attributes.

Marriage constitutes a critical life-cycle marker of brothers' differentiation. Their common parentage—a source of connectedness—is now complemented by different spouses and ultimately by different progeny as well. Astrology argues that each brother will influence and be influenced by the destinies of his wife and children, and even his wife's parents. Brothers thus assume divergent conjugal and parental destinies. Here astro-logic and socio-logic coincide perfectly: Brothers share a family of orientation but acquire their own families of procreation. A fortunate man gains a loyal, attractive wife who bears him many sons; his less fortunate brother may suffer a bad-tempered wife and see his children die prematurely. The important point is that the formal hierarchy of older brother-younger brother does not account for or control the complex vicissitudes of brothers' lives.

Adulthood also witnesses the ongoing manifestation of other facets of fraternal destinies. Similarities and differences continue to appear in brothers' intellectual abilities, artistic talents, spiritual pursuits, occupations and economic fortunes, and health and longevity. The father's death makes property and inheritance a central issue, and true to its practical orientation, astrology gives "wealth" (*dhan*) and "gain" (*labh*) a central role in brothers' relationship. "Wealth" and "gain" may be a pivot for "cooperation" and "support," on the one hand, and "conflict" and "fighting," on the other. However, from an astrological perspective, "wealth" is not inherently integrative or divisive; rather, its influence depends on brothers' personal circumstances and temperaments.

Brothers in the Landscape of the Family

The fraternal relationship assumes its full significance in the dynamic context of the family. North Indian texts on astrology, magic, and divination depict a spectrum of typical family-relational qualities.[12]

Five affective-interactional complexes stand at the center of the family's emotional landscape: (1) "devotion," "love," "happiness," and "passion"; (2) "pain" and "sadness"; (3) "cooperation"; (4) "trouble" and "worry"; and (5) multiple forms of "conflict" (Table 9.1). Surveying the range of emotional and interactional qualities that typify each relationship provides a contextual perspective on the fraternal bond.[13]

The parent-child tie is marked by the play of "happiness" and "pain" and the dynamics of "devotion" and "disagreement." Parents feel a nurturant "love" (*sneha*) for their children.[14] Sons and daughters may show "devotion" (*bhakti*) to their parents and do their "service" (*seva*), just as humans serve the gods. "Nurturance" and "devotion" are sources of "happiness" (*sukh*) for both parties. The parent-child relationship may also be filled with "pain" and "sadness" (*dukh, pira*). A man may "suffer in respect of happiness" from either or both of his parents. If his ideas do not "match" (*mel*) those of his parents—if there is "mutual opposition" (*parspar virodh*) between their thoughts—"family quarreling" (*parivarik kalah*) may occur. Relationships will not be "cordial," and a person may "remain distant" (*dur rahna*) from his parents. On the other hand, a person may remain devoted to his mother and father in spite of their "mutual disagreements."

The "love" (*prem, mahabbat*) and "happiness" (*sukh*) of husband and wife are expressed in "cooperation" (*sahayta*) and "passion"

TABLE 9.1. The Emotional Landscape of the Family

	Relationships with—			
	Children	Parents	Spouse	Brothers
"Devotion"		XX		
"Love"	XX	X	XX	XX
"Happiness"	XX	XX	XX	X
"Passion"			X	
"Pain" and "sadness"	XX	XX	X	X
"Cooperation"			X	XX
"Trouble" and "worry"	X	X	X	X
"Difference of opinion"	X	X	XX	X
"Quarreling"	X	X	X	XX
"Opposition"	X	X	X	XX
"Fighting"			X	XX
"Deception"				XX

X, common theme; XX, very common theme.

(*shringara*). Their counterpoints are "sadness" (*dukh*) and "trouble" (*kasht*) over "problems in the home." "Sadness" and "trouble" frequently attend "conflicts" that arise over "differences of opinion" (*matbhed*) and degenerate into "quarrels" (*kalah*) and "fights" (*larai*). Texts link these conflicts to problems with finances and family members' incompatible activities, but they also stress personal "temperament" (*svabhav, mizaj, tabi'at*) as a direct contributor to marital strife. A husband's or a wife's "bad temper," "laziness," "selfishness," "infidelity," and other character traits may threaten the marital bond.[15] The patriarchal orientation of the whole textual corpus gives rise to noticeably negative portrayals of "wifely temperament."

The relationship between brothers has its own distinctive construction. Brothers may give and receive "love" and "happiness" from one another. Texts mention "cooperation" in the husband–wife relationship, but they strongly emphasize its presence in the fraternal relationship. The theme of connectedness is central: Brothers as *sahaja* ("those born together") actualize their adult bonds through the connectedness of "cooperation" and the mutuality of "support." The all too common antithesis to these solidary ties is "conflict." Texts' lexical elaboration of "conflict" among brothers sets this relationship apart from other family dyads. While "conflict" occurs between parent and child and between husband and wife, it is considered more common and more intense among brothers. "Fighting" (*larai, jhagra*) and "deception" (*dhoka*) are its predictable expressions.

Texts also portray tensive interconnections among sibling, marital, and parent–child dyads. Problems between husband and wife may devolve from their own character and conduct or from the influences of "third parties." The couple's siblings, parents, and neighbors may resent their happiness and set out to destroy it, particularly through magical means. Likewise, troubled spouses may cause harm to their partner's siblings and parents. Often the wife is considered the likely malefactor. She is said to use amulets and incantations to create "opposition" between her husband, his siblings, and their parents. Her machinations destroy their "relationship of love" and the "harmony in their home." The term *bair-ke-rishte* ("hostile relations") refers to the conflictful relationship between a wife and her "natural enemies," including her husband's mother and sister (Platts 1982: 208). According to the texts, wives who are "envious" and "selfish" are likely to employ magical weapons to achieve their own ends. A woman may become so involved in her magic that "she is not even concerned with the terrible punishments of Hell" (Nuri 1972: 145). These accounts use an idiom of malefic influence to refract the family's internal dynamic and the problem of sibling conflict.

Advisory Sessions

A look at two advisory sessions will show how closely the problem-situations of everyday life mirror the models of fraternal relations in astrological and magical texts.

Session 1

A politician has decided to consult a Brahman astrologer about his electoral fortunes.[16] He and an associate have made their way through a maze of narrow lanes and are now seated on mats in the astrologer's drawing room. The astrologer uses the lines of the politician's palm to construct a horoscope, and the conversation revolves around the horoscopic interpretation of the man's career and chances for political success. First the astrologer offers the client advice on developing his own philosophy and keeping himself "pure." Then he identifies the central problem—the client's deception (*dhoka*) by adversaries in earlier political maneuvering. The politician and his associate concur, and together the three explore other aspects of the man's situation. Using horoscopic indications for "friendship" (*mitrata*), the astrologer predicts that the politician will get "help" from someone whose astrologically indicated qualities will offset his own "sadness" (*dukh*) and vacillatory ups and downs. The astrologer states that this unidentified person will provide "backing" for the client and also remove his "sadness." The astrologer's associate identifies this "friend" as the client's younger brother, and the client himself confirms that his brother has already made sacrifices (*utsarg*) for him. The astrologer recommends two courses of remedial action: a topaz ring to enhance the positive effects of Jupiter and the man's use of a personal astrological time schedule for undertaking professional activities and making political decisions.

This session shows the solidary aspects of the two brothers' relationship. The client's brother, of course, is not the problem here; on the contrary, his role surfaces when the astrologer refers to an unnamed "friend" and "supporter." This is a reflection of the positive strands of the fraternal relationship described in textual models: One brother "supports" another brother and contributes to his "happiness".

Session 2

A Muslim learned man (*maulvi*) is counseling a husband and wife about her illness and other problems in their family. The session

> is held in an antechamber of a small mosque; the *maulvi* sits behind a desk, and clients sit on nearby benches. Seated in front of the *maulvi*, the woman selects a labeled token from a dish, and the *maulvi* uses the token to begin his interpretation of her circumstances. First he describes the woman's symptoms, including nervousness (*ghabrahat*), insomnia (*nind bahut kam*), weakness (*susti*), pain (*dard*), heart palpitations (*dharkan*), and internal difficulties (*andaruni shikayat*). After considering the details of her illness, the *maulvi* states the "someone has done evil." The term *sihr*—broadly "evil"—is a euphemism for black magic or sorcery. The husband asks the *maulvi* to tell them the person's name, but the maulvi laughs and says that he cannot do that.
>
> The husband and wife shift the conversation to problems in the household. They describe the youngest brother's nervous (*ghabra*) condition and connect it with his lack of attention to the household. The wife says that until recently the brothers were "united" (*milap*), but trouble began after the youngest brother's marriage. It seems that he has become involved in some kind of secret financial dealings that he does not discuss with the other two brothers; moreover, he does not contribute any money to the household. The wife asks the *maulvi* to take a look at their houehold—"we have such a lot of worry" (*bahut zyada pareshani*). The discussion does not make it clear, and the *maulvi* does not explicitly indicate whether the person suspected of the "magic" that has caused the woman's illness is the younger brother himself, his wife, or the two of them. Clearly, in the sick woman's mind, the new wife is a key suspect. The *maulvi* tells them that there is no "badness" (*burai*) in their planets; rather, someone in the household has done something "bad." The *maulvi* concludes the session by preparing several charms (*ta'wiz*) to be worn by the woman and to be placed in the home. He assures her that these charms will change conflict to "mutual love" (*mel mahabbat*).

In contrast to the first case, the fraternal relationship here is very discordant. Formerly, it seems, "solidarity" (*milap, milat*) prevailed among the three brothers; then after the youngest's marriage, their relationship deteriorated. "Solidarity" changed to a lack of "support" and an absence of "responsibility." Now "a lot of trouble" afflicts not only the two brothers but the household itself, the family's livelihood, and one wife's health. These changes represent the "influence" (*asar*) of magic performed by a resentful or malicious member of the family—a textbook illustration of magic writ large.

These two cases show that the metaphors of "friend" and "enemy" capture the fundamental ambivalence of the fraternal relationship (see also Derné, Chapter 7, this volume). The hallmarks of friendship are "solidarity" and "support." The first session shows the brother as a "friend" and "supporter" who helps in the fight against adversaries—the "enemy others" who practice deception in their single-minded pursuit of political success. Divinatory texts themselves speak of "unity" (*milap*) between a person's kinsmen and his friends, thus indicating an expanded group of supporters.[17] They also warn that a charm placed to harm an enemy may "misfire" and actually injure a brother or friend. These references interlink the categories of "brother" (*bhai*), "kinsman" (*bhai-bandhu*), and "friend" (*mitra*) and place them in opposition to the category of "enemy."

The second advisory session casts into relief the full ambivalence of the fraternal relation and its transformation from friendship to enmity. The youngest brother has challenged the hierarchy of fraternal authority and failed to help support the family. In the eyes of his oldest brother, he has practiced secrecy and deception—the signature acts of an enemy. Of course, the youngest brother's own story may be quite different. Perhaps he regards his oldest brother as a domineering autocrat or a dull-witted impediment to the family business; perhaps his own fortunes have risen through his hard work and special talents. We can only surmise. But in any case, the general pattern of enmity is clear: the oldest brother and his ailing wife versus the youngest brother and his new bride.

The cultural qualities of the "enemy" are those attributed to this particular brother and also to the stereotypic brothers of the texts who "quarrel," "fight," and "deceive." A small divinatory pamphlet says of brothers' conflict: "There is no love (*prem*)—there is enmity (*dushmani*)" (Sharmana 1954:168). The idea of the brother as an enemy is a terrible yet very salient counterpoint to the "love" and "cooperation" founded on the innate connectedness of brothers. It is the ultimate assertion of sibling difference.

Astrologers and diviners offer clients an opportunity to discuss their problems and identify sources of trouble—this itself is therapeutic. But what other remedies can these counselors provide? The astrologer in the first case recommends a gemstone ring and an astrological time schedule. Indians explain that gemstones can magnify the beneficial rays of good planets and screen out the harmful rays of bad ones. The use of astrological time schedules rests on a belief that certain times (*muhurtta, sa'at*) hold ideal cosmic or "environmental" potentials for the success of an undertaking; local almanacs list many "auspicious moments" for events such as marriages and other life-cycle rites, journeys, agricultural activities, and school commencements.

The learned man in the second case gives the couple several charms to be worn by the woman and placed in their home. These commonly used remedies are considered to provide protective and ameliorative "influences" (*asar*), and they can be marshalled to improve health and assuage sibling conflict, as this case demonstrates.

Texts also describe remedies for other facets of family and sibling conflict. When a man suspects his wife of ruining his relationship with his siblings, he must try to establish "control" over her actions. In experiential terms, husband and wife have a multistranded relationship in which the wife has her own means of expression and sources of power, including her "temperamental" proclivities. Magical texts (for example, Garga n.d.) recommend a variety of charms to facilitate a husband's "control" (*vashikaran*) over his wife.

Charms are also designed to work directly on the relationship between brothers. One text reads: "This magic has been proven to create love (*mahabbat*), harmony (*ittifaq*), and friendship (*ittehad*) between brothers (*biradar*)" (Nuri 1972: 134). The magical procedure is this: Take a small piece (of unspecified measurements) from the clothing worn by each of the two brothers. Tie the pieces together, and while twisting the knot that joins them, read the following prayer seven times. An Arabic verse (*dv'a*) follows. The existence of this kind of charm indicates the vulnerability of fraternal "love" and "harmony." The "knot" symbolically reestablishes the "connectedness" of estranged brothers.

Conclusion

Astrology, magic, and divination give a wide-angled portrayal of brothers and their relationships. The local relevance of these models rests in a tangle of perceptions about society, personhood, and human existence, all strongly influenced by the subcontinent's religious and philosophical traditions. One set of notions revolves around the hierarchical, duty-oriented, group-centered values of Indian society; another set dwells on the uniqueness of each person's destiny and the unsettling vicissitudes of human existence. These two themes constitute a basic counterpoint in situationally shifting articulations of self and society.[18]

The dynamic of the fraternal relationship derives partly from the problematic interplay of these deeply held perspectives. The relationship between brothers is actualized in the "structure" of birth-order precedence and the "ideals" of duty, obedience, and cooperation; yet these actualizations are set in the unpredictable flux of life, where

"love" and "enmity" coexist, and brothers' differences are as striking as their similarities. Destiny's capricious influences and the flow of passing events may (1) act to alter brothers' personal situations, (2) encourage both solidarity and conflict, (3) randomize skills and talents with respect to birth order, and (4) disjoin brothers' temperaments and accomplishments from their formal positions in the family hierarchy.

From a Western point of view, astrology, magic, and divination may seem distant and unlikely mirrors for understanding the complexities of brothers' lives. Yet from an Indian perspective, these mirrors are real, attractive, and often compellingly accurate in their representations. Their widespread salience reminds us that the path to a cross-cultural understanding of sibling relations must accommodate the broad frames of social and personal experience in which siblings and other kinsmen conduct their lives.

Notes

1. This chapter is based in part on research conducted in Benares from January 1975–June 1976. I am indebted to the Social Science Research Council for an Overseas Dissertation Fellowship in support of this fieldwork.

2. Schneider's (1968) classic study of American kinship distinguishes between the person as a kinsman and the kinsman as a person.

3. This common anthropological distinction between norms and behavior, culture and conduct, and ideals and realities, recurs in studies of sibling relations in other world areas. See, for instance, Marshall (1983).

4. Mandelbaum (1970: 63–6, 125–30, 152–53) provides overviews of the fraternal relationship. See also Kolenda (1982) and Vatuk (1982).

5. In the past two decades, the study of ethnosociology has been an important enterprise in South Asian anthropology. Marriott (1990) offers a key statement on this approach.

6. The study of ethnopsychology has begun to raise critical issues in the study of person, affect, and cross-cultural experience. White and Kirkpatrick (1985) and Lutz (1988) contain representative samples of this work; Rosaldo's (1980) ethnography is exemplary.

7. For studies of siblings and birth order in Western society, see Dunn (1985), Sutton-Smith and Rosenberg (1970), and Zukow (1989).

8. The Census of India (1971) lists the population of Benares as 606,721.

9. The Census of India (1971) gives a breakdown of the population of Benares by religion, as follows; Hindu, 448,767; Muslim, 153,314; Christian, 2,006; Sikh, 1,712; Jain, 788; and Buddhist, 117.

10. Pugh (1988) analyzes the ideological uses of astrology, divination, and magic in Benares.

11. Well-known anthropological studies of twinship in non-Western

societies include Evans-Pritchard (1956) on the Nuer of the Sudan and Turner (1969) on the Ndembu of Zambia.

12. These texts include Sharmana (1954), Nilkanth (1972), Nuri (1972), Ojha (1972), Shrimali (1974), and an anonymous booklet entitled *Mahabir Prasnavali*. Nilkanth (1972) is the printed edition of a 16th century work.

13. Beck (1986) contains a useful survey of social dyads in Indian folktales.

14. Astrological texts' descriptions of the parent–child tie show striking parallels to Inden and Nicholas's (1977) account of Bengali views of this bond.

15. Nuri (1972: 129–31, 145) is a key source for these particular descriptions.

16. Pugh (1983b) provides a detailed discussion of this case.

17. See, for example, *Mahabir Prashnavali* (n.d.).

18. See Kemper (1979) for another perspective on astrology in Indian culture and society.

References

Beck, B. E. F. (1982). *The Three Twins: The Telling of a South Indian Folk Epic*. Bloomington: Indiana University Press.

Beck, B. E. F. (1986). Social Dyads in Indic Folktales. In S. H. Blackburn & A. K. Ramanujan (Eds.), *Another Harmony: New Essays on the Folklore of India*, (pp. 76–102). Berkeley: University of California Press.

Census of India. (1971). Part II-C. Social and Cultural Tables. Uttar Pradesh. Pp. 62–3.

Dunn, J. (1985). *Sisters and Brothers*. Cambridge, MA: Harvard University Press.

Evans-Pritchard, E. E. (1956). *Nuer Religion*. Oxford: Oxford University Press.

Garga, S. n.d. *Brihat Indrajal*. Delhi: Dehati Pustak Bhandar.

Geertz, C. (1973). *The Interpretation of Cultures*. New York: Basic Books.

Inden, R. B., & Nicholas, R. W. (1977). *Kinship in Bengali Culture*. Chicago: University of Chicago Press.

Kemper, S. (1979). "Sinhalese Astrology, South Asian Caste Systems, and the Notion of Individuality." *Journal of Asian Studies* 38: 477–97.

Kolenda, P. (1982). Widowhood among "Untouchable" Chuhras. In A. Ostor, L. Fruzzetti, & S. Barnett (Eds.), *Concepts of Person: Kinship, Caste, and Marriage in India* (pp. 172–220). Cambridge, MA: Harvard University Press.

Lutz, C. (1988). *Unnatural Emotions: Everyday Sentiments on a Micronesian Atoll and Their Challenge to Western Theory*. Chicago: University of Chicago Press.

Mahabir Prashnavali n.d. Varanasi: Thakurprasad.

Mandelbaum, D. G. (1970). *Society in India* (2 Vols.) Berkeley: University of California Press.

Marriott, M. (1990). Constructing an Indian Ethnosociology. In M. Marriott (Ed.), *India through Hindu Categories* (pp. 1-39). New Delhi: Sage Publications.

Marshall, M. (Ed.). (1983). *Siblingship in Oceania: Studies in the Meaning of Kin Relations.* Lanham, MD: University Press of America.

Nilkanth. (1972) *Tajik-Nilkanthi.* Varanasi: Thakurprasad.

Nuri, I. A. (1972). *'Aziz-ul-Khalaiq.* Bareilly: Rizvi Kitabkhana.

O'Flaherty, W. D. (1976). *The Origins of Evil in Hindu Mythology.* Berkeley: University of California Press.

Ojha, G. K. (1972). *Predictive Astrology of the Hindus.* Bombary: Taraporevala.

Platts, J. T. (1982). *A Dictionary of Urdu, Classical Hindi, and English.* Oxford: Oxford University Press.

Pugh, J. F. (1983a). Fate and Astrology: The Hindu and Muslim Experiences. In C. F. Keyes & E. V. Daniel (Eds.), *Karma: An Anthropological Inquiry* (pp. 131-46). Berkeley: University of California Press.

Pugh, J. F. (1983b). "Astrological Counseling in Contemporary India." *Culture, Medicine and Psychiatry* 7: 279-99.

Pugh, J. F. (1988). Divination and Ideology in the Banaras Muslim Community. In K. P. Ewing (Ed.), *Shari'at and Ambiguity in South Asian Islam* (pp. 288-306). Berkeley: University of California Press.

Rosaldo, M. Z. (1980). *Knowledge and Passion: Ilongot Notions of Self and Social Life.* Cambridge: Cambridge University Press.

Schneider, D. M. (1968). *American Kinship: A Cultural Account.* Englewood Cliffs, NJ: Prentice-Hall.

Sharmana, A. J. (1954). *Ramalnavaratnam.* Varanasi: Chowkhamba.

Shrimali, N. (1974). *Kundli Darpan.* Delhi: Anupam.

Sutton-Smith, B., & Rosenberg, B. G. (1970). *The Sibling.* New York: Holt, Rinehart & Winston.

Turner, V. (1969). *The Ritual Process.* Chicago: Aldine.

Vaidya, R. V. (1973). "Horoscopes for Twins." *The Astrological Magazine* 62: 58-60.

Vatuk, S. (1982). Forms of Address in the North Indian Family: An Exploration of the Cultural Meaning of Kin Terms. In A. Ostor, L. Fruzzetti, & S. Barnett (Eds.), *Concepts of Person: Kinship, Caste, and Marriage in India* (pp. 56-98). Cambridge, MA: Harvard University Press.

Wadley, S. (1976). "Brothers, Husbands, and Sometimes Sons: Kinsmen in North India Ritual." *Eastern Anthropologist* 29: 149-70.

White, G., & Kirkpatrick, J. (Eds.). (1985). *Person, Self, and Experience: Exploring Pacific Ethnopsychologies.* Berkeley: University of California Press.

Zukow, P. G. (Ed.). (1989). *Sibling Interaction across Cultures: Theoretical and Methodological Issues.* New York: Springer-Verlag.

Afterword
Perspectives on Siblings: A Developmental Psychologist's View

Judy Dunn

The question of how and why close relationships differ in different cultures is one that is increasingly acknowledged by psychologists to be important (e.g., Hinde 1979, 1987). We are—or should be—uncomfortably aware that our ideas and studies of relationships are based on a pitifully narrow section of the range of people's social experiences in different cultures throughout the world. It is from studies such as the diverse accounts of siblings in South Asia given in this volume that we begin to grasp just how far many of our assumptions about relationships may reflect the particular cultures in which the grand theories of psychology were formulated—the cultures of middle-class Vienna and Geneva at particular historical moments. The relationship between siblings provides a particularly vivid example of what can be learned by psychologists from listening to anthropologists. All over the world children grow up with siblings, in intimate, familiar, emotional proximity. Yet, as we have seen, their relationships can differ notably in different cultural worlds. And such differences highlight the importance of pursuing the question of how cultural beliefs and expectations, myths and narratives concerning siblings, and local patterns of social relationships within and beyond the family impact on the relationship.

However, the work on siblings described in this volume also highlights the *differences* between anthropologists and psychologists in perspectives, in goals, in questions asked, and in conceptual approaches, and it is these differences that inevitably leads to frustration and disappointment at what we *fail* to learn from each other. Developmental psychologists are interested in four sets of issues concerning siblings. What is the nature of the relationship between siblings and how does it change and develop as they grow older? How is this relationship affected by other familial relationships, by relationships outside the family, and by the wider cultural group in which the siblings are growing up? What is the developmental influence of siblings upon one another? And fourth, why do some siblings get along very well and others have conflicted or hostile relationships? We can look to the chapters in this volume for some illumination concerning the first and second questions, but not concerning the third and fourth. To answer these latter questions—probably the most central for psychologists—anthropological writing can provide intriguing anecdotes but is unlikely to give us the systematic material we need. On the first two questions, the documentation in this volume presents psychologists with important challenges, raises further questions, provides some provocative insights—and also some moments of surprise at the picture of psychological knowledge and research that is occasionally presented.

Most important are the challenges and questions raised by the anthropological material. There are, we learn from the chapters in this volume, striking differences between European and North American cultures, on the one hand, and those of South Asia, on the other, in the significance attributed to siblings in adulthood, in the time that siblings spend together, in the responsibility given to individuals for the care of their siblings, in the cultural expectations concerning the quality of that relationship, in the relation of economic and material issues in adulthood to the relations between siblings, and in the connection between individuals' sibling and marital relationships. These differences from our own culture are indisputable. For a developmental psychologist, the question these differences raise concerns their impact on the quality of the relationships between siblings—on what the siblings feel and think about each other, on the meaning of their relationship for each of them, and on their influence on one another. How do the shared cultural expectations of closeness and support between siblings affect the feelings that two individuals have for one another? How are those cultural messages sent and received, and what affects the degree of their impact? It seems *a priori* very likely that the quality and developmental influence of siblings' relationships would be affected by differences in cultural expectations, communicated in part in the mythology and folk narratives concerning siblings. And a theme running through several chapters is that the sibling relationship in South Asian cultures is in fact less dominated by rivalry and conflict than it is in the United States and in

Europe, in part, it is presumed, because of such differences in the symbolic meaning of the sibling relationship. A number of questions are, however, raised by such a claim.

First, is it appropriate to view the sibling relationship in the United States and Europe as dominated by rivalry? It is in fact a serious misrepresentation of psychologists' current ideas on the nature of the relationship between siblings to suggest that they are focused primarily on rivalry. For some clinicians, concerned with troubled individuals, this may be so. But the great wealth of current research on siblings, which has grown enormously in the last five years or so, examines a range of aspects of the relationship and documents the significance of intimacy, companionship, and support in siblings' relationships (for reviews, see Boer & Dunn 1992; Dunn & McGuire 1992). It is clear that for siblings in the preschool period, in early childhood, in middle childhood, and in adolescence, as well as later in the life span (Bedford & Gold 1989), these positive aspects of the relationship are both important and frequently found features of the relationship. This research shows, too, that it is important to distinguish between conflict and argument, on the one hand, and rivalry for parental attention and affection, on the other. It is clear from a number of studies that siblings argue and disagree for a variety of reasons, and that the extent of rivalry and of conflict are relatively independent features of their relationship. It is, of course, true that arguments and disagreements are frequent between many siblings in the United States and Europe during childhood, and that such quarrels are a source of irritation and concern to their parents. Psychologists are interested in such conflict partly because they would like to elucidate what accounts for differences between siblings in how much they disagree and fight. They are also interested in studying argument between siblings as a window on the nature of children's reasoning and their understanding of others. The question of whether children do in fact *learn* through participating in such conflictual exchanges (as proposed by Piaget and others) is, however, a matter for empirical enquiry, and it is certainly not assumed to be the case that they do (Shantz & Hartup 1992).

While the depiction of psychologists in the United States and Europe as focused on rivalry is far from accurate, the question of whether siblings in South Asia do in fact enjoy more harmonious relations than those in North America and Europe remains an intriguing one. Do siblings in India and Sri Lanka quarrel less frequently and form closer and more affectionate ties than those in our own culture? From my reading of the chapters in this volume, the question still appears to be an open one, at least for some of the cultural groups studied. While the limited observations described by

Beals and Eason (Chapter 4) suggest there is much less conflict in the families they studied in Karnatak State than in the Canadian families studied by Abramovitch and her colleagues (Abramovitch, Corter, Pepler, & Stanhope, 1986). De Munck's (Chapter 6) and Derné's (Chapter 7) contributions to this volume provide descriptions of conflicted sibling relations in South Asia. As a psychologist, I am now eager to learn about the impact of different cultures on this intimate relationship from a systematic comparison between sibling relationships in different cultural groups in South Asia and those of siblings in North America and Europe. Such a comparison would be based on the siblings' own accounts of their relationships, on observations of their interactions, and on the accounts of others who know them well. Thus, the chapters in this volume whet my appetite but don't satisfy it.

A third question concerns the extent of differences between the cultural groups in expectations and beliefs about the sibling relationship. Perhaps the most significant lesson for psychologists in this volume lies in the accounts of stories, myths, and expectations concerning siblings in the cultural groups within which these individuals grow up (see, for instance, Nuckolls, Chapter 8, and Pugh, Chapter 9). Developmental psychologists have, indeed, largely failed to pay much systematic attention to such shared representations in our own culture. What we now need to do is to look at the nature of cultural messages reaching children about the sibling relationship, and at the way such messages are linked to the children's own relationships. My impression is that one strong theme running through the transcripts of parent–child conversations collected in our studies of siblings in England and America is that parents stress that *siblings should like and support one another*. Consider the following two examples, recorded during observations of young siblings and their parents, the first in England, the second in Pennsylvania.

Example 1

> A 3-year-old sister complained angrily to her mother about her 7-year-old brother having teased her, saying: "I *hate* him! I wish he wasn't in this family!" Her mother responded: "Oh, you don't hate him! He's your brother! You don't hate your *brother*!"

Example 2

> An 8-year-old girl had a discussion with her mother on the issue of how she should stand up for her sister during neighborhood baseball games. Her mother commented to her on the importance

of loving and protecting her sister: "Well, your sibling is yours *for life* . . . your friends you only have around for a couple of years or so."

As psychologists, we should be grateful to anthropologists for alerting us to the possible importance of these messages to children in our own culture. And we should systematically explore not only such explicit admonitions and advice to children, but parents' beliefs concerning siblings, the portrayal of siblings in the media, as well as in common parlance. Here is how Ervin-Tripp (1989) comments on the meaning of the words "sisters" and "brothers" in our culture:

> When we say these words we think of camaraderie, intimacy, and support. In a recent letter to a newspaper a writer said, "She was my best friend. We were like sisters." These are treated as synonyms: she did not say "but we were like sisters," as though there is a contrast. If a man says "She's like a sister to me," we infer friendship without sexuality, and possibly protection and nurturance—not rivalry. These terms have been extended to fraternal orders, to unions, and to ethnic communities—all with the meaning of mutual concern rather than conflict. Everyday usage tells us that the image of rivalry is not dominant in the public prototypes of sisters and brothers even in our own society. (Ervin-Tripp 1989: p. 184)

As to the other lessons psychologists can learn from these chapters, they are as diverse as the very different approaches of the different contributors. The significance of economic pressures and stresses on adult siblings, which recurs as a theme in several chapters, has hardly been explored here in our own culture (see, however, Ross & Milgram 1982), yet is surely relevant. The question raised by Weisner (Chapter 7, this volume) on whether siblings in South Asia share a more similar environment than those in our own cultures, and are therefore more similar in personality and adjustment than siblings here, is of real significance for psychologists and deserves attention. The connections between siblings' relationships and individuals' marital relationships, another theme that recurs in several chapters, may also be worth exploring in our own culture, and may clarify the issue of what processes link close relationships—currently a "hot" topic for psychologists studying relationships (Dunn 1988a, 1988b).

At a more general level, the chapters bring home to us the significance of *cultural place* (to use Weisner's phrase) or *local scene* to the nature of close relationships. A recent comparison of parent-child relationships and children's fantasy play in Cambridge, England and Center County, Pennsylvania has demonstrated how early in childhood distinctive cultural expectations and priorities shape children's lives and their discourse (Dunn & Brown 1991). Examining how such aspects of *cultural place* are linked to the development of a relationship that is for most individuals the longest-lasting in their lives is surely worth our attention.

References

Abramovitch, R., Corter, C., Pepler, D. J., & Stanhope, L. (1986). Sibling and peer interaction: A final follow-up and a comparison. *Child Development*, 57: 217–29.

Bedford, V. H., & Gold, D. T. (1989). "Siblings in Later life: A Neglected Family Relationship. *American Behavioral Scientist*, 33: 3–126.

Boer, F., & Dunn, J. (1992). *Sibling relationships: Developmental and Clinical issues*. Hillsdale, NJ: Erlbaum.

Dunn, J. (1988a). Connections Between Relationships: Implications of Research on Mothers and Siblings. In R. A. Hinde & J. Stevenson-Hinde (Eds.), *Relationships within Families* (pp. 168–80). Oxford: Clarendon Press.

Dunn, J. (1988b). Relations among Relationships. In S. Duck (Ed.), *Handbook of Personal Relationships* (pp. 193–210). Chichester, England: Wiley.

Dunn, J., & Brown, J. (1991). Becoming American or English? Talking about the Social World in England and the United States. In M. Bornstein (Ed.), *Cultural Approaches to Parenting* (pp. 155–72). Hillsdale, NJ: Erlbaum.

Dunn, J., & McGuire, S. (1992). "Sibling and Peer Relationships in Childhood. *Journal of Child Psychology and Psychiatry*, 33: 67–105.

Ervin-Tripp, S. (1989). Sisters and Brothers. In P. G. Zukow (Ed.), *Sibling Interaction across Cultures: Theoretical and methodological Issues* (pp. 184–95). New York: Springer-Verlag.

Hinde, R. A. (1979). *Towards Understanding Relationships*. London: Academic Press.

Hinde, R. A. (1987). *Individuals, Relationships, and Culture: Ethology and the Social Sciences*. Cambridge: Cambridge University Press.

Ross, H. G., & Milgram, J. I. (1982). Important Variables in Adult Sibling Relationships: A Qualitative Study. In M. E. Lamb & B. Sutton-Smith (Eds.), *Sibling Relationships: Their Nature and Significance across the Lifespan* (pp. 225–50). Hillsdale, NJ: Erlbaum.

Shantz, C. U., & Hartup, W. W. (1992). *Conflict in Child and Adolescent Development*. Cambridge: Cambridge University Press.

Index

C

D